Fighting for Partnership

A volume in the series

Cornell Studies in Political Economy

Edited by Peter J. Katzenstein

A full list of titles in the series appears at the end of the book.

Fighting for Partnership

LABOR AND POLITICS IN UNIFIED GERMANY

LOWELL TURNER

CORNELL UNIVERSITY PRESS

Ithaca and London

For Ralph and Christine Turner

First published 1998 by Cornell University Press.
First printing, Cornell Paperbacks, 1998.

Printed in the United States of America.

Library of Congress Cataloging-in-Publication Data

Turner, Lowell.
    Fighting for partnership : labor and politics in unified Germany /
Lowell Turner.
        p.   cm. — (Cornell studies in political economy)
    Includes bibliographical references (p.   ) and index.
    ISBN 0-8014-3486-6 (cloth : alk. paper). — ISBN 0-8014-8483-9
(pbk. : alk. paper)
        1. Labor—Germany.   2. Industrial relations—Germany.   I. Title.
    II. Series.
    HD8541.T87   1998
    331'.0943—dc21   97-48683

Cornell University Press strives to use environmentally responsible suppliers and materials to the fullest extent possible in the publishing of its books. Such materials include vegetable-based, low-VOC inks and acid-free papers that are recycled, totally chlorine-free, or partly composed of nonwood fibers.

Cloth printing   10 9 8 7 6 5 4 3 2 1

Paperback printing   10 9 8 7 6 5 4 3 2 1

Contents

Preface

The history of the Federal Republic of Germany, commonly known as West Germany from 1949 to 1990, is a story of virtually unparalleled political and economic success. After the horrors of Nazism, West Germany produced an "economic miracle" of strong growth, beginning in the 1950s and continuing, in spite of recession and relative stagnation in the mid 1970s and early 1980s, right up through the unification of West and East Germany in 1990. Most remarkable, this export-oriented economic miracle was overseen by a well-functioning political democracy, in a country that had never known stable democracy before. And furthermore, the mechanisms of political democracy were extended to the workplace in an unprecedented way, to include a system of economic representation, with comprehensive collective bargaining, legally mandated codetermination for employees, and strong employer associations and labor unions in relations of "social partnership."

So far, so good. But can political democracy, economic growth, and social partnership endure in a unified Germany? Or is unification the beginning of the end for what the postwar world widely admired as the "German model"?

My own interest in these matters began when I lived and studied in Germany in 1968, as a participant in a semester abroad program organized through Pomona College and the Experiment in International Living. In the spring of that year, I spent two months doing independent study in Berlin. With an American friend, I made regular trips through Checkpoint Charlie into East Berlin and made friends there with some East German college students. We partied to rock-and-roll music one Saturday night in a small apartment, and I was surprised to discover (with my 1950s all-American, anticommunist upbringing) that both their parties and their concerns were very much like ours. These visits occurred during the brief "Prague spring" in neighboring Czechoslovakia. On our next visit some days later to the same apartment in East Berlin, we were met grimly at the door by one of our new friends, who told us that the secret police had arrested a fellow party-goer (an East German medical student) for handing out leaflets bearing the text of a Dubček speech. We were not to return, our friend told us sadly but in no uncertain terms.

That summer, after traveling through Czechoslovakia shortly before the Soviet invasion, I returned to the United States, demoralized by the brutality of Soviet suppression (and just in time to hear firsthand accounts from friends about police attacks on youthful demonstrators at the Democratic Party's national convention in Chicago). My life turned in other directions, and I did not return to Germany for twenty years. On that occasion, I spent a year at the Max-Planck-Institut für Gesellschaftsforschung in Cologne studying the politics of new work organization in West Germany, which compared most favorably to parallel processes I had studied and in which I had participated in the United States. Although I made two research visits to West Berlin, I did not enter East Berlin, my enthusiasm still dampened by those earlier sad events. When I returned home to the United States in the summer of 1989, like so many others I had no inkling of the cataclysm that was about to occur. I spent the next year absorbed in the writing of my book *Democracy at Work* (a comparative study of West German and American labor in an era of work reorganization), after which I intended to leave Germany behind, to move on to comparative studies in greener pastures: Paris, London, Brussels, and back home in the United States.

With disbelief, I watched from afar the events leading up to the collapse of the Berlin Wall on November 9–10, 1989. In February of 1990 I flew to Germany to give a talk at a conference in Wolfsburg, organized by the Volkswagen general works council. I had a few extra days and intended to visit friends and colleagues in Cologne before returning home, but again like so many others I found the pull of German unification overwhelming. I changed travel plans, flew to Berlin, took a cab to the Brandenburg Gate. From there I walked the length of the Wall along the western side to Checkpoint Charlie. Everywhere, people of all ages with hammers and chisels were tearing souvenirs from the thick concrete wall and jumping back and forth through now gaping holes, joking with teenage soldiers on the eastern side. For a few marks, I rented a hammer and chisel to hack out my own souvenirs. The frenzy of excitement and liberation unleashed powerful emotions and brought tears to my eyes even as I hammered away.

The next day I began the research that has culminated in this book. With Uli Jürgens, I interviewed the communist union leader at the large Oktober 17 (Niles) machinery plant in East Berlin and listened to his complaints about the new rank-and-file "free market liberation front" activists in his formerly satisfied and well-controlled workforce. This was high drama, and I was eager to know how things would develop. To satisfy the curiosity which gripped me that day, I have studied workplace transformation in eastern Germany ever since. My findings, along with a broader empirical and theoretical analysis, are presented in this book.

Most striking to me has been the overwhelmingly peaceful and at least to some extent successful nature of the transformation. Yes, there have been enormous problems, injustices, strong tensions between easterners and westerners— and there will continue to be for years to come. But as Claus Leggewie put it at a talk at Cornell University in February of 1996, "What the hell would you expect?"[1] On the whole, and to my great surprise, German unification, even at its most problematic in the workplaces of eastern Germany, has been a process of peaceful reform and adaptation; even at its most difficult, it has failed to destabilize German democracy.

This remarkably peaceful transformation, in a country notorious for its history of violence and repression, is what I seek to illuminate in this book. I think the explanation lies in the comprehensive transfer from West to East, and subsequent adaptation to existing circumstances, of the flexible and inclusive institutions of social partnership . The evidence presented in this book offers strong proof that institutions shape behavior and that at least flexible and inclusive institutions can be transferred from one society to another for adaptation to new circumstances. For some, this will be a controversial finding, one that I hope will stimulate both theoretical and policy debate.

In my presentation, I have tried to accomplish two in some ways contradictory tasks: to draw broader theoretical meaning from the evidence gathered, by way of careful social-scientific analysis; and at the same time to avoid the trap into which so many intellectual works fall, taking exciting real-life events and beating them into dry, lifeless academic constructs. To avoid this second pitfall, I begin the book with the dramatic story of the first great labor strike in postcommunist eastern Germany, which I hope will draw the reader into both careful and passionate consideration of the high-stakes drama played out in unified Germany in the 1990s.

Although it is impossible to remember everyone who has helped me (I always vow to write names down as I go along, and then unconscionably forget to do so), I would like to acknowledge invaluable research assistance from Martin Behrens, Mike Belzer, Owen Darbishire, Aline Hoffmann, Elena Atanassova Iankova, Matt Lyons, Dan Price, and Sally Schoen. Generous funding from the following sources has made this project possible: the German Marshall Fund of the United States in conjunction with the American Council of Learned Societies; the Institute of Collective Bargaining and Center for Advanced Human Resource Studies, both at the School of Industrial and Labor Relations at Cornell University; the International Political Economy Program and the Institute of European Studies, both in the Center for International Studies at Cornell; the Wissenschaftszentrum Berlin für sozialwissenschaftliche Forschung (WZB); and the Institut für Arbeitsrecht und Arbeitsbeziehungen in der Europaischen Gemeinschaft (IAAEG) at the University of Trier.

Neither the research nor the writing would have been possible without the support and constructive criticism of numerous friends and colleagues, including and especially Peter Auer, Uschi Backes-Gellner, Martin Behrens, Valerie Bunce, Alan Cheney, Peter Coldrick, Owen Darbishire, Michael Fichter, Bob Hancke, Roger Haydon, Charles Heckscher, Gary Herrigel, Elena Iankova, Ulrich Jürgens, Harry Katz, Berndt Keller, Horst Kern, Larissa Klinzing, Richard Locke, Manfred Muster, Jonas Pontusson, Dieter Sadowski, Nick Salvatore, Günther Schmid, Steven Silvia, David Soskice, Wolfgang Streeck, Kathleen Thelen, Karin Wagner, Kirstin Wever, and John Windmuller. Martin Behrens, Owen Darbishire, and Elena Iankova are also mentioned above as research assistants, in which role they each started out; all three, however, quickly evolved into colleagues who entered into the research and analysis, argued with me, and pushed me to make substantial changes and improvements. Jackie Dodge, Hannelore Minzlaff, and Dianne Porter provided valuable technical, administrative, and secretarial assistance. Thanks to Andrew Lewis for his fine copyediting work.

As always, my deepest thanks and appreciation go to those who put up with me, fight with me, love and inspire me the most: Kate Turner, whose preference for comparative French over German cuisine has only increased since the writing of *Democracy at Work*; Eric Turner, a veteran of kindergarten in Germany, now a wild and woolly Ithaca teenager; and Jennifer Turner, with a flair for the dramatic and an uncanny capacity to hold her own at home or abroad.

This book is dedicated to my dad, Ralph Turner, and my mom, Christine Turner—neither of whom I could ever thank enough for the opportunities they made available to me and for their lifetime of concern and support.

Lowell Turner

Ithaca, New York

The East in Open Conflict:
The Great Strike of 1993

When on November 9 and 10, 1989, hundreds of young Germans danced atop the massive and once impenetrable Berlin Wall, the world was forever transformed. The collapse of communism, the changes in eastern and central Europe and the former Soviet Union, and the agonizing efforts to construct a "new world order" have become defining political dramas of our era. At the center of these events stands a most remarkable and significant story: the peaceful and largely successful unification of the two postwar Germanys.

Countless books and articles have been written describing the collapse of communism in East Germany and chronicling the events leading up to formal German unification on October 3, 1990. Other writings emphasize the protracted difficulties and continuing conflicts and tensions (especially between easterners and westerners) in unified Germany in the 1990s. This book aims to round out the story by demonstrating that despite all the problems, the unification of Germany has been on the whole a rather remarkable success.

In a nutshell, German unification succeeded thanks to inclusive institutions and processes of negotiated adjustment. As a "social market" economy, West Germany maintained a dense web of regularized negotiations that shaped domestic policy in areas ranging from macroeconomic policy, to intergovernmental and industry-bank relations, to vocational training and company-level codetermination. When East and West Germany were unified on the one-sided basis of West German law and practice, West German institutions of negotiation were transferred wholesale to the East. Although fraught with difficulties and shortcomings, institutional transfer provided a new and surprisingly flexible framework for the transformation of economy and society in eastern Germany, and for the successful unification of modern Germany.

Because it is impossible in one book to examine all German institutions of negotiation, this book focuses on one important set of relations at the heart of social market regulation: the "social partnership" between labor and management. "Social partnership," a term widely used throughout the European Union but little known in the United States, refers to the nexus—and central political and economic importance—of bargaining relationships between strongly organized employers (in employer associations) and employees (in unions and works councils) that range from comprehensive collective bargaining and plant-level codetermination to vocational training and federal, state, and local economic policy discussions.

To some extent, I use "social partnership" in this book to represent other, parallel processes of regularized negotiation throughout the German political economy. From the perspective of economic citizenship and democratic participation, however, social partnership itself is the most critical of social market mechanisms of negotiation and inclusion. And what is most remarkable, social partnership has not only coexisted with but proactively facilitated the strong export-oriented economic performance of the Federal Republic of Germany ever since its founding in 1949.

Background to the Struggle

With the demise of communist trade unions in East Germany in 1990 and the subsequent collapse of the eastern economy in 1990–91, prospects for a western-style social partnership in the East appeared highly problematic. Many observers predicted that market liberalization in the East would bring the beginning of the end for strong labor unions, and hence social partnership, in unified Germany.

In a race to fill the vacuum of collapse, the sixteen unions of the western German Labor Federation (*Deutscher Gewerkschaftsbund,* or DGB) moved rapidly into eastern Germany to sign up new members and establish a presence in the eastern workplace. At the same time, western investors, employers, and employer associations moved rapidly into eastern Germany to establish ownership and influence. It was not long, of course, before these representatives of management and labor were face to face as each sought to secure influence in the new federal states.

Would the employer associations and the unions establish a strong presence, respecting each other's influence in western-style relations of social partnership? Or in the fluid and highly uncertain new situation would conflict break out, leading to predominantly conflictual relations in the East and perhaps even to a breakup of the social partnership back in the West, and in Germany as a whole? Would the unification of Germany result in an extension and expansion of strong interest representation and social partnership, or would it mean the beginning of the end for these institutions and practices?

The first great watershed for German social partnership in the post-unification era came in the spring of 1993, when employers in the metal industries of eastern Germany unilaterally refused to honor a previously negotiated collective agreement to raise workers' pay 26 percent. In a high-stakes effort to beat back the employer offensive, IG Metall (the German metalworkers' union) responded by calling eastern workers out on strike. The ensuing conflict and its outcome were to have major consequences for the future political economy of the East.[1]

The opponents in this confrontation were Gesamtmetall, the powerful employer association that encompasses a range of metal industries including automobile assembly and parts, machinery-building, shipbuilding, and electronics, and IG Metall, the equally powerful industrial union that represents the workforces, both blue and white collar, in each of these same industries. Throughout the postwar period in West Germany, collective bargaining agreements between Gesamtmetall and IG Metall (signed at regional levels but coordinated nationally) have both covered these industries comprehensively and set the pattern for negotiations in other sectors of German industry.

In 1990–91, Gesamtmetall and IG Metall each established a prominent presence in the new states of eastern Germany. Eastern employees joined IG Metall in large numbers, driving total membership in that union up from 2.6 to 3.6 million in the space of a year. Conscious of their pattern-setting role and eager to consolidate and stabilize western-style labor-management relations in the East, Gesamtmetall and IG Metall soon entered into negotiations and in March of 1991 signed similar three-year contracts for each region of eastern Germany, establishing basic pay levels and terms of employment for the metal and electronics industries.

These contracts provided for the phasing in, for eastern blue- and white-collar workers, of nominal wage parity with western workers over a three-year period (from 65 percent on April 1, 1991, to 100 percent on April 1, 1994; Bispinck 1993b, 470). Widely praised at the time, this arrangement offered eastern workers hope (above all to keep them from moving to the already crowded western labor market), promoted social stability in a precarious economic situation, and enabled employers and investors, who stood to gain by getting in early while wage costs remained low, to plan the rebuilding of the East in a rational manner—and at the same time protected western workers and employers from low-wage competition in the East.

The cozy relationships of early 1991, however, had evaporated by 1992 in the face of economic collapse in eastern Germany.[2] Although the pay raise of April 1, 1992, was paid on schedule, many employers, especially small-to-medium-sized ones, complained that the continuing phase-in of nominal wage parity would ruin them economically. Gesamtmetall knew that if it did not make a stand on this issue, its membership density in the East would suffer, since many firms would seek to go it alone in hopes of working out a better deal with their own threatened workforces (Silvia 1993, 22; Wever 1995).[3] Employer criticism focused increasingly on the scheduled 26 percent pay raise due on April 1, 1993.

After failed attempts at renegotiation and arbitration in the winter of 1992–93, Gesamtmetall seized the opportunity to "play hardball" in what looked like a sure-win situation in the spring of 1993. A hard-line view came to dominate within the employers' camp: with 40 percent real unemployment and massive job insecurity in the East, with no recent history of western-style collective bargaining or labor conflict, and with membership in IG Metall quite new and untested for eastern workers, mass mobilization and a successful strike in the East looked unlikely.

The employers announced their intention to cancel the contracts and proceed unilaterally with a 9 percent raise on April 1, instead of the scheduled 26 percent. IG Metall denounced the employer action as illegal and without precedent in the postwar period and filed a formal complaint with the labor court (not scheduled to be heard until May 14; Bispinck 1993b, 475–76). In the meantime, the union announced warning strikes, marches, and demonstrations beginning on April 1, to escalate toward a full-fledged strike throughout the metal industries of eastern Germany if no settlement were reached.

Employers denounced IG Metall as intransigent and out of touch with its membership in a desperate economic situation; the union accused the employers of breaking the postwar social contract and undermining the foundations of free collective bargaining.[4] Employers, backed by the business press and the broader employer community—through the Federation of German Employers (BDA) and the Federation of German Industry (BDI)—appeared unusually confident of victory. Eastern metalworking employees, for their part, obviously felt betrayed by the unilateral reduction of their scheduled pay increases; yet according to numerous journalistic accounts, they were also wary about going out on strike in a period of massive layoffs and economic crisis. Union representatives spoke militantly in public of the need to defend collective bargaining and free trade unionism but more hesitantly in private of their uncertainty regarding the viability of a strike in eastern Germany.

Press editorials called for reason on both sides, especially exhorting IG Metall to avoid leading its new eastern members into a labor-market disaster. In a front-page editorial cartoon, *Handelsblatt*, Germany's leading business daily, showed IG Metall president Franz Steinkühler sitting at the helm of a small boat, steering his eastern members over the crest of a great waterfall.[5] The *Economist* titled its article on the coming conflict "Mass Suicide."[6]

Although Gesamtmetall had signed a three-year contract in 1991, the temptation offered by mass unemployment proved impossible to resist. This was, after all, an employer's dream labor conflict: the new federal states were suffering 40 percent real unemployment (producing massive insecurity on the part of remaining job-holders); the need to hold down costs to preserve jobs was real and desperate; and the relationship between the (western) unions and their (eastern) members was new and untested. This was the ideal opportunity to show eastern employers (members and potential members of the employer associations) that Gesamtmetall could provide its constituents firm-level support during a labor conflict; a solid and aggressive united front against the powerful IG Metall; reduced labor costs and new wage flexibility as a bargaining outcome; and either a favorably reconfigured social partnership or a broader deregulation for unified Germany, with employers in the driver's seat at last. The stakes were high, but the prospects for victory bright.

April Warning Strikes: A Participant-Observer's View

On March 31, the day before the first scheduled warning strikes, I was sitting in the headquarters of the employer association in Berlin, listening to the explanations and predictions of a high-level employer spokesman.[7] According to him, and as other employers had explained in interviews in the preceding days, Gesamtmetall's hard line on contract cancellation and the unilaterally imposed 9 percent pay raise were necessary to rescue the eastern economy. Furthermore, IG Metall would come to its senses once it became apparent that easterners had no stomach for a real strike. Yes, there might be a few face-saving warning strikes, but no one could really believe either that eastern workers would vote to strike (with a 75 percent vote in favor required to authorize a strike) or that if they did, that they could hold out in a protracted conflict. From the employers' vantage point, this was the eve of a new era in which their own position would be consolidated in eastern Germany at the expense of IG Metall bargaining power. Although concerned about the imminent labor conflict, this employer spokesman was at the same time slightly flushed with the anticipation of a major victory.[8]

On the telephone that evening, I asked Manfred Muster, chairman of IG Metall for the city-state of Bremen in western Germany, what hope the union could have in such a desperate situation. Victory was widely predicted for the employers, who indeed seemed eager to push the union into a losing battle.

"I don't know what will happen," he replied. "We don't know if our eastern colleagues will strike. This is unknown territory, you know. We are in a position now where we have to fight, even if we may lose."

"What fall-back strategy is there if the strike doesn't work out? What compromise could the union accept?"

"The employers have broken the contract. We are willing to negotiate, but the employers must take back their contract cancellation and reinstate the principle of phased-in wage parity. Otherwise, collective bargaining is dead in Germany."

"But what if the easterners won't strike? So many of them have become disillusioned with IG Metall and other western unions for being unable to stop mass layoffs over the past two years. Will they follow you now? The papers say you are leading them into disaster."

"Listen, I don't know what will happen. I only know that we have our backs to the wall now and have to fight. Rostock is Bremen's sister city in the East, and tomorrow I go there to help organize the warning strikes. If you want to see for yourself what happens, meet me in Rostock."

And so at 6 A.M. on the morning of April 2, I found myself in an industrial district of Rostock, with a small group of IG Metall members and works councillors, shivering in the dark and cold outside a Siemens electronics plant. This group's job was to leaflet the morning shift at Siemens and other adjacent companies, to make sure that everyone knew about the warning strike scheduled for 11 A.M. Since this was a Friday, the plan was for everyone to walk off the job, march downtown for a rally at the shipyards, and then take the rest of the weekend off. The purpose of the warning strike was to demonstrate collective anger at the employers' cancellation of the three-year contract with its scheduled 26 percent April 1 pay raise; show worker solidarity with union demands; and give the employers a foretaste of the readiness of eastern workers to go out on strike. A strong showing would bolster the union position heading into a full-fledged strike, as well as increase the likelihood of a favorable settlement. A weak showing would cut the ground from under the union position.

Siemens seemed an unlikely place to produce a large strike turnout. In the first place, Siemens is an electronics firm, the least union-friendly sector that IG Metall organizes. At this particular plant, restructuring since unification (including the plant's purchase by Siemens) had meant a drop in workforce size from over 2,000 to around 600: the remaining employees were hardly likely to feel very secure about their individual job prospects. Finally, the "plant" here consisted mainly of a long, eight-story office building, occupied largely by white-collar workers, including many professional and technical employees and women, hardly the groups considered most highly organizable in traditional (and contemporary) western industrial relations.

My companions (two men and three women, all except Manfred easterners and members of Rostock IG Metall) handed out leaflets and talked with incoming employees. Most people were polite about taking leaflets and seemed genuinely interested in talking about the pros and cons of a warning strike—and would even stand out in the cold air for a few minutes to do so.

At one point, a Siemens manager (like almost everyone else at this plant an easterner) burst out of the lobby, demanding to know what these folks were doing there, urging his people to walk off the job.

"We are organizing a warning strike!" proclaimed Manfred. "This is our right under Article 9 of the Constitution."

The manager turned away and reentered the building. Manfred's eyes sparkled. "We are Germans," he said with a wink. "You have to tell them it's legal. In Italy or France it wouldn't make any difference whether it was legal or not, but here it matters."

"What does Article 9 say about warning strikes?" I asked.

"Freedom of association. We use it all the time. He will probably go look it up. There won't be anything in there about warning strikes, but it should keep him quiet."

The manager never reappeared. Incoming employees continued to take leaflets and talk at length with the IG Metallers. The sun finally came up and warmed the air a bit. When the morning shift was in and two adjacent companies had been leafleted as well, we drove back to union headquarters for breakfast. Rüdiger Klein, an easterner and head of the Rostock IG Metall, reviewed their plans for the day. With a stack of paperwork a foot high—member applications for various benefits, especially those related to unemployment—he never stopped examining and signing documents as he and his colleagues talked tactics and strategy.

At 10:00 A.M., the union office emptied out as groups headed off in different directions for various workplaces around Rostock. Back at the Siemens plant, the head of the works council, clearly concerned, met us with the news that top managers had gone through the offices, threatening employees with "dire consequences" if they joined the warning strike.

Manfred jumped into the IG Metall van and drove around to the side of the building. He turned on the loudspeaker. "This is IG Metall speaking," he said. "Today we are going out on a warning strike. 11:00 A.M. This is our right under Article 9 of the Constitution."

I looked up to see faces appearing from behind the curtains, windows opening on all floors. "The employers have illegally canceled the contract. You were supposed to get a 26 percent raise yesterday; instead you got 9 percent. This is a historic moment when we get to decide whether to accept such demeaning treatment or whether to fight back. The warning strike is the first step in standing up for what is rightfully yours. Without this step, no further steps are possible. If we let the employers walk over us now, there will be no stopping them. Colleagues, you have the legal right to join the warning strike, and we all have the duty to do so if we value collective bargaining and free trade unions in the Federal Republic of Germany."

Manfred paused for air and then continued. More faces appeared at the windows. "It doesn't matter if some boss runs through the building telling you not to join us. You won't defend your rights behind the curtains. You won't get a 26 percent pay raise by sitting at your desk today. Our peace obligation expired yesterday when the employers canceled the contract. Our warning strike rights are protected under the law. Come join us, colleagues, come join us!"

Manfred drove around to the other side of the building and repeated his exhortation, loudspeaker blaring. Again, heads appeared in the windows. But what weight could Manfred's words carry against the real threat of job loss? Could this be any more than Don Quixote against the windmills?

At 10:45, the lawn in front of the building was still empty except for a few anxious works councillors. At 10:50, two or three warning strikers (or just curious onlookers?) appeared. Manfred drove back and forth, from one end of the building to the other, escalating the intensity of his exhortations. At 10:55, a few more emerged, a small handful for what looked like a very lonely march into town.

And then something quite surprising happened. At 11:00 A.M., as punctual as the German trains, the white- and blue-collar employees of Siemens streamed out through the main door. There were twenty, then fifty, then a hundred, two hundred, and still the numbers grew. As the sidewalks overflowed on to the lawn, what was happening came suddenly into focus: these workers, despite the threats and uncertainty, and at great personal risk had in fact stood up for what they believed was right and shut their company down.

The crowd appeared quite uncertain about what it was doing. People tensed up noticeably as two police cars sped around the corner and pulled up next to the IG Metall van. Manfred flipped the loudspeaker on again and declared: "We greet the colleagues from the police department who have arrived to join the warning strike and escort us into town." People cheered, the police shrugged and waved back, and a squad car moved forward to clear traffic for the march. Manfred spun the van around and eased down the street, followed by a long line of warning strikers turned marchers, now several hundred strong.

Along the route, small crowds from several other workplaces waited to join the march. The sun blazed down on a cool but beautiful April day. An IG Metall youth group joined at the front of the march with a wide red banner calling for wage solidarity East and West. Spirits rose as the numbers grew, and by the time the columns passed under an elevated subway station and swung into the main corridor to the shipyards, there were a good one thousand marchers. At the approach to the square in front of the shipyards, our march was joined by an equally large group from another part of town. Columns approached from other directions, the workers had already spilled out from the shipyards, and there they were, about five thousand eastern workers (according to union and press reports) milling around in the crisp sunshine in front of a lashed-together stage, participating together in this history-making event: the first legally sanctioned collective bargaining work stoppage in eastern Germany since 1933.

TV cameras rolled as union leaders (Frank Teichmüller, head of IG Metall for the northern coastal region, Rüdi Klein of Rostock, and Manfred Muster from Bremen) gave speeches. The crowd roared at the announcement that twenty-thousand warning strikers in greater Rostock had shut down the metal, shipbuilding, and electronics industries of the area until Monday.[9]

In the aftermath, at a press conference in the shipyards, back at the union office, and later that evening over Rostocker beer in a smoke-filled tavern, these union leaders were quietly ecstatic. Although they recounted over and over the potential dangers ahead, they knew now that they had more support behind them than they had dreamed of. From that day on, the employers knew it too. The Rostock story was repeated in successful warning strikes all over eastern Germany on April 1 and 2. From then on, for the next six weeks, this first great eastern labor conflict since German unification, and the first major collective bargaining conflict in eastern Germany since the Weimar Republic—which Hitler had eliminated sixty years earlier along with free trade unions, codetermination, and collective bargaining—became a test of will and staying power.

THE MAY STRIKE

Successful warning strikes throughout the new German states April 1–2 and again April 14–15 shattered western preconceptions of eastern worker passivity. Even Michael Fichter, an astute, Berlin-based observer of eastern German industrial relations since 1989, had referred to "the widespread instance of lethargy and passive expectation . . . after years of being watched over, taken care of, and having favors and social improvements—when forthcoming—doled out to them, East Germans seem to be particularly prone to such behavior" (Fichter 1991, 35).[10]

For Gesamtmetall, the comfortable illusion that easterners, after sixty combined years of Nazism and command communism, would no longer stand up for their own interests when forcefully challenged vanished. For IG Metall, the demonstrative shattering of this same troubling preconception cast new light on the union's bargaining position in eastern Germany.

For a few days, an early settlement looked possible. Kurt Biedenkopf, prime minister of Saxony, offered his services as a mediator, leading to discussions between IG Metall and the employer association (VSME in Saxony) on April 4 and 5. An agreement was reached between the two sides, reinstating the scheduled April 1 pay raise but extending the timetable for full parity by one additional year. IG Metall headquarters in Frankfurt indicated its willingness to accept the compromise; Gesamtmetall headquarters in Cologne, however, turned it down, forcing the Saxon employer association chairman to resign his position. IG Metall pointed to this failed effort at compromise as evidence of Gesamtmetall's unreasonableness.[11]

Rumors of further behind-the-scenes discussions and possible compromise solutions circulated throughout the month of April and into May.[12] Publicly, however, both sides hardened their positions. After the second round of warning strikes on April 14–15, the first strike votes were scheduled for late April. Demonstrations of support for the eastern metalworkers organized by the DGB drew about 200,000 participants in both eastern and western Germany on April 24 and 25. The first strike votes, held April 26–28, yielded votes of 85 percent in favor in Saxony (the southern part of eastern Germany) and 90 percent in favor in Mecklenburg-Pomerania (the northern part, including Rostock). A parallel vote in the eastern steel industry, also organized by IG Metall but negotiating separately, yielded a vote of 86 percent in favor (Bispinck 1993b, 477).

The strike began in Saxony on May 3, with 7,000 workers at twenty workplaces, and in Mecklenburg-Pomerania on May 4, with 12,500 workers from twenty-four workplaces. The union raised the numbers gradually, so that by the second week, 30,000 workers from seventy-five workplaces had joined the strike (Bispinck 1993b, 477). Solidarity among the strikers, who received an average of DM 220–250 (about $150) per week in strike benefits from the union, appeared strong.[13] There were no signs at all of what the employers had expected: an early return to work by dispirited eastern workers.

On May 10–12, IG Metall escalated the stakes by holding strike votes in the remaining regions of eastern Germany, which produced votes of 81 percent in favor in Berlin-Brandenburg, 86 percent in favor in Saxony-Anhalt, and 85 percent in favor in Thuringia (Bispinck 1993b, 477). On May 12, 400,000 workers and their supporters demonstrated throughout Germany in support of the strikers, including over 50,000 western workers who briefly laid down their tools in solidarity.[14] On May 13, the IG Metall national executive board announced its decision to spread the strike to all of eastern Germany. By the end of the second week (May 14), 50,000 eastern metalworkers were on strike.[15]

Intensive negotiations resumed in Saxony, again with the mediation of Kurt Biedenkopf, finally yielding a settlement on May 14. The terms of this agreement served as a closely followed pattern for the other regions of eastern Germany and the steel industry as well. The parties agreed to the principle of phased-in wage parity for eastern workers but established a new timetable. In a symbolic but important gesture for the union, the 26 percent raise was reinstated retroactively to April 1. Effective April 16, the raise was dropped to 9 percent (plus anything else that individual firms had agreed to), then raised again in June, September, and December, so that the 26 percent level was reached by the end of the year. Further raises in 1994–96 were scheduled to bring wage parity between East and West by July 1, 1996. The employers issued a statement conceding that the extraordinary contract cancellation, used in this case only, was not an appropriate solution to collective bargaining problems.[16]

The union thus secured its main demands: a reinstatement of the 26 percent pay increase, an admission by the employers that the contract cancellation was inappropriate and could set no precedent for future labor conflicts, and a defense of phased-in wage parity for eastern workers. In addition, the union resisted the introduction of an "opening clause, " which would allow easy downward wage adjustment at specific firms (see below). Most important, perhaps, the union discovered in its new eastern membership a highly mobilizable force capable of conflict, solidarity, and personal sacrifice.

Employers secured considerable total labor cost savings for the period 1993–96 during the lengthened phase-in of wage parity.[17] In addition, Gesamtmetall was able to demonstrate a new bargaining aggressiveness on behalf of its members as well as to provide support services during a strike, to help convince skeptical eastern employers to join or remain in the association. But the employers, in the end, were forced to give in to the central union demands, including the concept of phased-in eastern wage parity; and they were forced to back down in the face of unexpectedly determined employee militancy.

Instead of an opening clause, Gesamtmetall settled for a new "hardship clause." While both allow for downward wage adjustment at designated firms, the distinction is critical. An opening clause puts the power to negotiate lower wage levels in the hand of firms and their works councils. In a period of economic crisis and mass unemployment, works councils would find themselves under great pressure to make substantial concessions. A hardship clause, on the other hand, puts the power of approval in the hands of a union-employer commission, effectively giving IG Metall the power to veto any attempt by an employer to defect from a settlement.[18] While the employers heralded this as a breakthrough in the direction of greater wage flexibility, the union vowed to use the new instrument selectively, to monitor and control carefully all temporary adjustments—a promise IG Metall has kept.

Striking workers clearly viewed the settlement as a victory. With only a 25 percent favorable vote required for ratification, yes votes totaled 78 percent in Saxony; a similar 61 percent in Mecklenburg-Pomerania, Thuringia, and Saxony-Anhalt; 46 percent in Berlin-Brandenburg; and 78 percent for the eastern steel industry.[19]

Explaining the Unexpected

Why did the employers provoke this labor conflict, which even they (at least off the record) admit that they lost? Why were they willing to gamble with the established system of social partnership, one that had worked so well for them for so long? The employer view, supported by many economists, was that economic collapse in the East had forced them into this strategy, given the uncompromising attitude of IG Metall. The survival of individual companies, especially the small and medium-sized, as well as the growth of the eastern German economy, required lower labor costs.

In itself, this argument rests on shaky foundations. As in the West, large firms typically dominate the employer associations in the East, and this is certainly true for Gesamtmetall. Most large firms in the East were owned either by western companies or the Treuhand (the government-established trust agency for industries formerly owned by the East German state, discussed further in Chapter

2) and had downsized drastically in the preceding years, thus substantially reducing the impact of any scheduled pay raise (medium-sized firms had also downsized drastically). Numerous large firms made this clear by promising their own works councils a premium over the imposed 9 percent April 1 raise; large firms in fact typically told works councils that they would like to pay the 26 percent but could not break ranks with the employer association and would match or exceed the final bargained settlement. As for the broader economic crisis and future development in the East, wage levels were hardly the dominant problem. Outstanding property claims, a weak infrastructure, and general economic uncertainty inhibited western investment in the East, even as unit labor costs dropped. With mass layoffs and the introduction of western production techniques, unit labor costs in eastern Germany, despite bargained wage raises, were on a rapid downward curve (Bispinck 1993a, 324–25).

A more plausible and complete explanation for the employer strategy highlights two factors. First, Gesamtmetall had not yet consolidated itself organizationally in the East, where membership levels remained considerably lower than in the West (Wiesenthal, Ettl, and Bialas 1992; Silvia 1993, 3, 22). Above all, it was the small and medium-sized firms who were not joining in the East, which not only undermined the association's membership base but also threatened its long-term finances and influence. Thus Gesamtmetall was more vulnerable to the demands of these firms than in the West, where companies had long experience with the benefits of membership, especially in the event of a strike.

Gesamtmetall therefore needed to show that it could be forceful, and wage restraint and downward wage flexibility were the handiest issues to be forceful about. And perhaps the association even welcomed a widespread strike as an opportunity to demonstrate to eastern firms the benefits of membership (including valuable financial and legal support for potentially isolated firms in the event of a strike). In addition, the chances of not only winning such a strike but strengthening permanently the position of German employers within or even beyond the social partnership seemed excellent. Given massive unemployment and near desperate job insecurity on the part of eastern workers, the temptation to go for a major win must have been irresistible.[20]

Neither of these conditions alone would have been sufficient to drive employers to their rather drastic course of action, the first midterm contract cancellation in the history of collective bargaining in the Federal Republic. Both conditions—labor market circumstances (massive unemployment) and institutional preservation (the need to expand and consolidate membership in eastern Germany)—appear necessary to explain the employer choice of strategy.

Why did IG Metall prove willing to strike against what even many unionists considered impossible odds? Newspaper editorials and employer and government rhetoric implied that the union's only interest was in its own power and the pay levels of its employed members. They accused the union of demonstrating a reckless disregard for the future of the eastern economy and catering only to the short-term interests of an eastern audience while defending the long-term interests of established western members (whose job security and pay levels could be undermined by lower wages in the East).

If this had been the case, however, the appropriate strategy would have been to find a face-saving compromise with employers, to avoid a possibly losing strike which would have had major negative repercussions in both the East and the West. A better explanation for what many saw as a counterintuitive (not to mention counterproductive) union strategy again highlights institutional preservation. IG Metall saw the contract cancellation as a possibly precedent-setting threat to the very rules and framework under which it had built up its influence in the German political economy. In choosing to strike, the union recognized that its own position in society was jeopardized if it failed to defend its institutional underpinnings, including collective bargaining and the binding nature of signed contracts. Even more important, the union was defending itself as an organization. In the wake of mass layoffs, there were already clear signs of eastern disillusionment with the promises of western-style unionism. If IG Metall had not been willing to fight to defend its contract and the principle of phased-in wage parity, a major hemorrhaging of eastern membership could have been expected. And if employers could go non-union (or weak-union) in the East, there was no reason to think they would not later move toward such an "Americanization" of industrial relations (as Germans put it) in the West.

The stakes were therefore high enough for the union to make gambling on a high-risk strategy worthwhile; institutional preservation was important enough to risk major defeat, which seemed quite likely at the time. In a way, the union needed a major strike in the East, just as the employers did, to demonstrate its commitment to the interests of its new eastern members and to mobilize eastern members behind a commitment to popular union demands. Even in defeat, such a mobilization could integrate eastern workers and forge an identity for them as union members in a way that no other activity could. And since unionized works councillors could be expected to play leading roles in organizing strike preparations at the plants, a strike could have the added benefit of solidifying union commitment on the works councils, drawing these important bodies more fully into the union orbit.[21]

And where did the eastern workers find such unexpected resolve and readiness for conflict? Why did they choose to go out on strike in large numbers in a high-risk situation? Their interest in higher pay was clearly an important factor. Expectations had risen dramatically after unification; and although living costs had risen rapidly toward western levels, income had not. For similar work, easterners were paid far less than western workers, and the 26 percent raise scheduled for April 1 was seen as a major step in the long-term move toward parity.

Wage interests alone, however, are clearly not sufficient to explain this high-risk choice. Periods of mass unemployment are typically times when union and worker bargaining power is low and the strike threat is least credible; at such times, worker militancy is typically restrained, despite interest in higher pay (Flaherty 1983; Katz and Kochan 1992, 222, 232).

There are, therefore, two other necessary parts to the explanation for eastern militancy. Worker mobilization in this case was fueled by extraordinary passion, a product of the combined frustrations and disillusionment that German unification had produced for eastern Germans.[22] In the rush to unification and the political campaigns of 1990, easterners had been promised prosperity to go along with their newfound freedoms. Instead, they found themselves plunged into an economic crisis complete with mass unemployment, rising prices, and great job insecurity and dispossessed by an invasion of western employers and government officials. For easterners in the metal industries, the unilateral employer cancellation of the scheduled pay raise was the straw that broke the camel's back. The bitterness and rage of what was in some ways a colonized people (Weiss 1991; Knuth 1993; Baylis 1993, 87) was channeled into this strike, much to the benefit of IG Metall.

The final necessary condition to explain eastern mobilization was the existence of a framework of credible institutions into which the passion could be funneled, with reasonable prospects of success. These institutions were largely imported from the West: codetermination based on elected works councillors who could, in their capacity as union members, provide strike leadership, and a system of comprehensive regional collective bargaining, which included the participation of a powerful, conflict-tested metalworkers union. The presence of these proven institutions, and the reassuring words of IG Metall that strikes were appropriate, legal, and winnable, provided the structure necessary for easterners to channel their passion into appropriate action (as opposed to either passive disillusionment and withdrawal or inappropriate action such as attacks on foreigners or other scapegoats).

Still unanswered, however, is the question, why did IG Metall and its eastern membership win? The employers were certainly quite sure, for good reason, that they and not the union or workers would win. The analyses of perceptive academics such as Mahnkopf (1991, 1993) and Armingeon (1991) pointed clearly toward declining union influence in unified Germany. If this were the case, it would hardly lead one to expect a major IG Metall victory in eastern Germany in 1993. Underestimated in such analyses, however, were two important factors: the passion and potential militancy of eastern workers; and the resilience and adaptability of the institutions of industrial relations in the Federal Republic, in particular codetermination and the system of comprehensive collective bargaining.

Under adverse circumstances, IG Metall won this strike because (1) it made the strategic and rather risky decision to strike, at a time when the most prudent course of action might have been some face-saving compromise; (2) eastern workers in large numbers made the courageous decision to risk future employment prospects for an issue in which they deeply believed (phased-in wage parity); and (3) western institutions of industrial relations, transplanted and adapted to conditions in the East, afforded a viable framework in which the strike could be fought and won. Codetermination law meant that most works councillors had received union training and thus provided a union base in most plants; comprehensive collective bargaining made it possible to mobilize widespread solidarity.

Not only was a union victory far from inevitable, the evidence suggests that a union victory would have been exceedingly difficult in the absence of any one of these three conditions.

IMPLICATIONS AND CONSEQUENCES

For IG Metall, successful mobilization of the eastern membership provided a much needed boost to union fortunes in the new federal states of eastern Germany. Precisely when generalized eastern disillusionment was broadening out to include the incoming western unions that so many had joined with high expectations but which had proven incapable of preventing mass unemployment, the strike solidified union commitment, at least in the pattern-setting metal industries. Here, at least, was an organization that would fight for eastern interests; here, at least, was a set of institutions that could offer some leverage for those interests. For many eastern workers, in fact, this strike may well prove to have been a formative experience. In the first major collective bargaining conflict in eastern Germany in sixty years, workers discovered that they could mobilize and defend their interests successfully. IG Metall became the beneficiary of this mobilization, in the organizational commitment both of eastern members, especially activists, and the works councils. Mobilizing works councils into bases of union support may have been the most important single effect of this strike for the union.

For Gesamtmetall, the hard-line strategy and effective dominance in the East that employers had sought was no longer viable, at least in the short run. But there was consolation in defeat for the employers. Because they were willing to provoke and sustain a strike, they did secure considerable labor cost savings over a three-year period. The hardship clause afforded a limited opening for downward wage adjustment. Most importantly, however, Gesamtmetall showed its members and potential members in the East that it would stand up to the union, fight for employer interests, and provide useful services in the event of a labor dispute.

What did the strike and settlement mean for the eastern economy? This is harder to gauge. Employers claimed, as a rule, that they could sustain the costs of phased-in wage parity, especially with the time period deferred. Union sources have presented persuasive data to indicate that labor costs were not the primary

15

cause of economic problems in the East (Bispinck 1993b, 472–74). The new contract brought stability to employer planning and investment strategies in eastern Germany, since in the wake of the settlement firms could now plan labor costs several years in advance. The consolidation of the principle of phased-in wage parity weakened the prospects for an economic and labor-market "polarization scenario" between East and West in Germany and strengthened the prospects that employers, if they invested, would take a modernizing, high-skills, high-quality approach to production organization in the East (Jürgens, Klinzing, and Turner 1993, 241–43). Whether the dominant reality in the coming years would be modernization or deindustrialization still depended on many factors, including government policy, economic growth in the West, the settlement of property claims, the development of infrastructure, and the opening of new markets in central and eastern Europe (as those countries either grow or stagnate).

For other sectors of the eastern economy, the settlement in the metal industries set an important pattern. In interviews in eastern Germany in March and April of 1993, I heard time and again from representatives of non-metal sectors that they were waiting to see what would happen in the metal industry conflict. Union representatives at ÖTV (the public sector) and DPG (postal and telecommunications workers), for example, said that if IG Metall lost the strike, their own bargaining partners could be expected to follow a similar hard-line, union-challenging strategy. For those unions, comprehensive collective bargaining contracts were set to expire within a few months of the metal conflict; as it turned out, IG Metall's victory established a pattern around which to negotiate settlements based on the principle of phased-in wage parity.

The conflict and settlement in the metal industries, in other words, were pattern-setting events that led to a widespread consolidation throughout the eastern economy of (1) nominal wage parity for eastern workers in the medium term,[23] and (2) western-style institutions of industrial relations, including considerable union influence along with comprehensive, region- and sector-based collective bargaining.

Although the crisis of social partnership was far from over, this strike and its settlement greatly increased the prospects for continuing social partner–style relations between employers and unions in eastern Germany.[24] It is still possible, however, that the union victory was a Pyrrhic one.[25] Much depends on economic and industrial development in eastern Germany as well as the outcome of future labor conflicts in both eastern and western Germany.

For Germany as a whole, however, the strike settlement of 1993 appears to have pushed forward the long-term development of a country truly unified, not just territorially, but economically, socially, and politically as well.

CHAPTER ONE

Social Partnership at the Crossroads:
Unified Germany in a World Transformed

The story told in the prologue is significant far beyond the borders of the new Germany. In a postcommunist era of market dominance, societies across the globe are confronted with burning questions of economic and social order: What kind of market economy? How much regulation or deregulation? What role for organized interests such as labor? Is there a viable social market alternative, organized around social partnership between business and labor, to Anglo-American deregulation?

In the unstable economic and political circumstances after 1989, the myth of the "end of history" quickly died.[1] The view that with the collapse of the Soviet bloc the world was now headed toward a new and enduringly stable order based on the triumphant partnership of liberal democracy and market economy was brutally undercut by the outbreak of a horrendous war in the former Yugoslavia and the rise to political prominence of nationalists and former communists in Russia after the failure of shock therapy. It soon became apparent that we had embarked not on a glorious era of peace and stability but rather on a turbulent and dangerous period of transformation toward particular national and regional outcomes not easily predicted in advance (Jowitt 1992).

In the new global economy, nations both East and West grappled with fundamental questions of institutional reform. In the former communist countries, existing institutions collapsed, launching prolonged, painful, and uncertain processes of reconstruction and transformation (Stark 1992). Among the "victorious" advanced industrial societies, contending models of political economy fought to survive and adapt, offering alternative models for the new democracies. Three models appeared most prominent and viable: Japanese "cartel capitalism," based on bank-centered alliances among groups of firms and close state-business relations; American "liberal capitalism," based on company-led economic development and growing deregulation, with only a weak role for government, business associations, and labor unions; and German "social capitalism," including a social market economy with relations of social partnership between strong employer associations and labor unions based on comprehensive, bargained relationships between management and labor, with important framing and negotiating roles for large banks and government (cf. Zysman 1983; Katzenstein 1989, 347–49; Hart 1992; and Albert 1993).

However, can fundamentally different models of political democracy and market economy coexist in the new global environment?[2] Or are common competitive and political pressures pushing all national economies in one direction (toward lean production and broader deregulation, or as some economists put it, "closer to the market")?[3] In particular, can social partnership, based on extensive webs of representation, negotiation, and codetermination, endure? This is an important question for many reasons, including the insight that it affords into a more fundamental question: Now that markets are global and communism has collapsed, is there a future for social-democratic efforts to regulate market economies?[4]

The political economy of contemporary Germany is an important test case for these concerns. Germany is the most prominent example of social capitalism in a large country today; the German economy stands at the center of the European Union and exerts a major influence on developments in Europe both East and West. Postwar West Germany was famous for its social market economy: a market economy accompanied by extensive social programs (from comprehensive pension and unemployment coverage to national health care and free university education) and regulated through negotiations among powerful actors, including government, banks, business, and labor. At the heart of the social market economy are relations of social partnership, the central concern of this book. Social partnership can be defined as a method of market regulation in which strongly organized business and labor (the "social partners") negotiate comprehensive agreements that frame the political economy from top to bottom. In Germany, this takes the form of peak agreements when necessary (e.g., Concerted Action in 1967, the Solidarity Pact in 1993), comprehensive industry-level collective bargaining, firm- and plant-level codetermination, and other important negotiations that shape, for example, vocational training and industrial policy. Together, these elements of social partnership and the social market economy add up to "social capitalism" in Germany.

The unification of Germany, however, has placed enormous strain on the institutions and practices of social capitalism, raising real questions about its future: Can the social market with its partnership relations in fact be transferred to the former East Germany, and thus continue on for Germany as a whole? Is the social market (in its various possible forms) a viable model for other full and associate members of the European Union, and for the EU as a whole? Or is social partnership part of an outmoded model of political economy, destined for obsolescence as global market pressures intensify? Is the social market a luxury affordable only in an earlier era of protected markets and bipolar international stability, or does social partnership offer an institutional framework in which major domestic (and perhaps even international) actors can negotiate the terms of appropriate innovation?

The answers to these questions are important not only for Germans but also for those in other countries committed to a measure of moderation, regulation, partnership, and equality for their market economies. In the United States and Great Britain, for example, experts on vocational training look enviously at comprehensive German apprenticeship systems organized by the social partners and ask what they can learn, what they can adapt to their own systems. Reflecting new stirrings of activity from the American labor movement, *Newsweek* tells us that it is now once again "hip to be union."[5] It is important to know, therefore, to what extent core relations of social partnership between strongly organized capital and labor can be flexible and resilient, capable of adaptation, reform, and continued success in the modern, post–Cold War global economy.

These questions are especially relevant as we head toward a new century and millennium. The German model is once again in crisis. Powerful voices, especially in the employers' camp, call for a dismantling of the social partnership, viewing it as an expensive relic of the past in today's much more competitive global market.[6] Unions battle to reform and preserve the system in which their influence is strong. The future of social capitalism depends on the outcome of these battles—for Germany, and by extension for the prospects of strong labor unions, social partnership, and social-democratic market regulation elsewhere.

The current crisis in Germany, a crisis of economic globalization, is distinct from, I would argue, the *previous* crisis, the crisis of German unification. These get confused in contemporary debates, and indeed the second crisis is magnified by having followed the first. It is important, however, not to let the current crisis (discussed in Chapter 6) obscure the successes of German unification, and especially the consolidation of new relations of social partnership in the East. Analysis of the unification crisis suggests the very real possibility of an outcome that validates and reinforces social partnership in the contemporary crisis and in the years ahead.

Dynamic Markets, Resilient Institutions, and Actor Choice

My argument assumes a model that incorporates the following sequence of events and responses. Dynamic market change puts great pressure on established economic institutions and actors. Actors (employer associations, employers, unions, workers, government) respond to this pressure with old or new strategies, which may or may not reform the institutions. Institutions may stagnate, collapse, be transformed, or show the resilience to adapt; in any case, institutions determine both the range of choice available to actors and the range of possible outcomes (for market regulation and the role and influence of particular actors). Although not all things are possible, different scenarios are plausible, especially in a period of market turbulence and political and economic change.

This approach is useful in examining a wide variety of economic, political, and social phenomena in societies impacted by dynamic market change: those with old and entrenched institutions, those with relatively new institutions, and even those with collapsed institutions in processes of building anew.[7] *Dynamic markets*, in this model, are the driving force for change as they impact both institutions and actors (Zysman 1983; Gourevitch 1986). *Institutions*, however, determine the direction of change and the actual outcome, since institutions both set the range of choice *and* shape actor preferences, interests, and power.[8]

The argument presented here, therefore, is a fundamentally *institutional* one, differing in important ways from explanations based on economic efficiency (neoclassical economics); political or personal preference (rational choice, pluralist interest group theories); culture, identity, and collective understanding (social or political constructionism); or economic and social structure (although the institutional perspective shares with these explanations an emphasis on the importance of the "structures" in which human agency operates).[9] The alternative arguments come up short, I believe, precisely in their failure to incorporate the central influence of institutions in shaping ideas, interests, identity, choice, behavior, and relations of power (Hall 1986; Steinmo, Thelen, and Longstreth 1992; Wildavsky 1994). While social or political constructionism contributes importantly to an analysis of the *origins* of dominant institutions (Dobbin 1994; Locke and Thelen 1997), these institutions, once established, embody ideas and the outcomes of past social conflicts as well as shape contemporary interests and identities.

I do not mean to imply that the other perspectives have no value. On the contrary, each makes important contributions. And some of the richest recent social science work crosses boundaries in the search for causation.[10] A synthetic view, however, attempts to position each of the pieces within a broader causal framework. In the perspective offered here, while *institutions* are identified as the primary independent variables shaping outcomes and the direction of change, *changing world markets* (broad economic and social forces and structures) are the driving force that makes change possible or necessary; *actors* (interest groups, voters, demonstrators, their interactions, conflict, and negotiation) are the proactive agents of change and institutional adaptation; and *collective understandings* and *ideas* become powerful precisely as they become embedded in institutions or in social movements that aim to reform, overthrow, or transform existing institutions.

Within the institutional model, it is important in particular to emphasize the proactive role of actors. Institutions are not only constraining but enabling for actor choice; and drawing upon political constructionism, institutions are to some extent malleable, capable of reform and adaptation by actors operating within the institutional context. Both the enabling and malleable aspects of institutions are critical in the analysis of German unification.

The institutional perspective is particularly persuasive in periods of relative stability.[11] An unstable situation, such as the unification of eastern and western Germany, therefore, offers a more demanding context in which to push (and test) the institutional perspective.

THE ARGUMENT: INSTITUTIONAL TRANSFER IN UNIFIED GERMANY

In the context of German unification, the argument is as follows:

The institutions of social partnership (well established in the postwar period in West Germany; transferred from West to East beginning with German unification in 1990) have given actors incentives to make decisions that are consistent with the survival and adaptation of those institutions.[12] It is important to emphasize this latter point: that actors (interest groups, associations, individuals), especially eastern actors, have not only responded to institutional incentives but have adapted the new institutions—more or less successfully—to their own particular circumstances and relationships.

The causal relationship here between institutions and behavior would not necessarily hold for any given or transferred set of institutions. Some institutions are more successful or appropriate than others; in particular, some institutions generate a dynamic tension that inspires creativity and innovation (Hall 1992, 24). In the case of German unification, the causal relationship holds both because (1) institutions shape understandings of individual and group interest, and (2) the institutions of German social partnership are flexible and resilient, affording each major interest group a place at the table (whether the table is national, regional, sectoral, local, or firm-level) when critical economic decisions are made (Katzenstein 1989; Wever and Allen 1993).[13]

Institutions, I contend, shape choice, either directly or indirectly. This was true for both West and East Germany from the late 1940s and 1950s (when postwar institutions were consolidated on both sides of the Cold War divide) through 1989–1990, when the institutions of East Germany collapsed. Unification scenarios in 1990 varied: dreamers on the right hoped for a shock therapy of rapid marketization to open up the East and in so doing undermine the extensive regulatory framework of the West; dreamers on the left hoped for a gradual unification in which both East and West would be reformed in a process of mutual exchange and learning. When eastern voters, by favoring the Christian Democrats (CDU) in elections of March 1990, in effect chose rapid unification within a western framework, Chancellor Helmut Kohl decisively orchestrated a third scenario: rapid and far-reaching institutional transfer from West to East.

Institutional transfer thus becomes the critical variable in this analysis. In the years following unification, in a highly volatile and in some ways wide-open economic landscape (westerners in the early 1990s commonly referred to the "Wild East"), actors in the East made decisions that were conditioned by the newly transferred institutions, often at the expense of economic efficiency, personal preference, "rational choice," apparent considerations of interest, or eastern political tradition and collective understandings. Outcomes of conflict and negotiation in economic and political arenas, therefore, were shaped to a large extent by institutional transfer, as the new institutions redefined actor interests, power relations, and choices.

The significant implication of this hypothesis is that not only do long-established institutions shape behavior, but new institutions can also quickly shape *and change* both behavior and outcomes. This is not to say that old ways or identities change overnight. One of the most fascinating findings of research in eastern Germany since 1989 concerns how old practices, attitudes, and relationships shape adaptation to (and of) the new institutions.[14] In so doing, as we will see at eastern workplaces, such attitudes generate pressures for innovation and reform *within* the transferred institutions, in some cases contributing to much-needed institutional change not only in the East but throughout unified Germany. The dominant reality, however, the shaping context in which behavior is changed, begins for eastern Germany in 1990 with institutional transfer from West to East.

Testing this argument for the demanding case of German unification requires both an examination of the processes of institutional transfer and an examination of empirical evidence in eastern Germany to determine whether behavior and outcomes are consistent with the newly imported institutions. Evidence considered includes plant-level case studies of labor-management relations in eastern workplaces, a watershed event (the eastern metalworkers strike of 1993, in the prologue), and an evaluation of aggregate data and the overall picture in eastern and unified Germany.

To preview the findings, the combined evidence points surprisingly and rather consistently toward behavior and outcomes that result in widely developing relations of social partnership in eastern Germany, while reinforcing such patterns for Germany as a whole (see also Webber 1994). Alternative explanatory frameworks could and did lead intelligent observers to predict behavior and outcomes quite different from those that actually occurred. Economic argumentation, for example, viewed economic collapse and massive unemployment in the East as reasons to predict low wages and weak unions incapable of strong, solidaristic action (Armingeon 1991). In fact, wages have risen rapidly toward western levels, union membership density is higher in the East than in the West, and eastern workers, as we have seen, have proven themselves capable of impressive and effective displays of solidarity. Arguments based on political culture and identity, to cite another example, have emphasized resistance to change and the legacies of workplace attributes such as passivity and demoralization (Fichter 1991, 1993; Mahnkopf 1991, 1993). Again, this view is undermined by evidence of wide-spread transformation, new work habits, active works councils and influential unions, and a surprising conflict readiness on the part of eastern workers.

In the face of established traditions, massive unemployment, and economic collapse, I would in fact suggest that the *only* way we can understand the surpris-ing outcomes in eastern Germany is to recognize how newly transferred western institutions have shaped choices and behavior on the part of workers and their representatives, company owners and managers, and government officials.

The picture, of course, is not all rosy. The political, economic, and social problems in the East in the wake of communism's demise and the collapse of the eastern economy are massive and enduring. Unions have suffered from declining membership after the initial upsurge in 1990–91, while employer association membership has remained low (placing new pressure on social partnership rela-tions throughout Germany), and unification has taken an extraordinary and ex-tremely unfair toll on important labor market groups, in particular women and workers over the age of 45 to 50. So severe has the crisis—and the injustice—been, that it has masked from the view of many German analysts and practi-tioners alike the remarkable and essentially successful transfer of western institu-tions of social partnership into the large and unstable territory of the former German Democratic Republic (GDR).

BEYOND UNIFICATION: THE PRESSURES OF EUROPEAN AND GLOBAL COMPETITION

Problems resulting from unification are not, of course, the only pressures on the contemporary German social market economy. Wolfgang Streeck, among others, is most concerned about the impact of European economic integration, with its potential to undermine the national institutions upon which strong unions and social partnership are based (Streeck 1991, 1997; see also Altvater and Mahnkopf 1993). The argument presented here, by contrast, suggests at least some grounds for a more optimistic perspective.

In the context of dynamic market change unleashed by the single European market as well as broader international competition and globalization of markets, existing German institutions of industrial relations (codetermination; comprehensive collective bargaining between industrial unions and employer associations) may well place the survival of social partnership in Germany within the range of possible outcomes. The institutions offer this possibility by providing unions and employer associations a solid footing at home on which to defend their national positions as well as a base from which to expand cross-national collaboration.

There are, in addition to German unification and European integration, other challenges facing German employer associations and unions that also tear at the fabric of social partnership. For employer associations, these include both the threat and reality of employer disinvestment in Germany, itself a product of high labor costs and declining competitiveness in an era of "lean production," intensified trade competition, and new reservoirs of low-cost skilled labor in central and eastern Europe, along with the tendency of many small and medium-sized employers (and a few large ones as well), especially in the East but also in the West, to go it alone, withdrawing from or failing to join an employer association (Ettl and Heikenroth 1996; Silvia 1997). For unions, the problems are legion, ranging from new production organization that includes extensive subcontracting to the need for internal reform to develop the kind of modern organization that can appeal to increasing numbers of new workforce entrants, especially young, highly skilled technicians, white-collar employees, and women (often with two or three of these characteristics rolled into the same employee). The relatively high cost of production in Germany today, along with stubbornly high unemployment, is a major concern for both social partners. Although all of these new challenges enter into the story of German unification, it is nonetheless also necessary to consider these problems separately to see which if any may now or in the future directly affect the outcomes considered here.

IMPLICATIONS: A SOLID FOOTING FOR SOCIAL
PARTNERSHIP IN THE MODERN WORLD ECONOMY

The central finding of this book is that social partnership in unified Germany, despite numerous, well-informed predictions to the contrary, has so far proven quite resilient. German unions, in particular, have stood up well against serious challenges to their influence in the short and medium term. Inclusive and flexible institutional structures were necessary but not sufficient conditions for this success. Equally important were decisions and adaptations made by employer associations, companies, workers, and unions—decisions and adaptations shaped importantly by the new institutional context in eastern Germany, as we have already seen in the eastern metal industry strike of 1993.

The implications, for academic analysis as well as for union, employer, and government policy, are considered more fully in Chapter 7. The point to emphasize here is that neither trade unionism nor social partnership (nor social democracy, by extension, of which social partnership is a key component) are dead in the post–Cold War world economy.

Well-argued explanations of union decline and demise are legion these days, from the pages of the mainstream press to the academic bookshelves. Indeed, in a capitalist world economy, especially one undergoing tremendous regional integration and globalization, the deck is stacked against nationally based trade unions.

We now find ourselves, therefore, in a period when unions everywhere face sharp new challenges, if not outright crisis. This is also true in Germany, the large industrial society in which unions have been most influential over the past two decades. As a result, predictions of the decline of unions in the Federal Republic, which began early in the postwar period (see Neumann 1951) only to be quickly disproved, and reappeared with new vigor in the 1970s, only to be discredited by the late 1980s (cf. Windolf and Hohn 1984; Hohn 1988; Thelen 1991), have emerged with new intensity and persuasiveness in the post–Cold War era (Armingeon 1991; Mahnkopf 1991, 1993; Streeck 1991).

The findings presented here, however, suggest that a social partnership that includes strong unions is very much alive in the new Germany. This is true because both unions and employer associations have so far weathered their stiffest challenge—unification. Success was made possible by existing flexible and inclusive institutions—above all codetermination and sectoral collective bargaining—and appropriate strategic choices and adaptations. Thus what Charles Sabel (1993, 145–53) has rather critically referred to as the "model of resurgent social democracy" may well be the reality in Germany.

This will depend, of course, on how German unions respond to the challenges of new production organization (that Sabel emphasizes; see also Herrigel 1997), new workforce characteristics (Armingeon 1989), and European market integration (Streeck 1991). Particularly intriguing in this regard is one of the central empirical findings of this study: that shrewd managers and works councillors in eastern Germany are now discovering that advanced forms of team and group work organization can be established on the basis of collective traditions inherited from the GDR. Case study evidence, analyzed in Chapters 3 and 4, highlights this finding. The expansion of western institutions into eastern Germany thus builds on existing material in ways that not only create something new (what Stark 1996 calls "recombinations") but may well reinvigorate the institutions themselves.

The persistence of the German model suggests that the "coordinated market economy" that David Soskice (1990) analyses and admires will continue to be very much a part of the modern world economy. The social partnership that is central to this model, particularly the strong union/social-democratic variant (as found in Germany), will continue to offer an alternative to the more deregulated market economies, an alternative that can be compared along dimensions of performance. And the resilience of the German model contrasted to the decline of the Swedish model suggests that a "softer" (and less centralized) version of social democracy may be more compatible than a "harder" version with contemporary globalization and dynamic market change.[15]

I would also suggest that the tension between more and less organized versions of the market economy has a positive side. The tendency in contemporary analysis is either to bemoan or to celebrate the contemporary collapse of market regulation—from the decline of democratic corporatism, especially the Swedish model, to the 1980s dominance of monetarism, Reaganism, and Thatcherism, to the onslaught of "lean production," to the single European market, to shock therapy in the East. Yet there are positive lessons to be learned across societies. Just as command communism in the East strengthened the hand of social-welfare advocates in the West in an earlier period, and market dynamism in the West later undermined command communism in the East, so in contemporary world markets, social capitalism in Germany is forced to become more productive, and this includes cost-cutting and a decentralization of production organization to which unions must respond (as Kern and Sabel 1991 rightly insist). At the same time, employees in "lean" Japan may be influenced by the gains of European labor to demand more vacation time, social benefits, and personal freedom.[16] And reformists in the United States, from the ranks of business, labor, and government, continue to consider innovations such as partnership, participation, and expanded vocational training (Appelbaum and Batt 1994; Commission on the Future of Worker-Management Relations 1994; Levine 1995).

The most important lessons to emerge from these findings, however, are that institutions can in fact be successfully transferred to new settings, that they can be adapted and reformed by new actors to accomplish new tasks, that actor choice is shaped by institutional contexts and does matter a great deal, and that in the post–Cold War era, different outcomes are possible.[17] Because we are living through what social scientists in the past have called a "critical juncture," contingency and choice are more the order of the day than usual. In such an unsettled context, the choices that people make—from elite actor choices, to election results, to popular decisions to protest or strike—may have a powerful impact on the course of events. Although an examination of available evidence may point toward likely outcomes (see Jürgens, Klinzing, and Turner 1993 on the eastern German case; see Streeck 1991 on the European case), alternative possible scenarios are an unusually central feature of this post–Cold War era.

Institutions may be resilient or they may be rigid. The European works councils considered briefly in Chapter 6 show that important new institutions can be built. The development of eastern German industrial relations since 1989 shows that old institutions can collapse and successful new ones can be established, if they are appropriately adapted and build on existing foundations. And institutional expansion—a point to be considered in Chapter 7—may well preclude continuation of the status quo, resulting instead in *either* institutional reinvigoration or institutional decline.

The strike of 1993 demonstrates that established institutions can be reinvigorated in new settings, especially when these institutions are adapted in ways that win popular support. In social science work of the past two decades, we have brought back the state (Evans, Rueschemeyer, and Skocpol 1985), highlighted the importance of organized labor and capital (Schmitter and Lehmbruch 1979; Berger 1981; Swenson 1991), and refocused on the importance of institutions (Hall 1986; Streeck 1992; Steinmo, Thelen, and Longstreth 1992). Perhaps now it is high time to bring back "the people" as well: those in East Germany, for example, who brought down the GDR through both mass migration and protest (exit and voice) in 1989;[18] who unexpectedly voted Christian-Democratic in the East and thereby speeded unification in 1990; who chose to strike in large numbers in highly risky circumstances in 1993; and whose collective workplace traditions have laid the groundwork for innovative production organization in an eastern German economy now struggling for takeoff.

People, however, do not make choices in a vacuum. The most important lesson for reformers in Germany, the United States, and elsewhere is that *crucial institutional developments* have a powerful shaping influence on strategic as well as tactical actor choice. For the outcomes described and explained in this study, for the survival, reform, and even resurgence of trade unionism and a social market organized around relations of social partnership, proactive strategies, including those fueled by popular passion but in every case strongly influenced by framing institutions—including new ones—have been and will continue to be decisive.

Chapter Two

Worlds Apart, Thrown Together:
New Institutions and Economic Collapse

To most people in West Germany, life looked good in 1989. The economy boomed at the center of broad West European growth, spurred on by the developing single European market. Many West Germans in this relatively egalitarian society considered themselves prosperous; in blue-collar and white-collar circles alike, talk often turned to individual and family plans for the paid vacation period (four to six weeks per year): millions of Germans vacationed each year in places such as Greece, Italy, Spain, Portugal, the Austrian Alps, or by a lake in Bavaria. If the "two-thirds society" had not yet opened its doors fully to all—foreign workers, women, the young and unskilled were disproportionately represented in temporary and part-time jobs and among the unemployed—generous social benefits, from comprehensive health care, to long-term unemployment compensation, to universally adequate retirement income, were widely available. Reasons for economic prosperity and world market success were many and included a highly skilled workforce, an industrial relations system of social partnership that generated labor peace and steady production, and a well-deserved and hard-earned reputation for high quality and well-engineered capital goods and consumer durables.[1]

SNAPSHOT: SOCIAL PARTNERSHIP IN A STABLE WEST GERMANY

Underpinning West Germany's economic and industrial success was a comprehensive framework of partnership relations among the major interest groups and actors, including banks, government, employer associations, and unions. Although this was very much a market economy, enough coordinated bargaining occurred at enough important levels for analysts to use descriptive terms such as "democratic corporatism" (Wilensky 1983; Katzenstein 1985) or to refer to this as a "bargained political economy" (Zysman 1983). Of particular importance were long-term and interlocking relations among major banks and large firms (Shonfield 1969; Zysman 1983, 251–66; Hall 1986, 234–42). David Soskice characterized West Germany as a prime example of the "coordinated market economy," whose incentive structures encouraged firms to make long-term plans, develop employee skills, and move upmarket, and juxtaposed this type of political economy to the less coordinated and on the whole less successful British or American-style capitalism (Soskice 1990).[2]

Critical to the broad framework of coordination was regularized bargaining among industry and labor, the so-called "social partners." Most large and medium-sized companies belonged to employer associations organized along industry lines at regional and national levels. These powerful associations lobbied for business interests at federal, state, and local governments and provided information on product and labor markets and investment opportunities (under the umbrella federation BDI); and engaged in nationally coordinated collective bargaining with corresponding industrial unions, providing an array of related support to individual firms, including strike support and codetermination and legal advice. West German employees were organized primarily into sixteen industrial unions, which negotiated comprehensive regional-level contracts with employer associations for entire industry sectors. With union membership density fairly stable in the 1970s and 1980s at around 35 to 40 percent, with most large and medium-sized employers belonging to employer associations, and with one industry, metalworking, setting widely followed wage patterns, collective bargaining contracts established fairly universal terms of employment for West German employees (blue and white collar) and companies. Nonmember firms typically followed the patterns, and where they did not, the Minister of Labor was empowered under certain circumstances to declare contractual provisions universally binding.[3] As a result, around 90 percent of the West German workforce was covered by the terms of collective agreements (Bispinck 1993a, 311).

Although a great deal of public debate and blustering often preceded bargaining rounds, including union-led warning strikes to demonstrate support and resolve, strike rates were quite low, mediation was frequent, and the two sides generally arrived at results acceptable to both (including gradually rising wages that nonetheless preserved high profits for successful firms).[4] Weak firms were squeezed out in this high-wage economy, which kept investment flowing into strong sectors and firms; displaced workers were provided for with "social plan" severance pay, retraining opportunities, and, if necessary, long-term unemployment compensation.

Along with comprehensive collective bargaining coverage, social partnership was reinforced by a legislated system of codetermination. At large firms, employee representatives were entitled to at least one-third of the seats on supervisory boards.[5] More importantly, at every firm with five or more employees, blue- and white-collar workers together were entitled to elect a works council, with legal rights to information, consultation, and in key areas of personnel and compensation policy full codetermination (veto) rights. Since most elected works councillors were union members, the system of works council–based codetermination effectively drew unions into close consideration of the concerns and decision-making processes of management at individual firms.[6]

From industry-wide collective bargaining to daily shopfloor negotiations between managers and elected works councillors, West German industrial relations produced a dense network of social partnership relations. In largely constructive ways, these relations influenced everything from company investment decisions, to supplier relations, to working conditions and skill levels. Employers and unions participated together, with government support, in a national system of apprenticeship training that linked skills formation to product and technology development, and arguably produced the world's most skilled workforce (Streeck et al. 1987; Berg 1994). Innovation and restructuring succeeded within the constantly evolving framework of social partnership relations (Schettkat and Wagner 1990; Weiss 1991).

Although Germans complained about the deficiencies of their system and argued for critical reform (cf. Windolf and Hohn 1984; Hohn 1988; Hoffmann et al. 1990), foreign observers, with the benefit of a comparative perspective, waxed increasingly enthusiastic in the 1980s (see, for example, Flanagan, Soskice, and Ulman 1983; Coriat 1990; Soskice 1990; Thelen 1991; Turner 1991; Crouch 1993; and Wever 1994, 1995). Wolfgang Streeck (1987, 1992) describes the "virtuous circle" of production, politics, and social partnership that produced high skills, active internal labor markets and flexibility, and market-successful "diversified, quality production (DQP)." Kathleen Thelen's lucid analysis of "negotiated adjustment" in the metal industry offers concrete evidence for the constructive interaction between management, works councils, and unions in the 1980s push for new and more flexible work organization (Thelen 1991). My own research in West Germany demonstrates the linkage between workplace codetermination (through works councils) and the survival and adaptation of national unions in the difficult circumstances of contemporary global markets (Turner 1991). In a similar argument, Anthony Ferner and Richard Hyman (1992, xxiv) point to the integration of cohesive national unions with solid workplace representation as a source of union resilience in the contemporary period; and Colin Crouch (1993) refers to the strategic use of the works councils by German unions as a "particularly sophisticated form of articulation" (213), helping to account for the "robustness" of German unions (287–88).

In the industrial relations arena, this long-term West German industrial success was grounded in horizontal relations of social partnership at numerous levels. To Americans of the 1990s, social partnership may sound like some "feel-good" cooperation approach designed to replace an earlier adversarial relationship. This is not the case, and the polarization of the American discussion into cooperation versus adversity obscures what social partnership is and what makes it work. Social partnership begins with the recognition that there are legitimate, contrasting interests within the workplace, the firm, and the broader economy. To make legitimate, "win-win" compromises possible, these interests need to be organized and recognized and provided with forums in which to exchange information and negotiate. Because both sides recognize the other's legitimacy (underpinned by legislation such as the Works Constitution Act, which mandates works councils) and neither side "goes for the throat," a partnership based on mutual strength becomes possible.

Social partnership thus recognizes and includes opposing positions, adversity, occasional strikes and lockouts, and much hard bargaining and negotiation. Yet the essence of social partnership is that the negotiating partners typically reach commonly acceptable solutions based on full information and an understanding of each side's needs. Through the 1980s, social partnership West German–style proved itself compatible with industrial success in turbulent world markets; with major employer initiatives to rationalize, increase functional flexibility, and reorganize production; with works council efforts to protect workforce interests and maintain high skill levels; and with union efforts to maintain membership and secure collective bargaining gains such as rising wages and a shorter workweek.[7]

CHALLENGES AND STABILITY ON THE EVE OF TRANSFORMATION

Critical to the success of social partnership throughout the postwar period was its ability to adapt and change in the face of new challenges, as part of successful overall West German patterns of "incremental adjustment" (Katzenstein 1989). The efforts of the new conservative chancellor Helmut Kohl after 1982 to engineer a major change ("die Wende") toward freer markets and less union influence failed to alter either industrial relations or economic policy very much (Webber 1992).[8] Institutions were resistant to change, the unions proved too strong to dislodge, and even the employer associations thought Kohl was going too far. After the impressive strike victory of IG Metall for the shorter workweek in 1984, relations between the social partners remained stable through the economic boom years of the late 1980s.

By the end of the decade, however, it was clear that significant adjustments were necessary. For employers, the growing costs of production in West Germany provoked threats to disinvest, debates about the long-term viability of *Standort Deutschland* (Germany as a production site), and new initiatives to move toward Japanese/American–style "lean production" (Hans-Böckler-Stiftung 1992; Roth 1992; Turner and Auer 1994, 47–51; Streeck 1996). The problem was exemplified by increasing Japanese import penetration of the West German auto market and the emergence on North American markets of high-quality, lower-cost Japanese competition for upscale German products such as BMW and Mercedes-Benz. German employers began to study more efficient Japanese methods of production and to launch strategies, sometimes quite controversial and threatening in the eyes of the unions, to increase flexibility, raise productivity, and cut costs.[9] By the late 1980s, for example, employers began with some regularity to make new investment in plant equipment dependent on more flexible working hours, thereby hacking away at union "sacred cows" such as prohibitions against night and weekend shifts. The drive to reduce costs of production in West Germany relative to its major competitors had become a major preoccupation even before unification.

Although the union response was instinctively defensive, bargaining positions became increasingly flexible for issues such as shift work and new work organization. In part, unions gave ground under intensified employer and market pressure. Opel management, for example, threatened to relocate production unless works councillors agreed to allow a new stamping facility at the Bochum auto assembly plant to operate around the clock (Turner 1991, 127–28). The works council, in conjunction with the local and national IG Metall, agreed to round-the-clock production in return for specific commitments for new jobs, protections, and bonuses for night workers. In addition, however, unions traded new flexibility in working hours for long-sought-after gains such as the shorter workweek. IG Metall, in nationally coordinated regional bargaining, made such trade-offs in the 1984, 1987, and 1990 bargaining rounds (Thelen 1991, 155–59).

In addition to defensive strategies and trade-offs, some West German unions began to adopt a more proactive position on issues such as new work organization. The best example is again afforded by the pattern-setting IG Metall, which in the mid-1980s developed its innovative and forward-looking principles of group work for the auto industry (Muster and Wannöffel 1989; Turner 1991, 111–17). By 1988, works councils at most of the major West German auto plants had introduced group work proposals to management and were involved in active negotiations and the establishment of pilot projects. In the history of modern unionism, this was a remarkable step: a union-led, nationally coordinated campaign for innovative work organization in response to changing world markets, managerial drives for rationalization, and shopfloor demands for more responsibility and autonomy.

The labor drive for new work organization did not go uncontested within union ranks. Innovators in IG Metall and other unions faced opposition from traditionalists of both radical and conservative orientation. The traditional radicals feared that proactive collaboration with management on new issues such as work organization would dilute working-class consciousness and union resolve for the class struggle. More conservative traditionalists (perhaps the German equivalent of U.S.-style "business unionists") shared the concern that a proactive campaign could weaken the union's real strength: its ability to promote worker gains and defend worker interests in the face of management opposition.

By the late 1980s, such debates within union ranks had become part of a broader discussion concerning internal union reform (Hoffmann 1988; Armingeon 1989; Hoffmann et al. 1993; Silvia 1993). Although West German unions, unlike those in many other countries, maintained their membership density throughout the 1970s and 1980s, they did so by deepening membership in core manufacturing sectors where they were already strong (Armingeon 1989; Jacobi, Keller, and Müller-Jentsch 1992, 232). It was clear, however, that they were approaching the limits of this strategy, as occupational structures changed and the workforce increasingly included new entrants such as women and young professional, technical, and white-collar workers. Debates broke out within the unions over how to recruit such workers and how to reform the unions as organizations to make them more attractive for the new groups of employees.

By the late 1980s, therefore, major debates and in some cases campaigns of one kind or another were under way for internal union reform. Demands raised in such processes included greater union democracy; a more vital participatory culture; greater participation of women, foreign workers, and white-collar (professional, technical, and service) employees in union leadership and organizational life; and the move beyond traditional wage and benefit demands to new issues of work organization, responsibility, autonomy, enhanced training rights on the job, and new "green" environmental considerations. Another issue promoted by international-minded unionists in the context of the broader reform discussion was the need for West German unions to become more engaged in cross-national labor efforts, especially within the developing single European market.

All of these issues were prominent on the agenda of the DGB and important individual unions by the late 1980s. In some cases, the pressure for reform appeared to come from the top of the union (as at IG Metall and IG Chemie); in other cases pressure came from the rank and file (as at ÖTV; Silvia 1993, 40–45). For many activists, these were campaigns for union renewal against the weight of inertia and traditional resistance to change, and the outcomes of these campaigns would have a major impact on the future influence of organized labor in West Germany.

Despite the pressures for change within both employer and union camps by the late 1980s, relations of social partnership appeared stable. In the pattern-setting metal industry, the 1987 bargaining round (the first since the major 1984 strike) was peacefully resolved in the continuing trade-off between a shorter workweek and more flexible working hours, underpinned by moderate wage gains in a three-year contract. As late as the summer of 1989, neither employers nor unions appeared to have any inkling of the earthquake about to hit. Talk in the metal industry was of a tough bargaining round and possible strike in 1990, as IG Metall prepared its final push toward the 35-hour week while employers grew increasingly resistant in the face of rising costs. In the event, the 1990 round was settled peacefully in the spring, after the wall came down but before unification, in a compromise that extended the general lines of the 1984 and 1987 agreements.[10] As the economy boomed in the late 1980s, employers and unions shared the fruits of social-partnership relations and showed little inclination to attack the other's position. The best predictions were that successful incremental adjustments would continue through processes of negotiation marked by occasional conflict and considerable consensus (Katzenstein 1989).

Social partnership and prosperity moved along nicely together under the Cold War umbrella of international bipolar stability. Germany, like Europe and the world, appeared permanently divided into opposing camps (Gowa 1989). The Iron Curtain sheltered both sides from excessive interaction with different economic systems and levels of development; behind the Wall in the West, momentum toward a single European market gave an added boost to West German prosperity, which appeared to ensure that successful institutions of social partnership would continue to thrive.

THE GROUND TREMBLES

Prosperity in the West not only stabilized existing institutions there but contributed to the demise of the command economies on the other side of the bipolar divide. By the mid-1980s, at precisely the time when western European leaders were worried about "Eurosclerosis" and crafting their single market response, Soviet elites became increasingly aware that their own planned economy could not keep up with dynamic economic development in the West. Gorbachev came to power to loosen up the system with glasnost and perestroika, to pursue reforms that would revitalize the economy. When such reforms eventually deprived other central and eastern European elites of military backing for their repressive regimes, the Iron Curtain crumbled.

The hard-line Honecker regime in East Germany held out as long as it could; once deprived of Soviet backing, however, it collapsed upon its decaying foundations in the face of popular opposition with a suddenness that stunned the world (see, for example, McFalls 1992, 1995; Torpey 1992; Hanhardt 1993; and Hancock and Welsh 1994). In the summer and fall of 1989, East Germans voted with their feet: by the thousands they crossed the border into Czechoslovakia and Hungary, demanding passage to West Germany; additional thousands joined the Monday demonstrations in Leipzig, in bold new public demands for political, economic, and social freedoms.[11] As public opposition mounted in the absence of Soviet intervention, the East German regime finally ran out of options. In a last desperate bid to retain power, the regime allowed the opening of the Berlin Wall on November 9, 1989.[12]

The world changed forever. East and West Berliners greeted each other with champagne, they danced along and upon the wall and chiseled off chunks for souvenirs, they partied all night on New Year's Eve at the Brandenburg Gate. Despite leadership changes, a succession of announced reforms, and highly publicized roundtable discussions among representatives of different groups, the East German regime crumbled quickly. In local elections in March 1990, in their first opportunity to vote in free, western-style elections, East Germans voted for Helmut Kohl's Christian Democratic Party and its promise of quick unification and early prosperity (Singer 1992, 80–81; Hanhardt 1993, 226). On July 1, 1990, currency union between East and West Germany laid the groundwork for formal unification on October 3. The Soviet Union agreed to unification and a graduated schedule for troop withdrawal from East Germany in return for large payments to cover resettlement costs, including new housing for the troops back home. The almost unthinkable had occurred with unimaginable speed.

In this dizzying year euphoria, hesitation, and foreboding stalked the land. Euphoria, because the two Germanys were reunited, families came together, the cruel arbitrary separation was ended, drab daily life under "Realsozialismus" opened up, the stranglehold of the party bureaucrats over political, economic, and social life was broken; hesitation, because no one had planned for this, no one really knew how to put these two now very different parts of Germany back together again; and foreboding, for the westerners because this cataclysmic event threatened to destabilize a well-functioning and prosperous society, and for the easterners because their economy, communities, and social props threatened to collapse as they were thrown into a new market society in which westerners had a huge head start.

This was, in fact, an extraordinary social experiment. As the command economic and political systems of central and eastern Europe collapsed, as new leaders proclaimed faith in political democracy and market economy, large questions arose. Could these countries effect a smooth transition? To what extent would they have to sweep the slate clean of old institutions and actors to start anew; or to what extent could they build on what was there? How long would the necessary reforms take? Could they ever catch up with the West? Different approaches based on different legacies emerged in Poland, Czechoslovakia (soon to divided into two countries), Hungary, Romania, and Bulgaria.[13] Yet here in Germany, while the questions were the same, the situation was unique.[14] Could economically powerful and socially stable West Germany (population 60 million) absorb one chunk of this former Eastern bloc (East Germany, population 16 million)? Could this be done without undermining Western prosperity and stability? Could easterners quickly learn the lessons of political democracy and market economy, adapt them to their own circumstances, and catch up with the West in short order? Would institutional transfer prove to be a viable option?

Many were hopeful and optimistic in 1990. Helmut Kohl and his Christian Democrats won the national elections in December, in the wake of formal unity, on the promise of easy unification, no tax increases in the West, and a "blooming landscape" in the East. Opposition Social Democrats, their candidate Oskar Lafontaine and others, voiced doubts about the cost, the haste, and other possible difficulties of unification. Some suggested that a more gradual approach might make it possible to reform both East and West in a process of compromise that would draw on the strengths of each system. But voices of caution were drowned out in the rush to unification in 1990.[15] The window of opportunity had been opened by Gorbachev, for how long no one knew, and Chancellor Kohl stepped forward to force the pace. Hesitant Social Democrats, Greens, and others came across as naysayers in the face of unprecedented historical opportunity; they were soundly defeated in the 1990 federal elections.

While Kohl may have been right to seize the moment, the Social Democrats and others proved right in their doubts.[16] The costs of unification soon far exceeded the easy promises of an election year. For the West, costs included a massive transfer of institutions, resources, and cash from West to East ($100 billion per year from 1990 on through the decade, paid for by tax increases and massive public debt); for the East, costs included a collapsed economy, mass unemployment, and widespread social dislocation. As became apparent early in 1990, especially after the Christian Democratic election victories in March in the East, this would be no unification of equals or even senior and junior partners. The formal process of unification consisted of the dissolution and dismemberment of the German Democratic Republic (East Germany) into five "new states," which were then incorporated into the German Federal Republic (West Germany). Unification occurred on West German terms, on the basis of West German laws and institutions (Weiss 1991).

THE MODEL: INSTITUTIONAL TRANSFER

The historic task in the years immediately after 1989 was to unite East and West Germany on the basis of political democracy and a market economy. The model chosen was institutional transfer from West to East: a clearing away of existing eastern institutions so that a virtual "colonization" of the East by western institutions could take place (Weiss 1991, 16–17; Baylis 1993).[17] Reality, however, was more complex: institutions were in fact transferred on a large scale from West to East, but this happened in a context of economic collapse, mass unemployment, and the continuing legacy of eastern practices and institutional remnants. Outcomes were various and uncertain, including simultaneous and contending scenarios of prosperity and disaster, of modernization and polarization, of social partnership reinvented in the East and open conflict or demoralization and defeat (Jürgens, Klinzing, and Turner 1993).[18]

Western government, law, banks, employers, and unions moved eastward and implanted themselves quickly in 1990–91.[19] In retrospect, and certainly in comparison to the rest of central and eastern Europe where no such transfer obtained, eastern institutions gave way with extraordinary speed. Local, state, and national governments were rapidly replaced with western structures. The *Treuhandanstalt* was established (originally by the East German regime in its dying months) as a trust agency to take over most of the eastern economy, formerly state owned, for purposes of privatization, restructuring, and liquidation (Kern and Sabel 1991; Seibel 1994). Western banks established branches all over eastern Germany to accept deposits of the lifelong savings of easterners, now converted into western deutschmarks. Western employer associations moved in to organize eastern employers (many of them westerners buying companies from the Treuhand). Western unions, after initial hesitation, moved quickly into the vacuum after the eastern labor federation (*Freier Deutscher Gewerkschaftsbund,* FDGB) collapsed in the spring of 1990. In various ways, each actor facilitated the parallel efforts of others, joined by a common understanding that western institutions and practices should be replicated as closely as possible in the new eastern frontier (Soskice and Schettkat 1993, 117–26).

On paper, the new eastern states quickly achieved political democracy and an institutional framework for the West German variant of a market economy. And for the social partners, the institutions mattered a great deal. Unions, for example, could carry around the Works Constitution Act, ensure that works councils were being set up at firms throughout eastern Germany, and offer their services as trainers and advisers for the new works councillors, most of whom quickly joined the western unions. The institutional framework offered the necessary leverage for the social partners to begin to replicate western practices and their own influence in the East.

There were, however, critical obstacles to smooth institutional transfer.[20] For one thing, western institutions were not designed for the monumental tasks faced in the East, including a complete overhaul and restructuring of the economy (Wiesenthal, Ettl, and Bialas 1992, 29–30). For another, old institutions, their legacies and remnants, continued to exert important influence, from networks of formerly communist managers and unionists to the established practices and expectations in factories and offices. And finally, people do not change their ways overnight. Western employers and unionists who moved eastward to invest or organize found as much trouble adapting their own behavior to the realities they found as did eastern managers, employees, and unionists in the effort to adapt to the new demands of a market economy.[21]

Western Unions Drive Eastward

As soon as the wall came down, West German unionists began to intensify contacts with their counterparts in the East. Initially, the expanded contacts were tentative and exploratory, based on individual and group meetings at various levels of workplace and union interaction. Like all other actors, West German unions were unprepared for the collapse of the German Democratic Republic and the coming unification. Officially, the DGB and its member unions hesitated, unsure of the right strategy in the new circumstances, not wanting to be seen as intervening in the internal affairs of a still sovereign nation and its recognized labor organizations.[22]

Eastern labor union structures, however, gave way quickly in the face of rank-and-file opposition. While workers initially played little role in the upheaval and popular protest of the fall of 1989 (Fuller and Bridges 1992), the opening up of society soon drew them into processes of protest and change, especially in the workplace.

The two essential structures of labor organization in the GDR were the FDGB, the comprehensive labor federation, and the BGL (*Betriebsgewerkschaftsleitung*), the plant union committee. Both were controlled by communist party (SED) members and served as transmission belts for bringing party and government decisions to the workforce. The BGL worked with plant management to meet established goals of production and full employment, as well as servicing worker needs (such as access to vacation homes and childcare) and helping to resolve worker grievances. As the party and government collapsed, these structures were no longer viable, especially as centralized organs of authority.

At an extraordinary congress on January 31–February 1, 1990, the FDGB attempted to save itself through reform, decentralizing its structure into autonomous industrial unions. As a counterpart to the western IG Metall, for example, the FDGB established IG Metall-Ost. DGB unions in the West then negotiated cooperation agreements with their counterparts in the East, to begin to influence the direction of change. As the pace of unification escalated after the March elections in the East, debate intensified within the new union structures. Old leaders were pushed aside or changed their thinking quickly, and in May 1990 the industrial unions in the East withdrew from the FDGB and called for fusion with their western counterparts. The FDGB formally dissolved itself on September 30, 1990 (Fichter 1991, 23–28).

The DGB unions of the West rejected the strategy of fusion, fearful that their ranks would fill up with communists and former Stasi (state police) agents. Applicants for union jobs in the East were processed on an individual basis and were required to sign an oath that they had not worked for the Stasi. From the summer of 1990 through the summer of 1991, the DGB and its sixteen member industrial unions opened offices all over eastern Germany, signed up new members in the millions, and essentially completed the process of formal organizational expansion by mid-1991 (Fichter 1991, 27–28). While western unions pursued various approaches, ranging from close ties with the reformed eastern unions and virtual absorption to exclusion and the building of a wholly new union structure in the East, all of the unions pursued an expansionist strategy as opposed to an amalgamationist one, and all attempted to screen carefully their new eastern hires (Fichter 1993, 4–6).[23]

Formal organizational expansion was an overwhelming success. Indeed, it is hard to think of a historical parallel in which a labor movement so successfully expanded its membership into new territory so rapidly. In hopes of combating pervasive employment insecurity and improving wages and working conditions, eastern workers flocked into the arriving western unions. By the end of 1991, DGB unions had signed up 4.2 million new members in eastern Germany. Although the rapidly changing employment structure in the East made precise union membership density figures for employed workers impossible, it was clear that by 1991 union membership density in the DGB unions in the East exceeded levels in the West (Wiesenthal, Ettl, and Bialas 1992, 23; Fichter 1993, 9).

Meanwhile, in the workplace, rank-and-file activists throughout eastern Germany began efforts, as early as the spring of 1990, to set up western-style works councils. In some cases, old communist BGL leaders were able to change tunes quickly to lead the new initiatives. In most cases, however, BGL leaders were dethroned and new union committees were established or elected to lay the groundwork for works councils and new western-style local unions. With formal unification on October 3, the Works Constitution Act took effect in the East, granting employees there the same rights as existed in western Germany to information, consultation, and codetermination through elected works councils at the plant and firm levels. In the ensuing year, workers established the new works councils and held their first elections at workplaces throughout eastern Germany.

In overwhelming numbers, eastern DGB union members were elected to these new works council positions. In many cases, these were individuals who had been union officials under the communist system, typically (but not always) at the lower or middle levels where they had retained close ties to their fellow employees. For the western DGB unions coming into the East, it would be hard to overestimate the importance of codetermination law and the new works council structures. Western unionists and newly hired eastern staff representatives in the DGB unions received instant access to the eastern workplace through the works councils. Under the law, unions are authorized to train works councillors while employers are obliged to give elected employees time off for such training. Beginning in the fall of 1990 and continuing through the present, the DGB unions have invested major resources in the training of elected eastern works councillors. As is true in the West, these works councillors themselves have typically become the key union activists in the eastern workplaces, thus affording DGB unions important access points both to company decision making and for workforce union recruitment in eastern Germany.

Employer Associations and Collective Bargaining

As western German firms began to buy up chunks of the former East German economy in 1990–91, western employer associations moved in to establish offices in the East. Just as the unions recognized the necessity to organize the East, employer associations understood early on that if they did not move eastward, they could eventually lose their bases in the West (Bispinck 1991). Already in February 1990, the BDA began a broad initiative to move eastward, either by expanding existing western employer associations or by supporting the establishment of new branches. On March 9, the BDA and DGB issued their first joint statement calling for the transfer to the East of the West German collective bargaining system, whose basic structures were in place for the first bargaining rounds in May and June. By the end of 1990, employer associations were established throughout eastern Germany, each affiliated with appropriate sectoral organizations of the BDA (Wiesenthal, Ettl, and Bialas 1992, 11–12).

By contrast to the unions that quickly established higher membership density rates in the East than in the West, employer association membership lagged. In part, this occurred because it took time for private firms to emerge from the former East German economy, either as spin-offs of the Treuhand, management buyouts, or new start-ups. But more importantly, membership problems reflected a lesser need or desire on the part of eastern firms for employer associations, as a result both of high unemployment (which made union strike threats less credible) and the dominance of western leadership in the associations (which made it questionable to many eastern employers, especially the small and medium-sized, just how vigorously eastern interests would be represented).[24] Although membership density data remained confidential, association officials did not dispute the obvious fact that membership rates were too low in the East. In 1993, as we have seen, the shortfall in membership as well as the dissatisfaction of many member firms with their representation in the eastern associations would push Gesamtmetall into an unprecedented collective bargaining campaign against IG Metall.

By the spring of 1991, however, eastern branches of both Gesamtmetall and IG Metall were in place and ready to negotiate a pattern-setting contract for the East. At the core of their discussions, they faced a choice of momentous implications: to hold down wages in the East to maintain employment and encourage western investment, or to bring wages up to western levels quickly to discourage mass migration and prevent the possible permanent polarization of Germany into a high-wage West and a low-wage East. As negotiations developed in these uncharted waters, Gesamtmetall and IG Metall came rather quickly to a consensus around the latter alternative.[25] Unions supported the parity strategy under pressure from their new eastern members and to inhibit the consolidation of a low-wage East that could be used by employers to undermine wages and other labor standards in the West. Western-dominated employer associations backed the parity alternative above all to protect their member firms from low-wage competition in the East. In effect, the agreement to raise eastern pay levels rather quickly up to western levels meant the acceptance by the unions of medium-term high unemployment in the East, to be cushioned by the massive application of active labor market policies (Bosch 1993, 5–6; Soskice and Schettkat 1993, 119–20).[26]

With a minimum of typical strike and lockout threats, Gesamtmetall and IG Metall signed patterned agreements for the five new states of eastern Germany along with eastern Berlin in the spring of 1991. The three-year contracts set nominal wage levels in the East at between 62 and 68 percent of western pay levels, with wage parity to be phased in by 1994 (Bispinck 1993b; Jürgens, Klinzing, and Turner 1993, 233). Given low productivity in the East and a collapsing economy, these pay levels were clearly above what economists refer to as market level (Soskice and Schettkat 1993, 121). On the other hand, these contracts ensured that real wage parity would take a decade or more. Work hours parity was not to be reached until 1998, while actual wage levels in the East remained considerably below the nominal 62–68 percent. This was true because workers in the East were often placed in lower job categories than comparable workers in the West, and because western works councils typically negotiated an additional plant or firm premium of 10 to 15 percent. Real wage parity remained an elusive goal, provoking widespread dissatisfaction among employed eastern workers (Jürgens, Klinzing, and Turner, 233–40).[27]

Parallel negotiations in other sectors followed the general outlines of the metal industry approach, with nominal wage parity to be achieved between 1994 and 1996 (Bosch 1993, 6). The broad pattern of these agreements provoked the same criticisms noted above (and these criticisms from both sides would grow in intensity in the ensuing years): from investors, economists, and the federal government, the criticism that rising wages would stifle investment and generate mass unemployment; from employed eastern workers and union members, the criticism that, although their numbers were being rapidly reduced and they were being asked to work at western standards of performance, they would remain second-class citizens in terms of real wages and working hours. Indeed, both criticisms proved valid. In part because of high unit labor costs in the East, the pace of investment lagged. At the same time, higher pay levels in the West contributed to a much feared exodus of labor from eastern Germany, so that by the end of 1991, 1.1 million (out of 9.8 million formerly employed) easterners had taken jobs in the West (Bosch and Knuth 1992; Bosch 1993, 6).

Institutional Leverage

It is important to reemphasize the leverage afforded western unions by the transfer of the institutions of industrial relations from West to East in unified Germany. The transfer of codetermination law and the election of works councils all across eastern Germany in 1990–91 made the unions immediately capable of offering resources, training, and other benefits of union membership to newly elected works councillors. These individuals, both before and after their election as works councillors, often became the key union activists in the workplace, signing up their fellow workers and establishing a union presence. Under codetermination law, the new eastern works councillors could claim a formal and protected position in the workplace, from which they could both negotiate with management on behalf of the workforce and build up the union.

In a similar vein, the spread of region-based, sectoral collective bargaining to the East served to solidify and legitimize union presence. Although many small and medium-sized employers did not join the employer associations at the outset, most large firms taken over by western investors did. By negotiating regional contracts early on in virtually all sectors for all of eastern Germany, the unions established an important reference point and extensive (if not full) comprehensive collective bargaining coverage for eastern workers. Given the attraction of high wages in the West, rising wage levels in the East, and the easy availability of cushioning labor market instruments (especially unemployment insurance and short-time pay), employers who offered pay levels substantially less than the bargained rates would be hard pressed to find and keep employees, even in circumstances of high unemployment. In the eyes of eastern workers, the new unions quickly became identified as primary advocates of rising living standards.

In the absence of these institutional anchors, it is quite possible to imagine a virtually non-union eastern Germany, given the widespread disillusionment of eastern employees with the communist transmission-belt unions they had known. With the benefit of codetermination law, works councils, and the transfer of sectoral collective bargaining structures, however, unions were in a position to prevent widespread employer adoption of a U.S.-style non-union "southern strategy" approach (Katz 1985, 88–90). If active employee participation was necessary for the rebuilding of the eastern economy (Cheney 1991), the transfer of codetermination rights and union representation established a framework in which such participation could occur.

Economic Collapse

Economic disaster, at least in the short run, was the dominant post-unification reality in the new German states. The collapse of production and employment in the former GDR began with economic and monetary union on July 1, 1990, after which eastern German firms had to sell their products for western deutschmarks (Singer 1992, 88–91). Traditional protected markets in central and eastern Europe and the Soviet Union disappeared. By winter of 1991, vast permanent reductions in personnel had taken place throughout the economy, especially in manufacturing; and in major branches of the economy, over 50 percent of the workforce was on "short-time work" (*Kurzarbeit*), most of these still paid but not working at all.

It would be hard to overestimate the extent of the economic collapse in eastern Germany and its effect on the population there. Between November 1989 and early 1992, industrial output dropped to 30 percent of its former level (Hitchens, Wagner, and Birnie 1993, 86). Real GDP (gross domestic product) for eastern Germany dropped in the same period by 42 percent, and 3 million people lost their jobs (Dornbusch and Wolf 1992, 239–40). By July 1991, 40 percent of the formerly employed eastern workforce was either unemployed or without regular work (Baylis 1993, 83–84).

The collapse in eastern Germany, in contrast to Chancellor Kohl's election-year "blooming landscape" predictions, was linked directly to the sudden coming of the market economy. Thomas Baylis called this "shock without therapy": the economic effect of currency union and rapid unification was "to catapult the GDR's firms and their workers, virtually unprotected, into competition with one of the most efficient and technologically advanced western economies" (Baylis 1993, 80). Eastern industry faced simultaneously the collapse of eastern markets (because currency union priced eastern German goods too high for their formerly most important markets, and because these economies also declined), an implicit revaluation of the East German mark by over 300 percent (the effect of currency union; Herr 1992, 3), and powerful new competition at home from more desirable western products. It was the particular way in which the market economy came to eastern Germany (currency union, revaluation, rapid unification) that ensured economic collapse and serious deindustrialization.

In the short-to-medium run, government economic and labor market policy exacerbated the crisis of production and employment.[28] The *Treuhandanstalt* hoped to stimulate market-led firm restructuring by an emphasis on privatization and massive personnel reduction. Although the Treuhand did succeed in privatizing or liquidating most of the eastern German economy within a few years, the economic and employment crisis persisted.[29]

The biggest short-term problem, and the key factor undermining Kohl's glowing predictions, was the shortage of private capital investment in the eastern economy. Reasons commonly cited for low investment levels fall into three categories: the uncertainty brought on by millions of property claims against eastern plant and real estate (itself a product of government policy that favored restitution of property over compensation); weak infrastructure and institutions of support for a modern market economy; and high unit labor costs, a function both of low productivity and rising wages. German state investment, at DM 54.5 billion in 1992, far exceeded the total private investment, at DM 32.5 billion; at a time of unprecedented need in the East, private investment per capita was actually one-third less there than in western Germany (DM 6,000 versus DM 9,000 in 1992).[30]

Early optimism about the economic and social effects of unification had vanished by 1992 (see, for example, Herr 1992, 3, and Baylis 1993) and showed no signs of an early rebound.[31] Mass unemployment (estimated at 35–40 percent in real terms, including both those covered by government programs and those forced from the labor market) was accompanied by widespread employment insecurity for the remaining workforce (Hickel and Priewe 1994). The disastrous labor-market situation afforded little bargaining power to workers or unions, opening a vacuum of uncertainty and despair in which neo-Nazi skinheads and others could seek out foreign-born scapegoats on which to blame the economic crisis.

In this desperate situation, hopeful developments were hard to find. Unemployment, to cite the most important example, was cushioned by the massive application of active labor market policy: by late 1991, 400,000 people in eastern Germany were participating in government-subsidized training programs, an equal number held temporary positions in job creation schemes, 700,000 had taken early retirement, and another one million had their jobs subsidized by the government through "short-time" work allowances (Herr 1992, 4). More important still in the long run, productivity appeared to be rising rapidly. In a comparative study of thirty-two sample plants in eastern Germany, Hitchens, Wagner, and Birnie (1993, 19) found that underlying productivity increased by 50 percent between June 1990 and June 1991.[32] As a result, unit labor costs, although still higher in eastern Germany than in the West, dropped rapidly in the years after 1990 (Bispinck 1993a, 324–25). A strong case could be made that eastern Germany's skills base (or "human capital stock") allowed for successful development-oriented industrial policy, in contrast to failed long-term efforts in other places such as Northern Ireland and southern Italy.[33]

In a major institutional innovation, representatives of government, business, and labor agreed in July of 1991 to support the development of Employment and Training Companies (ETCs).[34] The idea, developed and promoted by the unions, was to employ laid-off workers at unused plants to set up production and training facilities that could lead to permanent new jobs (in small spin-off firms or on the open labor market) for the displaced. In the wake of the July agreement, ETCs were set up throughout eastern Germany, funded primarily by the Federal Labor Bureau (*Bundesanstalt für Arbeit*, or BA). It remained to be seen whether these ETCs would result in real job creation and training, or mainly serve to disguise long-term unemployment (Knuth 1993, 1997).

Despite the glimmerings of potentially favorable developments in the long term, labor-market realities in the early years after unification remained extremely grim for much of the population. As one would expect in such an unstable situation, the major actors proposed contrasting solutions. Employers, as we have seen, backed away from phased-in wage parity and launched a new offensive to hold down labor costs; at the same time, they demanded incentives and guarantees from the government for increased private investment. Unions demanded comprehensive industrial policy to halt deindustrialization and rebuild the eastern economy; to maintain eastern membership, they also demanded employment security and rising wages. Workers clung to their jobs, often willing to do whatever management asked, and at the same time demanded greater protections and higher wages from their unions and works councils.

A truce of sorts, or a set of mutual understandings, was reached among the major actors in "Solidarity Pact" negotiations that occurred under government auspices between September 1992 and March 1993 (Sally and Webber 1994). The federal government, already committed to massive spending in the East for infrastructure development (roads, railroads, government offices, and the like) and an active labor market policy, extended new investment incentives to business and, in a major concession to the unions, agreed to protect the eastern "industrial core" (Silvia 1993, 9; Nolte, Sitte, and Wagner 1993). Industrial companies that the Treuhand had been unable to sell would be placed into a government-supported holding company rather than liquidated. Local government, unions, and employer associations would participate in decisions concerning which firms to promote and temporarily subsidize in a transition toward market self-sufficiency, to protect both employment and industry in eastern Germany. The federal government in effect agreed to proactive restructuring through industrial policy for the East along the lines of the innovative Atlas program in Saxony (Sally and Webber 1994; Kern 1994; Nolte 1994; Behrens 1995).

In return, unions indicated a readiness to hold down wage demands in both East and West as well as to give full support to the restructuring and realistic market-oriented development of the protected industrial core. Employer associations made explicit commitments to increase investment in and especially orders from eastern firms, and also agreed to participate in regional projects such as Atlas. Chancellor Kohl, who organized the Solidarity Pact negotiations originally proposed by the opposition SPD, agreed with the SPD on tax increases to reduce the budget deficit and in return accepted the SPD's demand for basic protection of welfare-state benefits. In the background, the Bundesbank, critical of the government's failure to cut spending, nonetheless lowered interest rates in response to the prospects of future deficit reduction.

As the actors moved toward broad agreement, there nonetheless remained major areas of conflict in specific policy and implementation. We have already seen the major employer attempt to break through established patterns in the eastern metalworking conflict of 1993. And no matter what was finally (or temporarily) agreed to at the macro level, eastern Germany, even with collapsed institutions and economy, never offered a "clean slate" for economic development. As elsewhere throughout central and eastern Europe, actors found it necessary to build on remnants of the old system (Stark 1992). This was true for institutional transfer from West to East, as employer associations, unions, and government faced new realities and entrenched interests in the East to which organizational policy and structure had to be adapted. It was especially true in cases of major institutional innovation such as Atlas-type industrial policy efforts and the new ETCs: in these cases, new institutions were built directly upon surviving structures from the eastern economy. And it was even true at the level of the individual: as we will see in the case studies presented in Chapter 3, the expectations and habits of both the "old red socks" (former communist functionaries) and the general population stood as embedded realities to which firms and unions would have to adapt.

At the firm and plant levels, employers pursued a variety of strategies in their efforts to build successful enterprises in the new context. Some employers followed a sweatshop approach, treating eastern branches as extended assembly lines for western-directed mass production (Voskamp and Wittke 1991). Other firms saw eastern Germany as a fertile field for experimentation in the most advanced production innovations. In both cases, as well as numerous cases in between, employers increased the pressure on eastern workforces to speed up the pace of work and raise productivity. This pressure, combined with the threat and reality of massive layoffs and unemployment, left employees vulnerable, angry at employers, government, and even unions and works councils unable to provide better protection.

In these uncertain and high-pressure circumstances, conflict ranged widely beneath the surface, even when it did not break out into open warfare. As actors tried out different strategies, coalitions and patterns of conflict shifted, rising and falling. Both eastern and unified Germany appeared to have reached a moment in history in which quite different outcomes were possible. Unlike the postwar decades of relative institutional stability, the early-to-mid 1990s stand out sharply as a period of contingency, in which outcomes became unusually dependent on the decisions and strategies of major actors and their processes of conflict and negotiation.

"Plant egoism" concerns, for example, intensified. In the West German dual system of industrial relations, the interests of plant and firm-oriented works councils could easily diverge from broader working-class and union interests (Streeck 1984a, 1984b; Berghahn and Karsten 1987, 135–39; Hohn 1988). With this system transferred to the East, tensions between works councils and unions could only be magnified when the former were elected from the eastern shop floor while the latter moved in from the West. Contrasting political and economic backgrounds, in other words, aggravated an already present structural tension. Kirsten Wever, among others, argued that East-West tensions were to some extent replacing class or labor-management conflict (Wever 1995, 168–75). The persistence of such centrifugal forces threatened the fabric of social partnership.

"Which way for unified Germany?" became the burning question, from politics, to economics, to civil society, to foreign policy. Workplace case studies presented in Chapter 3 demonstrate the intensity of conflict and negotiation, the ever-present contingency of this moment in German history, as well as various, divergent, and predominant outcomes for economic restructuring and industrial relations.

CHAPTER THREE

Transformation in the East:
Labor-Management Case Studies, 1990–1995

Workplaces in eastern Germany have undergone a profound transformation since 1990. There have been massive layoffs. Publicly owned facilities have been privatized. Middle managers are being retrained. The old union structures have collapsed, to be replaced by western unions. There have been free works council elections. Work has been reorganized. And labor-management relations have been totally reconfigured. The case studies presented in this chapter chart these developments at ten firms in eastern Germany. Although definitive conclusions cannot be drawn from a limited sample of case studies alone, close empirical examinations are essential for getting inside the causal processes at work and uncovering patterns that can be tested more broadly (Mitchell 1983; Belanger, Edwards, and Haiven 1994).

The cases presented here are drawn from the automobile, machinery, and electronics industries. IG Metall is the union that organizes these sectors (known broadly as "metalworking"); Gesamtmetall is the corresponding employer association. Negotiations between IG Metall and Gesamtmetall typically established economy-wide patterns for West Germany in the decades preceding unification; bargaining between these two parties has continued to play a pattern-setting role in eastern Germany and in Germany as a whole since 1990. All but one of the firms examined here was once part of a large conglomerate[1] in the German Democratic Republic; processes of transformation are thus elucidated in these case studies. The cases presented show a range of diversity in process and outcome for firms that survived through the mid-1990s.[2]

ABB Kraftwerke Berlin (Bergmann-Borsig)

Located on the border between East and West Berlin in tree-lined Pankow, Bergmann-Borsig was considered a "model plant" in the German Democratic Republic. As the flagship for a larger conglomerate known as VEB Bergmann-Borsig, this plant had a long and venerable history. A brass plaque on one of the main buildings still proclaims: "At this spot in the November revolution of 1918 Karl Liebknecht called the workers of Bergmann Electrical Works out in support of the movement against militarism and reaction. . . . The working class today carries on toward fulfillment the work of our earlier class heroes" (author's translation).

Producing power plant machinery such as turbines and generators, this sprawling complex employed 4800 when the Treuhand took over in 1990. In September of that year, Bergmann-Borsig was fully privatized when it was purchased by the large multinational firm Asea Brown Boveri (ABB). Downsizing—through layoffs, early retirement, resignation (especially of highly skilled workers who found better-paying jobs in western Berlin), and placement in an employment and training company located on the premises—continued through 1995, at which time 950 employees remained. By 1993, having lost the production of generators and much other equipment, the plant produced mainly turbines and had become, in the eyes of the works councillors, an extended assembly line for the main western German plant at Mannheim.

New top management came in from the West, signed Bergmann-Borsig up for membership in Gesamtmetall, and signaled its intent to follow western industrial relations patterns, including phased-in wage parity and cooperative relations with a newly elected works council. Most middle managers kept on the books were veterans of the old system, the so-called "old red socks," many of them former communist party members or leaders. As at most other privatized firms in eastern Germany, former managers were reemployed, despite their political histories, because the new owners lacked alternative sources for new management. As one works councillor put it, shopfloor workers, especially those laid off, were bitter at the sight of their old bosses still on top; some said the revolution had been too peaceful. On the other hand, according to the same source, many of these people had been "*Scheinkommunisten*" (phony communists), opportunists who could adapt to the new system as they had to the old.

Incoming top ABB management made a commitment to train the remaining workers, bring in new technology, and transform Bergmann-Borsig into a smaller but viable firm in a market economy. Forced to compete with other ABB companies for orders and long-term survival, Bergmann-Borsig was nonetheless given a quasi-monopoly within ABB for its products in eastern Germany. The intent was to improve its prospects for short-term survival by giving it the time it needed for restructuring. Employees were sent to Mannheim to learn modern production techniques, some of them for up to six months. The employees who remained after downsizing were, according to management, highly skilled and eminently trainable in the latest technology and work organization.

Although prospects for firm survival and the remaining jobs appeared good, employees bemoaned the changes that had taken place in their workplace and community. No longer the core workforce of a conglomerate, they felt decidedly subservient to the needs of the Mannheim plant. They claimed that much of their product range had been taken away to protect the viability of the Mannheim plant. Proud of rising productivity and product quality and hopeful that their production would be allowed to increase, they nonetheless felt hemmed in by internal (especially East-West) company politics. While the old socialist "brigade organization" remained to some extent in place, especially its leadership structure (based on the *Vorarbeiter*, or advanced worker who takes the lead in production), employees claimed that the team spirit of the old problem-solving "musketeers" had broken down. Modern production organization at Bergmann-Borsig seemed to these employees to bring a shift *away* from team-work, as each worker sought to do his or her own job well, to shore up personal employment security, to survive in the new capitalist "elbow society." Female employees felt especially hard pressed, as their numbers dropped from 40 percent (in the old days) to 10 percent of the Bergmann-Borsig workforce by 1993. And everyone, it seemed, bemoaned the loss of the extensive community relations and networks that had surrounded this once large and prominent plant.

When the opportunity was presented in 1990, over 90 percent of the workforce joined the incoming western IG Metall. In the first works council elections that same year, twenty-three works councillors were elected and provided training for their new representation work by IG Metall (which all of them had joined). The new works council was composed of a mixture of former union leaders and new faces from the rank and file, and was headed up by Herr Schaffenberg, a veteran of the old union leadership (the BGL) at Bergmann-Borsig. Schaffenberg, a lifetime employee of the plant, was in some ways typical of the type of person who often stepped forward into leadership positions in the new eastern Germany. Although he had served on the BGL for many years, he had never joined the communist party (SED)—because, as he put it, he liked to play organ music in church on Sunday. In 1989, as the corruption of national union leadership became known, Schaffenberg resigned his position on the BGL in protest; his election as head of the first works council at Bergmann-Borsig reflected both the services he had provided and the trust he had won in his past BGL work as well as his principled stand in 1989–90 and the way in which he, so to speak, had joined the revolution. He served as head of the works council until his retirement in 1992, at which time he was replaced by a younger, soccer-playing skilled worker named Wolfgang Bayer, a "new face" who had played no leadership role in the former plant union or management hierarchy.

Because of workforce downsizing, a new, smaller works council of fifteen members, three of them full-time, was elected in 1993, with Bayer reelected as chair. Works councillors expressed great misgivings about their inability to prevent massive layoffs, and they were critical of the new (western) codetermination law that left them powerless to stop severe downsizing. Union membership density dropped from 90 percent in 1990 to 76 percent of the remaining workforce in 1994; and many of those laid off also quit the union, bitterly disappointed at IG Metall's inability to save their jobs. While the drop in union membership density may indeed reflect a corresponding drop in morale as well as faith in the union, works councillors nonetheless pointed with pride to the 76 percent level as one of the highest in Berlin (eastern or western).

Although works councillors spoke harshly about some of the "old red socks" in management (and claimed to have better working relations with top management from the West, who at least understood codetermination rights), the works council and management worked closely together to improve production, secure orders, and save the remaining jobs. According to works councillors, much of their work involved collaboration with management to facilitate changes in production and organization that would increase the prospects for continuing western investment in the plant as well as secure new markets for their products. Five years after the revolution, however, elected works councillors still criticized the authoritarian leadership style of many (old red sock) middle managers, who in their opinion needed both better screening and more retraining in modern leadership styles.

As at many eastern plants, the imperative for labor-management collaboration caused tensions between works council and union in the years immediately following unification. Bergmann-Borsig works councillors in the early 1990s complained that western union leaders and organizers did not fully understand the life-and-death situation faced by eastern firms and workforces. Union calls for militancy and opposition against weekend and night-shift work fell to some extent on deaf ears for a works council in need above all of western investment. Extensive negotiations were required before IG Metall would approve the three shifts management demanded to justify the costs of new machinery. But here as in many other cases in eastern and western Germany, the union proved flexible when faced with economic necessity and company willingness to protect jobs.

Although they belonged to IG Metall and appreciated the support of the union, especially the training provided for their codetermination work, works councillors criticized the union on two grounds. First, they viewed the union as too bureaucratic and undemocratic. They resented some of the directives issued and appointments made by Frankfurt headquarters, which they perceived as often out of touch with their needs. They also objected to the local union (*Verwaltungsstelle*) voting rules, which gave easterners and westerners in Berlin each half of the votes, although eastern membership was considerably larger. Second, they were unhappy with the 1991 contract, as well as its renegotiation in 1993, in which wage, benefits, and working hours parity were to be phased in over the course of the decade. In the view of Bergmann-Borsig workers and their representatives, they were being asked to pay western prices and work at western standards of production at considerably lower rates of real compensation for the foreseeable future.

Works council–union relations within the plant, however, were quite good. Bergmann-Borsig workers were among the first in eastern Germany to establish a working shop steward structure in 1990. Although the size of the steward group dropped with employment numbers, active stewards continued to play an important shopfloor role in cooperation with works councillors (calling problems to the attention of the works council, working out shopfloor problems with management, communicating with the local union). The steward group, in fact, became an important source of innovation when the first steward leader, Gerd Seidel, established an Employment and Training Company (ETC) in 1991 to train and reemploy laid-off Bergmann-Borsig workers. One of the more successful of its kind, this company kept hundreds of workers in the labor market and by 1994 had spun off two innovative production ventures, employing a total of 500 former Bergmann-Borsig employees.

Like many large firms in the East, ABB Kraftwerke Berlin had indicated its willingness to pay the scheduled 26 percent pay raise on April 1, 1993, above all to retain its highly skilled workforce core. Because Gesamtmetall abrogated the contract and unilaterally announced a pay raise of only 9 percent in early 1993, however, the company announced its intention to pay only the 9 percent, in solidarity with other employers. The workforce shocked the company, however, with a successful warning strike, in which two-thirds of the workforce participated, and a large, noisy march on the Pankow town hall. In behind-the-scenes negotiations, company management promised the works council that the 9 percent would be quietly raised to 21 percent.

This left the works council somewhat torn. Employees appreciated the strong stand that IG Metall was taking in defense of eastern pay parity and wanted to back the strike. On the other hand, why mobilize the workforce for a risky strike effort when an acceptable pay raise had already been promised at Bergmann-Borsig? In the end, although this plant was on IG Metall's A list for the strike, the full May strike never came to Berlin-Brandenburg, much to the relief of the works council. But IG Metall's willingness to strike in support of eastern demands impressed many and helped to sustain high union membership at a time when free fall seemed likely.

One of the biggest changes for this plant in the transition to a market economy and the accompanying process of privatization was the shift from core-plant status in a large conglomerate to the much-reduced status of one among many, competing for orders within a large multinational corporation. Earlier, the works council at the German "mother" plant had secured an agreement that protected production and jobs in Mannheim. But this worked to the detriment of the workforce at the former Bergmann-Borsig, a new player within the multinational, who watched Mannheim get the production orders. In 1994, the head of ABB Berlin's works council, now also a member of the company supervisory board, viewed negotiation of an employment security agreement for the remaining employees as a top priority.

KNORR-BREMSE BERLIN (BERLINER BREMSENWERK)

When Germany was divided after the second world war, Berliner Bremsenwerk remained in East Berlin while the parent firm, Knorr-Bremse—a railroad brake parts manufacturing firm dating back to 1905—relocated to Munich in the West. For much of the postwar period, Berliner Bremsenwerk produced mainly locomotive, freight, and passenger car brakes for markets in the Soviet bloc, employing 1600 blue- and white-collar workers in 1990. In February of 1991, Berliner Bremsenwerk was privatized through repurchase by its old parent Knorr, still based in Munich but now a multinational concern.

As was the case at many eastern manufacturing firms, the new eastern Knorr-Bremse branch faced two critical problems: the collapse of eastern markets and, by western standards, obsolete technology and production organization. Between 1990 and 1995, Knorr-Bremse in eastern Berlin was modernized with new machinery, employment dropped from 1600 to 400, and production was reoriented toward markets in the West, especially for locomotive brake production required by the Bundesbahn and other western firms. By 1994, the former Berliner Bremsenwerk was hardly recognizable, having moved to a new location where modern production techniques relied on new equipment—94 percent of it under five years old (contrasted to 86 percent of the machinery over five years old in the former plant). Productivity levels had risen dramatically, as 400 workers delivered approximately the same total production in 1994 as 1600 workers had in 1990. And new production levels included a continuing commitment to training and retraining; Knorr-Bremse Berlin in 1994 counted forty apprentices among its workforce.

A few top managers from the West came in to oversee production reorganization and to rehire and retrain many of the former eastern managers; by 1994, it had become clear to all that the easterners themselves could manage Knorr-Bremse's rejuvenated operation in the East. As elsewhere, eastern workers resented many of the old bosses and their positions of power in the new system. By the mid-1990s, however, this tension eased as both workers and managers internalized their new rights and responsibilities and worked together to raise productivity and keep investment flowing into the plant.

According to management, an important element of stability in labor-management relations at this plant was derived from the election of the former head of the BGL, Bodo Krause, as chair of the new works council in 1990. Although referring to himself as an "old red sock" and admitting that he would never have the full confidence of the workforce, Krause changed with the times, argued for the interests of the workers during the transition to the new system (as he claimed to have done under the old system), and won enough trust from the rank and file to get elected and reelected to lead the works council through the traumatic years of downsizing, relocation, and reorganization. In May of 1994, Krause was reelected works council chair by a 74 percent vote.

An energetic and engaged leader, Krause passed information back and forth between management and the workforce, pushed management to reorganize and accept new ideas and policies, and helped to mobilize the workforce for the new commitment to high production levels that was now expected. His efforts variously brought him into conflict with the union as well as particular managers and workers. Krause, for example, in 1990–91, actively supported management's drive to raise production levels; this meant a willingness to work three shifts and weekends to make the investment in new machinery pay off, and to demonstrate that such investment in the future would be cost effective. The willingness of the works council to accept such long working hours, however, brought it immediately into conflict with IG Metall, which Krause and most of his fellow workers had joined in 1990. Although resentful of union pressure (both from westerners and from easterners now employed by IG Metall), Krause fought his way through to win the support of the union for the short- to medium-term expansion of working hours at Knorr-Bremse.

With downsizing, the works council had dropped from fifteen members to nine by 1993, including four white-collar and five blue-collar workers and a mix of "old red socks" and new people. Both works councillors and managers claimed to have close working relations with each other and a good ability to resolve problems both formally and informally. Works councillors were particularly proud of the substantial "social plan" payments secured for laid-off employees; based on age, years of service, and pay level, these payments averaged DM 11,000, with some employees getting up to DM 30,000. Of the original 1600 employees at Berliner Bremsenwerk in 1989, 400 had been temporary foreign workers (from other socialist countries such as Cuba, Mozambique, Poland, and Vietnam). They were the first laid off (many to return home); the rest left for better jobs in the West, took early retirement, or were laid off with social-plan payments. As a result, argued works councillors, there had been no need for an employment and training company at Knorr-Bremse in eastern Berlin. In January of 1994, the works council and management signed an agreement guaranteeing the remaining 400 jobs through 1995.

Having developed good working relations with the local union, works councillors in 1993 helped establish an elected shop steward structure in the plant, although it was difficult to find people to step forward for these positions in a period of continual workforce downsizing. Driven by disillusionment both with union inability to prevent layoffs and a contract that kept them underpaid compared to western Berliners, union membership density dropped to around 50 percent of the workforce (a bit higher among blue-collar workers, a bit lower among white-collar) by 1993. Meanwhile, Bodo Krause was elected as one of two eastern members of Knorr-Bremse's general works council, itself composed of representatives from all eight company plants in Germany (five in the West, three in the East).

In early 1993, the works council at Knorr-Bremse Berlin negotiated with management for implementation of the 26 percent raise scheduled for April 1. As a member of Gesamtmetall, however, the company soon found itself under pressure to pay only the 9 percent and announced its intention to stand with other metalworking industry employers. As elsewhere, workers here were furious about this perceived betrayal, the rescinding of a promised pay raise that would help push them up toward western levels. At Knorr-Bremse Berlin, where they had worked long hours to secure the latest equipment, employees and works councillors argued that their productivity approached and even sometimes exceeded that of the Munich flagship plant; the highly skilled and productive employees who made up the remaining workforce of 400, many of whom had been retrained at Munich and who could therefore see the comparison first hand, bitterly objected to their second-class treatment. Krause predicted that if IG Metall surrendered on the pay-equity issue and/or lost the coming strike, union membership density at his plant would collapse.

Although not called upon to strike in May of 1993, the workforce here nonetheless worked closely with the local union office to put on an impressive display of solidarity in a brief warning strike on April 15. The union's willingness to fight for eastern workers in April and May, and the growing strike in Saxony and Mecklenburg-Pomerania that looked set to spread to Berlin-Brandenburg in mid-May, impressed the workforce at Knorr-Bremse. Although people were not happy with the strike settlement and its two-year extension of phased-in wage parity, the strike nonetheless strengthened IG Metall ties to the works council and, according to works councillors, helped stabilize union membership density in the year following the strike.

In 1993 and 1994, the works council and management at Knorr-Bremse Berlin signed several agreements to establish and regulate a new structure of group work for all 400 employees. Groups included eight to ten members and a group leader jointly selected by management and the works council. Extensive negotiations concerning pay levels for group members proceeded on two principles: that no one should receive less pay than before when placed in a group, and that bonuses would be based on group (not individual) performance. The group work experiment here was viewed by the company as a pilot project for the 6,000 Knorr-Bremse employees worldwide.

Works councillors were enthusiastic about the coming of group work. Krause claimed strong workforce support for this partial return to a more collective form of work organization, building on the spirit of the old brigades. The Berlin workforce, he argued, could adapt to this new structure much faster than workers at the Munich flagship plant, accustomed as the latter were to more individualistic traditions in the workplace. The legacy of a collective spirit and history, joined to modern skills, technology, and work organization, placed this plant in a potentially forerunner role for coming group structures of production. Of the cases considered in this study, Knorr-Bremse Berlin provided the most explicit and comprehensive example of modern production organization building not from scratch but upon practices inherited from the preexisting system of organization.

By the mid-1990s, Knorr-Bremse Berlin could be characterized as a modern plant with advanced technology and work organization, run fully by eastern management and a highly skilled and productive eastern workforce, with close and cooperative labor-management relations, a moderate level of union membership density with reasonably good relations between the works council and the union, and good prospects for future market success as the economy climbed out of recession. The main elements of both successful production and firm-level social partnership appeared to be in place. Developments here offered support for Krause's prediction that the East would in time be the site of unified Germany's most modern industrial production.

NILES

The 7 Oktober Kombinat, based at the "Niles" plant in East Berlin's Weissensee district, was a highly regarded producer and exporter of modern machine tools. The flagship plant, known informally throughout the GDR's history by its earlier British name (Niles), employed 2250 people in 1989. When the core plant was separated from the Kombinat to become a Treuhand enterprise in 1990, "Niles" became the official name, and employment dropped to 1750. Because most of its export markets were in the West and in Japan and other Asian countries (with only 35 percent of its export markets in eastern Europe and the Soviet Union), this plant was considered a good prospect for continued success in a market economy. Nonetheless, Treuhand negotiations with various groups of western investors dragged on, fell through, and started up again, so that Niles was not finally privatized until May of 1993.

During the three-year Treuhand period, uncertainty about future ownership made it difficult for the company to secure credit for new machinery or to find new markets for its products. Waves of workforce reduction accompanied prolonged negotiations with prospective buyers, so that by 1994, total employment at Niles was down to 410. Although little new machinery had been added since 1990, most of the equipment was reasonably up to date (since this flagship plant had been a major source of hard currency investment under the GDR), and the remaining workforce was highly skilled. Although worldwide demand for Niles products had fallen in half (with recession and the collapse of eastern markets), the company continued to sell machines in thirty-five countries while actively attempting to locate and open new markets.

As at other surviving eastern plants, downsizing occurred through early retirements, layoffs that included social-plan payments, and attrition as workers left for better-paying jobs in the West (mainly western Berlin). Works councillors spoke proudly of their successful efforts to apportion social-plan payments upward and downward from a base of DM 5,000, according to years of service, skill levels, and other criteria.

In addition to clearing out "nonproductive" service workers (in areas such as food service, library, recreation, and administration), eastern management at this plant studied advanced production techniques, paid for advice from western consulting firms such as McKinsey, and pushed the productivity of its remaining workforce steadily upward. Turnover per capita increased from DM 60,000 in 1991 to DM 100,000 in 1994, with plans on the books to raise it further to DM 200,000.[3] The productivity-enhancing reorganization of work included new concepts such as production islands and group work, among a well-informed and highly skilled workforce bound together in a common struggle for survival in a market economy. Managers and works councillors alike claimed that new group-based organization functioned well on the base of the former brigade spirit.

Unlike Bergmann-Borsig and Berliner Bremsenwerk, Niles was not taken over by a western parent firm. Throughout its Treuhand years and even after it was purchased by a group of investors in 1993, this company retained eastern top management along with a consciously "eastern" labor-management collaboration intent on proving itself in the new circumstances. Works councillors expressed faith in the remaining eastern top management and personnel directors, people with long plant histories and good technical skills. The former head of the union BGL now worked in personnel, an example of the "old red socks" middle manager who knew the company and its workforce well and with whom works councillors claimed to have good working relations. In a case study of Niles that focused on production organization, Gerlinde Dörr and Stefan Schmidt identified the "production intelligence" of these technically skilled plant veterans as a major asset in the transformation to new work organization (Dörr and Schmidt 1992). A successful transformation, they argued, such as the one at Niles, must not only clear out the obsolete but must above all build on the strong "innovation and know-how potential" of the inherited skilled workforce. Although uncertainty and lack of investment during the Treuhand years had undermined much of the potential, Niles continued to find strength in the surviving managers who had come up through the skilled ranks and understood the shopfloor potential for innovation and teamwork.

The original works council elected in 1990 had fifteen members, three of them full-time. As a result of substantial downsizing, new elections in November 1992 established a council of nine members, only one full-time. Although all works councillors belonged to IG Metall, relations between the Niles works council and the Berlin IG Metall proved difficult. The works council saw its main mission very clearly as working with personnel, top, and middle management as well as the workforce to ensure the survival of Niles as a company in the market economy. Although respectful of the union and its broader perspective, the works council commitment to IG Metall and its policies clearly came second after the close relationship to the company.

Niles demonstrates the tension within the dual system that has long been identified in western Germany as "plant egoism": the tendency for works councils to place the needs of their own companies above the more general class interests promoted by the comprehensive industrial union. In contrast to countless predictions (from Neumann 1951 to Hohn 1988), this tension did not seriously weaken unions or undermine industrial relations in West Germany. Not only did the tension prove manageable, the dual channels of representation, collective bargaining outside the company and codetermination inside the company, offered the resilience of negotiated adjustment to companies, unions, and German social partnership (Thelen 1991). In eastern Germany, however, where the unions came in from the West to interact with newly elected eastern works councils, contrasting political and economic histories as well as contemporary interests threatened to exacerbate the tensions inherent in the structures of social partnership (Jürgens, Klinzing, and Turner 1993, 239–40). This is exactly what has happened at Niles.

Although at the time 70 percent of the workforce, including all nine works councillors, belonged to IG Metall, the Niles works council did not support the strike actions of April and May 1993. The works council chair went so far as to block attempts within the plant to organize a warning strike for April 1. At a subsequent IG Metall meeting, the Niles group was denounced as the only one in its area that did not join the mass actions of April 1.

In the face of such pressure, the works council chair stood firm, claiming that the plant had orders to fill, that a strike would be a disaster for both sides, and that at Niles they were fighting for the jobs of their workers, most of whom were over forty and would have few other opportunities for employment. Although Niles belonged to Gesamtmetall, the company, in order to preempt a strike, "split the difference" between the employers' unilateral reduced raise of 9 percent and the contractual 26 percent, giving the employees a 16 percent raise (the 9 percent plus a plant premium of 7 percent negotiated with the works council).

Ordinarily, an important plant such as Niles would have been on the union's A list of plants to be targeted in the opening wave of May strikes. Given the opposition of the Niles works council, however, IG Metall placed Niles on the B list, to be called out later if and when the strike escalated beyond the A list. As it happened, the strike was won by the solidarity of A list plants in Saxony and Mecklenburg-Pomerania, while the employees and their works council at Niles worked right on through without even a warning strike, defending the plant's reputation for a highly skilled and cooperative workforce worthy both of the orders it was getting for its products and its imminent sale by the Treuhand to a group of private investors.

Although the workforce at Niles benefited from the new contract signed as a result of the strike (since Niles is a member of Gesamtmetall), union presence at the plant remained weak. As of 1994, there was still no shop steward structure in the plant, although union membership density had stabilized around 70 percent. Reflecting the popularity of its plant-based strategy, all nine members of the works council were reelected in 1994; the incumbent works council chair received a strong endorsement with a vote of over 80 percent. Relations between the company and its works council, by contrast, remained close. Although conflicts arose regularly and were hammered out in negotiations, the relationship continued to be characterized as collaborative, held together by a common interest in company success. By 1994, the CEO and works council chair had established a pattern of regular weekly meetings to discuss company and workforce concerns. With its world market position and its highly skilled and motivated workforce, Niles appeared a good prospect for future success as a streamlined plant reorganized around advanced production techniques.

EL PRO

Pulled together from several pieces of a large electronics company in eastern Berlin's Marzahn district (part of the former Kombinat VEB Starkstrom), El Pro survived the obsolescence of many of its industrial electronics products as a much streamlined company specializing in plant construction (especially hot and cold rolling mills).

Siemens and AEG, two large and well-established western firms, each negotiated with the Treuhand for a possible purchase of El Pro in 1990–91. When both efforts came to naught, these companies, as potential competitors, left El Pro employees convinced that they had been used: Siemens, in particular, in the eyes of works councillors and others, had used the time to delay other possible investment at El Pro, to learn all about the company, and to lure away some of the best managerial and skilled talent, before purchasing a competing VEB Starkstrom plant in Rostock instead of El Pro in Berlin. After an employee effort to organize a management buyout (MBO) failed to win support from the Treuhand, El Pro was finally sold to an investment group organized by the McKinsey consulting firm in 1992 and restructured as a so-called Holding, subdivided into a Control and Power group, another group called El Pro GmbH, and other smaller groups including two outside firms added to the new complicated structure.

With total employment down from 7400 to 1600 by 1994, El Pro's workforce was a highly qualified mix of skilled workers, engineers, and a streamlined staff of clerical employees and administrators. Like most eastern manufacturing firms, this company faced immediate market problems as a result of the collapse of eastern markets, recession in the West, and the unsuitability of many of its products for western markets. Sales dropped dramatically from 1991–92 levels, before rising substantially again in 1993. Employment stabilized after privatization, while sales shifted from eastern European markets to eastern and western Germany. Major efforts were made to develop new markets in countries such as China, South Korea, Russia, and Ukraine.

High-level managers were hired from the West to help turn the company around, especially by reorganizing production and developing new market strategies. As everywhere in the East, however, the great majority of middle managers and some top managers as well were in the beginning the same people who had run the plant under the old system. In the eyes of incoming western managers, elected works councillors, and the eastern managers themselves, these people proved adaptable, above all because of their professional competence: they were for the most part engineers and/or highly trained technicians.

In the two years prior to privatization, however, considerable tension developed between these remaining managers and the newly elected works councillors. The latter, made up mainly of highly trained employees who had not been part of the communist union structure, criticized the "old red socks" in management for their willingness to go along with whatever Siemens, AEG, or other potential western investors demanded. Some works councillors, by contrast, from new bases in IG Metall and the local Social-Democratic Party, pushed in the broader political arena (especially city government) for a state-supported industrial policy that would develop a modern electronics sector in eastern Germany. Such activists supported the idea of a management buyout and a broad vision of the company's future size and market position.

Works councillors claimed that by the time privatization took place, these efforts had failed for a number of reasons: lack of support for such industrial policy from the federal government in Bonn; the efforts of Siemens and AEG, working through the Treuhand, to prevent the rise of strong, competing firms in the East; the failure of IG Metall to develop a strong politics of industrial policy for the East and lead mobilizations in defense of eastern jobs; the passivity of El Pro managers in negotiations with western investors; and the inadequate co-determination rights granted the works council under western law. By 1992, highly motivated works councillors with an expansive vision for the company's future expressed great disappointment at their inability to influence the company's strategic development and direction. In particular, the works council resented its marginalization from key negotiations and decisions by the Treuhand concerning the company's future.

The "old red socks" problem was finally solved in a distinctive way at El Pro. As a result of corporate downsizing, a considerable number of western managers from competing AEG became available (either because of layoff or the fear of layoff). Top management at El Pro decided that although El Pro middle managers were trainable, the company would do better to buy them out (with severance payments) and hire AEG people, who were already fully trained and experienced in the cost-accounting techniques of a capitalist enterprise in a market economy. Within a year, most of the "old red socks" managers had been replaced in this way, so that by mid-1994, top management as well as the ranks of upper middle management consisted with only a few exceptions of experienced western managers.

By 1993–94, works councillors, managers, and remaining employees appeared to have accepted the company's more modest size and market aspirations. Future employment and sales prospects were enhanced by the commitment of the western owners to construct a new plant at a new location, scheduled to open for production in May of 1995. Sales continued to rise as the recession in the West ended and new markets were developed.

Union membership (in IG Metall) had been close to 100 percent in the early months after unification. As elsewhere, however, support waned as the union was unable to prevent massive downsizing and layoffs. In contrast to the situation at Niles, however, works councillors maintained close relations to the Berlin IG Metall office, reserving their criticism for national and regional union levels where strategy was seen as inadequate for the restructuring of eastern industry and where decisions such as the development of policy and the appointment (rather than election) of district leaders was seen by many at El Pro as undemocratic. Works councillors were enthusiastic when the local IG Metall hired a full-time expert on restructuring and new technology to advise works councils in Berlin; but they viewed this as a drop in the bucket compared to the need.

It is a telling statement on the perceptions of the works councillors regarding their own inability to influence the course of events in a period of dramatic change that by 1993, two engineers who had played central roles on the works council ever since the first election in 1990 were considering not running for re-election. Both saw their futures at the company, but one intended to become more active in the local IG Metall and the other planned to pursue a parallel political career through the SPD. The former carried through on this decision and in 1994 was both a group leader (lower-level management) at work and an elected member of the IG Metall local council; the latter changed his mind when the company restructured and was elected head of the works council at El Pro GmbH (one of the companies that made up the new El Pro Holding). The new group included nine elected works councillors, all IG Metall members; in the wake of company restructuring, this body worked with other El Pro Holding works councils to build a general works council to represent the common interests of the diverse groups within the larger corporate structure.

Employees at El Pro shared the common eastern anger at Gesamtmetall's cancellation of the scheduled 26 percent pay raise on April 1, 1993. Although the company belonged to the association, employees viewed the betrayal as an external one, dictated from the West. They supported IG Metall in its mobilization efforts, with large-scale participation in one-hour warning strikes at El Pro on both April 1 and April 14. Reflecting the collective spirit of company loyalty at El Pro and the need to fulfill orders to keep the company's production growing, however, most employees worked an extra hour without pay in the evening to compensate for the work lost. In a pattern not at all uncommon in eastern Germany in the period after unification, El Pro employees showed strong support *both* for the company and for the union during the labor conflict of 1993. El Pro was on the union's A list; expectations among both managers and works councillors indicated that employees would have overwhelmingly supported the strike had it spread to Berlin-Brandenburg in mid-May as anticipated.

Although the solidarity of the warning strikes and subsequent strike preparation strengthened commitment to the union through the remainder of 1993, continued downsizing soon led to renewed disillusionment; by mid-1994, IG Metall membership had dropped to 60 percent of the workforce, high by the standards of the electronics industry in western Germany but a substantial drop from virtually full unionization in 1990.

SIEMENS IN ROSTOCK

The new Siemens branch in the northern port city of Rostock was formed by combining two established plants, one specializing in electrical installation, the other in radio and telecommunications installation. Like El Pro, these plants had been part of the East German conglomerate VEB Starkstrom. After a brief period as Treuhand firms, both plants were taken over by Siemens in the fall of 1990 and purchased (and severed of the Treuhand connection) in March of 1991. Where before these plants had employed 2200 between them, the total by 1994 had dropped to 870 blue- and white-collar workers employed in the preparation, installation, and servicing of electrical systems for factories and office buildings.

For the highly skilled workforces at these two Siemens plants, the biggest problem in 1994, as for so much of eastern industry, was business: forced to compete for orders with modern Siemens plants in the West, the Rostockers found their low-cost and location advantages undercut by much lower costs to the east in Poland and south in the Czech Republic. To head off further layoffs in a continuing economic recession, the works council embarked on negotiations with management in 1994 for a new agreement (following the widely publicized "VW model"—see Chapter 6) to reduce both working hours and pay temporarily in exchange for employment security.

The big story at Siemens in Rostock, however, and a continuing source of pride for the works councillors, was the successful strike action of May 1993. As at other eastern workplaces, the strike here was the first major test since German unification of the ability of IG Metall to mobilize the workforce, as well as a test of the relationship between the works council and the union.

Elected works councillors at Siemens in Rostock included several blue- and white-collar workers who had played activist roles against the old company leadership during the economic and political transformation of 1989 and 1990. Some of the newly elected works councillors had been unionists under the old system, but none of them had been BGL leaders. They had all joined IG Metall and developed close relations with the local union office. At the same time, their primary tasks had been to work with management for the benefit of the firm, to promote the upgrading of workforce skills, and to negotiate the terms of large-scale downsizing. As all successful works councillors must, they had learned to work with and acquire information from multiple sources, including plant management, the local union (where they had secured elected representation on the

63

executive committee), the company supervisory board (where they also had representation under codetermination law), and the Siemens general (company-wide) works council, to which their works council chair had been elected. At a time of major restructuring during which they had to learn their new responsibilities under fire, works councillors found themselves in highly stressful jobs from the very start in 1990.

One of their few secure anchors was the three-year wage-parity agreement negotiated by IG Metall and Gesamtmetall in 1991. When that agreement was unilaterally broken by the employer association in early 1993, when Siemens, an active member of Gesamtmetall, announced its intention to pay the much-reduced pay raise on April 1 (down from 26 percent to 9 percent) with no supplemental plant premium (as Rostock shipyard workers, for example, had been offered), works councillors along with most of the workforce at Siemens in Rostock reacted with anger and disillusionment. What was the point of all their information, discussion, planning, and negotiation, they asked, if such a pivotal agreement could so easily be broken? Siemens, they knew, was a highly profitable firm with a strong voice in Gesamtmetall. The works councillors in Rostock, several wearing new hats as strike committee members, channeled their frustration and anger into preparations for the coming warning strikes, strike votes, and full-scale strike action.

They received important support in the form of advice, training, and logistics from the local IG Metall, whose elected chair Rüdiger Klein was an easterner (unlike the majority of imported western local chairmen in eastern Germany in this period) and strong supporter of the strike. Nonetheless, because this was a first-time event for all of them—there had been no legally sanctioned collective bargaining strikes in eastern Germany since Hitler's rise to power in 1933—the strike organizers at Siemens really had no idea what kind of support they could expect from their members. They stood before the main door on April 2, 1993, a few minutes before the scheduled 11 A.M. warning strike, having heard that management that morning had tried with thinly veiled threats to persuade employees not to participate, wondering if their colleagues would in fact come out on strike. As we have seen, large numbers, around 250 according to the works council, emerged at the appointed hour to join the march to the shipyards and subsequent mass demonstration. According to works councillors a year later, this event and the subsequent strike tied workforce representation at Siemens in Rostock to IG Metall in a relationship of loyalty and mutual commitment far exceeding that found at most western Siemens plants (given typical relative union weakness in the electronics industry).

A second warning strike in mid-April yielded a similar result in numbers and an even more impressive effect: warning strikers this time drove their cars to the shipyard rally in an enormous traffic-blocking, horn-honking parade, followed by a march on foot through the neighboring coastal town of Warnemünde, to the widespread spontaneous applause of local residents. Now viewed as a bastion of IG Metall strength, the Siemens workforce was rewarded with a high spot on the union A list for the upcoming strike. After a strike vote of over 90 percent (according to works council estimates)[4] in late April, the Siemens workforce was called out on May 4 for a strike that would last here for twelve working days until the return to work on May 19.

About two-thirds of the Siemens workforce joined the strike, with the overwhelming majority of these remaining on strike until the end. Crucial to the success of the strike was a massive demonstration of 300 employees in front of the main door on the first day, followed by daily displays of spirited picketers wearing bright red strike mantels. Since several of the leaders of the strike at Siemens were women, they made a point of standing each morning directly in front of the entrance, reasoning that it would be harder for strikebreakers to push women out of the way than men. To the very end, the personnel director stood directly behind them, attempting to persuade people to come back to work. Women on the front lines were taunted by aggressive strikebreakers, who reminded them, for example, that Joan of Arc had ended up on the stake.

In circumstances of daily conflict and with minimal strike pay taking its toll in adverse economic conditions—in which most families now lacked a second income at home to fall back on—equally crucial to the success of the strike was outside support. On the second day of the strike, Franz Steinkühler, national president of IG Metall, and Heinz-Werner Meyer, president of the DGB, visited the picket line at Siemens in Rostock to show their support. More important still, local Rostock supporters arrived daily with food and money. From the non-striking Siemens plant in Greifswald, for example, ten buses, bearing 400 warning strikers, arrived one day to demonstrate their solidarity.

All of this support was necessary, according to strike leaders at Siemens in Rostock. When the settlement came, it came none too soon for strikers whose personal finances were in shambles and who were nearing the breaking point. Although workers at Siemens voted to accept the settlement and return to work, the agreement did not contain all that they had hoped (above all wage parity by 1994). Shipyard workers wanted to reject the settlement and stay out on strike. Debate was spirited within the local IG Metall among representatives from many different workplaces who had fought hard for this victory; the agreement was finally accepted by a vote of around 60 percent in Rostock.

Employees at Siemens returned to work not celebrating but nonetheless proud of what they had accomplished. As is often the case in such situations, tensions endured between the two-thirds who had gone out on strike and the one-third who had not. In one assembly shop, for example, out of a workforce of twenty-five, three had crossed the picket line to continue to work; a year later, these three continued to eat lunch at a table where no one else joined them.

Despite what was widely perceived as a victory for IG Metall but a mixed outcome for employees (with wage parity for eastern workers defended but stretched out from 1994 to 1996), the strike clearly cemented union loyalty among activists and works councillors while solidifying their base among the rank and file. As a result of cumulative downsizing over the preceding three years, new elections were held for a smaller, consolidated works council in the fall of 1993. Where there had previously been two works councils—with fifteen members at one plant and nine at the other—there was now one works council for both plants with a combined total of fifteen members. Although three contending slates of candidates were put forward in the consolidation vote, all of those elected were IG Metall members and all had supported the strike. Through the mid-1990s, they remained committed unionists, working closely as a group with the local IG Metall office. For the entire workforce, union membership in 1994 was 65 percent, a level considerably higher number than that at comparable Siemens plants in western Germany.

By the summer of 1994, however, the luster of strike victory had worn thin in the eyes of works councillors, in the face of two so far intractable problems. The first of these was the continuing prevalence and insensitive authority of the "old red socks" throughout the ranks of middle management. Works councillors spoke favorably of top managers from the West who pushed reorganization and a modern logic of proactive participation and teamwork for the workforce. Although they also claimed to work well with younger western managers sent to prove themselves in troubled locations (such as central and eastern Europe, developing countries, and Rostock), they resented the temporary, "carpetbagging" nature of these assignments in which authority at their plant was given to twenty-five-year-olds. But above all, they resented the authority of the former communist bosses who had managed to hang on at Siemens. These men had been shaped in a system in which they received and passed on orders; works councillors claimed that this is what they continued to do in the new system, thereby undermining attempts by top managers, workforce representatives, and employees to build a new participatory culture on the remains of the old.

The second and most serious problem was continuing market weakness and a corresponding downsizing that knocked off another 20 percent of the workforce in the eighteen months following the strike (bringing it down to 870). Although the works council promoted social-plan payments and insisted that people had to leave voluntarily, the pressure of continuing workforce reductions took a heavy toll on the morale of works council and workforce alike. To stop the hemorrhaging of a skilled workforce and preserve an adequate core upon which to build for the future, the works council in 1994, with the support of the local IG Metall, entered into negotiations for an employment security agreement. For 300 of the remaining workers, the idea proposed was that management could reduce working hours by up to 20 percent along with pay by a corresponding but somewhat lower amount. In return, workers would have their jobs protected for a two-year period; if they were laid off after that time, they would receive the total amount of foregone compensation in a lump sum. This new employment security agreement at Siemens, a possible forerunner of a future region-wide IG Metall–Gesamtmetall framework agreement, was based on both the reduced working time agreement at VW of fall 1993 and the employment security provisions of the western metalworking settlement of spring 1994 (see Chapter 6). Viewed as the best possible outcome by Siemens works councillors in 1994, the agreement was nonetheless a bitter pill to swallow for employees facing a reduced income. While the union and works council pursued these negotiations in order to save jobs, they would also share responsibility for resulting lower incomes.

Rüdiger Klein, head of IG Metall in Rostock and a close ally of the works councillors at Siemens, could take credit for leading an impressive strike victory in his area in 1993 and greatly boosting the prospects for his union. At the same time, it was clear to him a year later that continuing downsizing with its corresponding job and income insecurity was an issue that swamped all others. If employment numbers continued to drop, if the union was forced to negotiate widespread job-saving agreements as at Siemens, the union, although temporarily strengthened by the strike, would surely get weaker—both in numbers and in workplace influence. Downsizing and deindustrialization had caused IG Metall membership in Rostock to drop from its peak of 26,000 in 1990–91 to 16,000 by 1994; and of the remaining 16,000, half were unemployed (thus paying only token dues while contributing nothing to union influence in the plants). In severe labor market circumstances, firms could continue to make demands on their works councils, bringing the latter more and more under firm influence and farther away from the reach of the union, who could only help negotiate the terms of layoffs or conditional employment security. At the same time, there was little to prevent small and medium-sized firms from leaving or failing to join the employer association, thereby escaping from the terms of IG Metall-Gesamtmetall contracts and undermining the future of social partnership regulation.

With these continuing dangers in mind, Rüdi Klein threw his hat into the ring as a candidate for the Rostock city council in 1994, to strengthen the political influence of IG Metall. Inspired by the success of projects such as the active employment and training companies in Rostock and the new Treuhand holding concept designed to save core industrial firms, Klein and his union saw their best future hope now in expanded policy influence in broader local, regional, and national political debates. In the absence of larger framework agreements for expanded development and funding in areas such as labor market and industrial policy, the union remained vulnerable to a future decline of influence.

At the Siemens plant in Rostock, union strike success had secured the loyalty and commitment of a core of eastern activists, centered in the elected works council. In the absence of broader political support in the form of policies to boost industry and employment, however, the base that such loyalty would provide for future union influence and successful social partnership in the Rostock area could very well continue to shrink.

Volkswagen in Saxony

One of the more dramatic and highly publicized western investments in eastern Germany was the early move by Volkswagen to establish a major new production site in Saxony. Starting with plant and equipment from the old VEB Sachsenring, producer of the now discontinued Trabant automobile, as well as former Trabant plant workers, VW aimed to play a major role in the development of a modern industrial area centered around the city of Zwickau (between Dresden and Leipzig). The state government of Saxony, as well as the federal government, IG Metall, and the industrial workers of Saxony, had high hopes for this investment.[5]

As East Germany began to open up in late 1989, VW had moved quickly to establish a joint venture with the East German producers of the Trabant. Included in this investment was a new plant, scheduled to open in 1994 in the town of Mosel, just outside Zwickau, to produce small VW's (Golfs) for western and eastern markets. In the meantime, at an adjacent older plant, Volkswagen, by June 1991, had rehired 1250 former Trabi workers to begin final assembly of VW Golfs and Polos from bodies supplied by the flagship VW plant in Wolfsburg.[6] Because the original low labor-cost strategy was undermined by currency union in 1990 and by the wage-parity agreement in 1991, plans for success at the Mosel plant were soon founded on planned innovations in production and work organization.

Both management and labor viewed the Mosel experiment as a sort of German NUMMI or Saturn—two GM projects in the United States designed to prove that advanced organizational innovation based on labor-management cooperation is possible with domestic workforces.[7] VW management at Mosel was quite explicit in its intent to introduce at this semi-greenfield site innovations that would be much more difficult at western plants, where established practices and interest representation are entrenched. Management planned early on, for example, to outsource as much possible, and to hire only skilled workers, organized from the start in production teams of eight to twelve members.[8]

Communist union structures at the Trabi plant collapsed in 1990; and in April 1991, the smaller, rehired workforce elected its first works council under provisions of the Works Constitution Act. Prior to the election, rehired union activists from the Trabi era joined the western IG Metall (as did most of the workforce) and sought an experienced VW works councillor to assist them in negotiations with experienced VW top management brought in to Mosel from the West. Through IG Metall sources, the union group in the plant located Dieter Riemann from the VW Kassel plant, who impressed them with his knowledge and nonauthoritarian style. Mosel management was persuaded to put Riemann on the books; he was elected to the new works council in 1991 with the highest number of votes (about 600 out of 800 cast).

The remaining elected works councillors had all been workers at the Trabi plant, most of them former union activists from the middle and lower ranks, some of them former party members and some of them not. This mixed group, including both blue- and white-collar workers, elected Riemann as head of the works council and set out to build an effective bargaining team. Working in a plant receiving major new investment from the West, they were optimistic at the start (1991–92) about their prospects for the future. They supported VW's modernization strategy (with elements of "lean production," including an advanced stamping plant for quick die changes) and saw in it the opportunity not only for rising workforce wages and future employment security but for better, more humane working conditions. They supported, for example, management's intention to establish plant-wide teamwork; but they planned to use IG Metall's twelve principles of group work (Muster and Wannöffel 1989, 39–54; Turner 1991, 113–14) to push for the human-side benefits of innovative work organization. They expressed commitment to the concept of an "engaged worker" (*mitwirkender Mitarbeiter*) with shopfloor autonomy and problem-solving responsibility.

There were elements in management's strategy, however, that they did not like. Management, for example, planned to run the plant round-the-clock on three-shift production, which would mean night work and no hiring of women.[9] This was an important issue both because West German unions have long fought against night and weekend work and because about half the workers in the old Trabi plant were women, many of them skilled. In subsequent negotiations, the Mosel works council, with IG Metall support and after securing concessions on break time and night premiums, gave its consent to a three-shift production schedule in which every worker rotated through a night shift once every three weeks. As elsewhere in eastern manufacturing, however, the percentage of rehired women remained disproportionally small.

Works councillors were also opposed to the continued presence in management at the Mosel plant of so many "old red socks." VW management, for its part, claimed that many of the old middle managers did well on assessment tests and showed the capacity to learn, adapt, and manage in the new environment. Workforce representatives disagreed, claiming that too many of the rehired

bosses lacked both the trust of the workers and the capacity to develop nonauthoritarian relations and innovative labor-management practices. This percep-
tion appeared just as strong in 1995 as it had in 1991 and 1992; elected works
councillors remained convinced that order-dispensing old red socks in middle
management were undermining the democratic potential of modern teamwork.

By far the biggest problem for the works council, however, was the decision
made at VW headquarters in Wolfsburg in late 1992 to delay full production at
Mosel until 1996. This decision meant that by 1994 there were still only 2500 employees at Mosel, with planned hiring of the total 4500 deferred for at least two
years, contingent upon final assignment of a new VW model for the Mosel
plant.[10] Although workers at Mosel experienced this decision as a betrayal by the
western "mother" at Wolfsburg, the postponement was clearly linked to deep recession in the West, including a major economic crisis for Volkswagen and the
urgent search for ways to cut costs, production, and investment on all fronts (a
cost-cutting effort which, as we will see in Chapter 6, would include a reduction
of the workweek to 28 hours at all western VW plants by 1994). In the Wolfsburg
view, it would have been unfair to continue hiring at Mosel while laying workers
off or involuntarily reducing hours at other plants.[11]

The crisis of deferred expansion at Mosel demonstrated the concrete link
between recession in the West and continuing economic crisis and slower-than-
expected growth in the East. Another consequence of this recession/slow-
growth dynamic was the eastern metalworking strike of 1993. As we have seen,
Saxony turned out to be the pivotal region where the strike was waged and the
final pattern-setting agreement was reached. At IG Metall-Saxony headquarters
in Dresden, it was clear that a successful strike would require the active participation of large and highly organized plants such as (and perhaps above all) the
VW plant at Mosel.

As part of VW's new strategy in eastern Germany, the company had joined
the employer association in Saxony; instead of going it alone and signing an individual firm contract (*Haustarifvertrag*), a practice that had proven very expensive
for VW in the West, VW-Saxony aimed to use the regional contract to help keep
costs down. The company was thus fair game, and high on the list, as a strike
target in the spring of 1993. To undercut the strike threat, management offered
to pay a plant premium that would bring the April 1 pay raise up to the previously agreed upon level of 26 percent. While the workers and works council at
Mosel (as well as at supplier plants in Chemnitz and Eisenach owned by VW-
Saxony) would have been happy with such an arrangement, IG Metall quickly
saw the danger of its activist core being removed from the strike. IG Metall-
Saxony announced the following position: if firms wanted to pay the 26 percent,
that was fine; but to be removed from the strike list, such firms must sign a separate, enforceable agreement with the union (and not just with the works council).

When VW-Saxony refused to do this, since a key part of its strategy in the East was to avoid the expensive *Haustarifvertrag*, IG Metall announced that the terms of the pay premium were unacceptable. VW at Mosel took a prominent position on the A list of first-round strike targets.

It was left to Dieter Riemann and colleagues on the Mosel works council (all of them IG Metall members) to explain to the workforce why a strike was necessary even though the company had offered to pay the demanded amount. As one can imagine, this was an uphill battle at first. When a busload of western VW workers arrived to support the first warning strike on April 1, management pointed to the "Wessi" presence as added proof that this was a strike orchestrated in the West, against the mutual interests of labor and management in the East, to impose western unions and their bargaining practices and settlements on a reluctant eastern workforce. Highly organized Mosel shop stewards and works councillors countered with the argument that the western VW colleagues were there on their own unpaid time, to demonstrate solidarity with eastern IG Metallers and aid the struggle to bring strong union representation and enforceable wage parity to the East.

As the strike in Saxony unfolded, the latter point of view won the day at Mosel. On April 1, the shop stewards pulled a substantial majority of the workforce out of the halls and into a warning strike march to the main gate. A year later, stewards still spoke with passion of the sight of distinct groups of workers (in blue uniforms from the body shop, white uniforms from the stamping plant, yellow uniforms from assembly, and so on) marching together for the first time, experiencing firsthand the solidarity of a strike, the sense of collective success in a labor conflict that could not be put down by Soviet tanks, with the support of seasoned western colleagues. After an equally successful warning strike of two hours on April 15, 90 percent of the blue-collar workforce at Mosel (joined by a substantial number of white-collar employees) went on strike on May 3 and remained out until the settlement was reached on May 14. The Mosel workforce thus fulfilled its IG Metall–assigned role as an activist center of strike activity, from which strikers fanned out for support actions at other strike targets in the area.

The terms of the strike settlement were disappointing to the workforce at Mosel, since workers there (as elsewhere in Saxony and eastern Germany) would not reach the previously agreed-upon 26 percent raise until the end of the year, and since wage parity with the West was deferred from 1994 to 1996. Both Dieter Riemann of the Mosel works council and Hasso Düwel, chief negotiator and head of IG Metall in Saxony, gave presentations to the assembled workforce at Mosel, emphasizing the accomplishments of the strike: successful mobilization, East-West solidarity, and guaranteed (if delayed) pay raises leading to wage parity within three years—as opposed to the offer by management of a company–works council agreement of uncertain duration. Although ratification votes are tallied not for plants or firms but for regions, Mosel workforce acceptance of the agreement was indicated by (1) union membership that climbed at Mosel from 74 percent before the strike to 91 percent by mid-1994; and (2) the reelection of the works council one month later in June of 1993, with (unofficial) strike-leader Riemann receiving the highest number of votes.[12]

A year later, works councillors at Mosel maintained that union consciousness and commitment (in addition to high union membership) were the most important by-products of the strike. By 1994, over 100 shop stewards represented the workforce on the shop floor and in the office, in networks based in part on union activism from the old Trabi plant days, reinforced by the experience of the prolonged and successful strike in 1993. Modern work organization appeared also to have played a role, as production teams took pride in their common participation in the strike. As for the 500 strikebreakers (compared to 2,000 strikers), union leadership at Mosel made a strategic decision not to isolate or attack them but to win them over—since this had been a first-time experience for all of them. As a result, many joined the union in the year following the strike, including the one strikebreaker who had been elected to the works council in June of 1993.

By 1994, therefore, all nineteen elected works councillors at Mosel were IG Metall members.[13] As at VW and other auto assembly plants in western Germany, the works council had consolidated a strong position of codetermination in management decision making, in a process that was at times conflictual but for the most part cooperative and well attuned to the organizational and market needs of the firm.

The works council, for example, had consistently supported the introduction of innovative work organization at Mosel. With works council support, the workforce was organized throughout in teams of eight to twelve members, with considerable responsibility in each team for the division of labor, work, and vacation scheduling and continuous improvement of production processes. Three years after the introduction of teams in 1991, however, the works council was still negotiating the terms of a plant agreement on teamwork with management. Team leaders had so far been appointed by management; the works council was demanding democratic election by the team. Management claimed that the existing system (with appointed team leaders) was working fine, while nonetheless professing a willingness to compromise with works council demands and confidence that a formal agreement would soon be reached. Works councillors argued that elections would root out authoritarian team leaders who lacked the trust of their members and would therefore make the system work better, both for production and for employee morale.[14]

Although Volkswagen had explicitly designed Mosel as a greenfield to take advantage of innovations in production and work organization, legacies of the past continued to play an important role. Most of the workforce, blue-collar, white-collar, and middle management, were eastern veterans of earlier Trabi production. This was problematic in cases where workers perceived their bosses as unreformed order-givers transplanted from the old system into the new; works councillors and shop stewards argued that the election of team leaders by the teams themselves would go a long way toward solving this problem. In addition, works councillors and top managers agreed that collective practices from the earlier time had been harnessed at Mosel: in team production as in union and strike solidarity.

So far at Mosel, the blending of elements of the VW model (such as strongly organized interests, full information exchange, and cooperative social partnership relations) with advanced production innovations (teams of highly skilled workers, just-in-time parts delivery) and the collective orientation of the former Trabi workforce had proven successful. Mosel production ranked at the top in quality and productivity comparisons with other VW plants. Long-term prospects looked good here in the mid-1990s, pending new model assignments within VW, as management at Mosel professed itself ready to hire an additional 2,000 employees by 1997 to bring the new plant up to full production.

VW SUPPLIERS IN SAXONY: SACHSENRING, VW-CHEMNITZ, HELLA

An important question raised by the VW experience in Mosel was to what extent this investment would stimulate industrial development and modernization in the greater Zwickau area. As the rest of the large VEB Sachsenring collapsed, the pessimistic prediction that outposts such as Mosel would remain "cathedrals in the desert" appeared plausible (Grabher 1992). And Mosel's deferred production and hiring schedule made it possible that even the "cathedral" itself would be of limited size and duration (thus hardly qualifying as a cathedral at all).

After Volkswagen peeled off the Mosel site for VW-Sachsen, workforce representatives and managers at what remained of Sachsenring in Zwickau pursued numerous survival options in negotiations with the Treuhand and various potential investors. The idea in 1990–91 was to survive as a large parts supplier for Mosel and other auto plants in eastern and western Europe, such as the Skoda plants in nearby Czechoslovakia and other VW and Audi plants in western Germany, and at the same time to spin off a large employment and training company for displaced Sachsenring workers.

A militant campaign in 1991, supported by both the IG Metall local and the Sachsenring works council and including a lengthy plant occupation by over 1,000 workers, forced the Treuhand to establish and help arrange financing for one of eastern Germany's largest employment companies, SAQ (Sächsische Aufbau- und Qualifizierungsgesellschaft). This company, financed to a large extent by the Federal Labor Bureau, created jobs and training opportunities for thousands of displaced Sachsenring employees for up to three years in areas such as environmental cleanup and the removal of obsolete buildings. For many, SAQ provided a bridge to future jobs at Mosel or elsewhere in the Zwickau area; for many others, however, the employment company provided an important but only temporary respite before the descent into prolonged unemployment.

In the attempt to build a core auto-parts supplier company, however, Sachsenring management and works council were less successful. The sprawling size of Sachsenring (spread across three large plants in Zwickau) made both potential investors and the Treuhand wary. As prolonged negotiations failed to bear fruit, total employment at Sachsenring dropped from 11,500 in 1989, to 6,500 in 1991, to 2,200 in 1992. Reductions took place through early retirement, transfer to SAQ, resignations (as, for example, skilled workers sought better jobs in the West or were hired at VW-Mosel), buyouts, and layoffs with substantial social-plan payments. By 1992, works council and management were proud of the role played by SAQ, which they had helped to found, and still had high hopes of attracting investors to keep Sachsenring alive as a company employing at least 1500 workers.

Even this scaled-down aspiration, however, failed to materialize. By 1994, one piece had been privatized as Sachsenring Automobiltechnik (SAT), a parts supplier employing 325 workers, projected to hire an additional 100 along with twenty-five apprentices by 1995. About 1,000 remained in the employment company, SAQ, while the remainder of the once-mighty Sachsenring remained a Treuhand firm, now employing only 320 workers, facing continuing liquidation while still seeking buyers to privatize more bits and pieces.

The surviving SAT was a highly unionized firm, represented by several newly elected works councillors who had moved over with the workforce from the old Sachsenring. Labor-management relations were cooperative as the new firm fought for market success; the new western owners encountered and worked with a highly skilled workforce along with a works council that had already known extensive mobilization and negotiation. At the same time, the many former Sachsenring workers who had gone through SAQ had seen the value of mobilization and appreciated the consistently supportive role played by the IG Metall local. Although the old Sachsenring was now set to disappear, the surviving pieces, including VW-Sachsen, SAT, and SAQ, contributed to a reservoir of union membership that made the Zwickau IG Metall local the largest in Saxony.[15]

Beyond the immediate Zwickau area, Volkswagen also made a substantial investment in the purchase from the Treuhand in 1992 of a motor plant in Chemnitz, one hour away on the autobahn. Here again, the decision was made to use advanced innovations in production organization, including outsourcing, just-in-time production, and shopfloor group work. Down from a peak of over 4,000 employees, VW-Chemnitz in 1994 employed 483 blue- and white-collar workers in the production of engines for VW in Mosel as well as for VW-owned SEAT in Spain. In addition, another 400 former motor plant workers were employed on the premises in numerous small supplier and service companies for the surviving VW engine plant.

Managers and works councillors at VW in Chemnitz were convinced in 1994 that they had reached a recession-induced trough in production and employment numbers. In their view, innovations such as group work based exclusively on skilled workers, along with high productivity and product quality, put the plant in good position for the anticipated economic upswing. At this plant, representatives of both labor and management claimed that their past history together, including the tradition of collective working relationships, contributed to the success both of group work in production and close cooperation in works council–management relations. So close were these relations, in fact, that the works council had opposed participation in the 1993 strike (and was therefore not called out on strike by IG Metall). Nonetheless, along with 87 percent of the workforce, all works councillors were IG Metall members and claimed to need a strong union presence for plant-level representation and relations of social partnership with management. Here at Chemnitz, works councillors traced a direct line from inherited collective practices from before unification to effective labor-management cooperation in a market economy, high levels of union membership and loyalty, and successful modern group work organization.

At another VW supplier, the Hella plant in Meerane about ten kilometers from Mosel, workers and managers saw the same connection between earlier collective practices and modern work organization. Ominously for IG Metall, however, this connection did not include high levels of union membership or even any works council at all. With only forty-three employees, Hella is not atypical of small firms, which even in western Germany usually have low union membership and often do not have works councils.

Hella is a well-known western auto supplier that was approached by VW about setting up front-end assembly and delivery for the Mosel plant. In 1991, Hella began construction of a brand new plant in Meerane, followed by production start-up in August of 1992. The plant produces only for VW-Mosel, in tightly scheduled and orchestrated just-in-time production and delivery. The orders come at three-minute intervals for each front-end assembly (including bumper and headlights), each order received by computer printout exactly 440 minutes before the part is required on the Mosel assembly line. As at Mosel, the Hella plant operates round-the-clock, three-shift production.

The core workforce for each shift is a team of seven workers and a foreman, with job rotation and full quality responsibility within the team. All employees are skilled workers, and all of them, including the plant manager, are easterners.

In a 1994 interview, the plant manager was emphatic that the eastern tradition of *Zusammenarbeit* (working together, or common effort), as opposed to the western preoccupation with rights and status, was well suited to the needs of modern team production. In an increasingly common perspective on the part of eastern managers and works councillors in the mid-1990s, this Hella plant manager saw the East as one day becoming the most modern part of Germany. He also predicted a continuing important role for unions, works councils, and social partnership, despite the reluctance so far of any of his Hella employees to step forward for a works council election at this small plant.

The biggest problem facing the Hella plant was the deferred production schedule at Mosel. Producing 400 pieces per day in 1994, and limited to this number through the end of the model run in 1996, the plant was built with a capacity of 800 to 1,000 pieces per day. Expansion at Hella, as with much of production around Zwickau, awaited stronger economic growth in the West, upswing in the East, and a firm VW commitment to expanded production at Mosel.

The supplier plants at Chemnitz, Hella, and even Sachsenring nonetheless show a process of modernization occurring in eastern Germany, in this case linked through supplier networks to the new VW production site and future expansion at Mosel. The big danger for industrial development in this area is that Mosel production will remain small. The larger (and more "cathedral"-like) it gets in the years ahead, the more positive impacts are likely in Saxony for employment, modernization, and social partnership.

Opel in Eisenach: NUMMI-East

Even more so than VW in Saxony, Opel's new plant in Eisenach (in Thuringia, not far from the old East-West border) launched production in 1991–92 to great media and public relations fanfare.[16] Quite explicitly from the start, Opel-Eisenach was designed as a showcase of high-productivity lean production, to show the way for Opel at other plants in Germany as well as for General Motors plants throughout Europe and the world. According to Peter Enderle, Opel's executive directive for manufacturing:

> Opel combined the know-how of its Technical Development Center, the experience from the Model Shop [pilot projects at West German plants], and the knowledge acquired by General Motors in various joint ventures with Japanese manufacturers in North America, to plan and establish its new plant in Eisenach. This resulted in an automobile plant in the federal state of Thuringia which is one of the most modern in the world in terms of environmental protection, production technology, and systems. Eisenach is showing the European automobile industry the way to the future.[17]

Until 1991, Eisenach was the production site for the East German Wartburg automobile. Along with Zwickau's Trabant-producing VEB Sachsenring, Automobilwerke Eisenach (AWE) belonged the huge IFA Kombinat, which produced both East German automobiles (the low-cost Trabi and the slightly "upscale" Wartburg). Although reorganization had made it possible that Wartburg production would be in the black by mid-1991, the Treuhand announced the decision to liquidate AWE, in what was widely seen as a political decision to prevent overcrowding in the German auto market (and thus reduce the pressure on low-cost competitors such as VW, Opel, and Ford).

After having agreed to a joint venture with AWE in March of 1990, Opel bought a piece of AWE land, built an all-new, state-of-the-art assembly plant, hired former AWE workers, and built up to full production speed by early 1993. Producing Corsas and Astras for western and eastern markets in processes based on just-in-time parts delivery and shopfloor teamwork, Opel-Eisenach claimed to have reached world-class (i.e. Japanese) levels of productivity and product quality by 1994.

The 10,000 former AWE workers faced early retirement, layoff, relocation, and for the lucky ones new jobs in the Eisenach area. Less than 1,000 of them would find jobs at the Opel plant; former AWE employees comprised 40 to 50 percent of the workforce of 1,800 at Opel-Eisenach in 1994. Those hired had to go through a lengthy assessment test that evaluated not only formal training, experience, and skill levels, but the capacity for teamwork and group problem-solving as well. So selective was the assessment process that Opel could not find enough workers for its new team production in the Eisenach area; the company advertised throughout eastern Germany and even recruited a small number of workers (about twenty) from the West.

The first 200 workers hired elected a works council of seven members in March 1991, with former AWE skilled maintenance worker Harald Lieske chosen as council chair. As workforce numbers expanded, a larger works council of fifteen, all easterners, was elected two years later in March 1993, to hold office until 1998. Four of these were full-time, including Lieske, who was reelected as chair. From early on, Lieske and his colleagues on the works council played an important role in building the new production system at Opel-Eisenach.

In a refrain that has become increasingly familiar throughout eastern Germany, works councillors at Eisenach claimed to build on eastern legacies in the development of the most modern team production. As Lieske put it in a remarkable public talk in October of 1992:

> In many respects, the post-Fordist production system developed at Eisenach is based on a skillful extension of long-practiced methods of auto production in the GDR. Technical and organizational characteristics of automobile production in

the GDR, necessarily viewed from a western perspective as constraining for productivity growth, are now proving themselves extremely advantageous for the implementation of teamwork concepts. Auto factories in the GDR were not nearly so Fordist in structure as their western counterparts.[18]

Lieske then elaborated on the characteristics of East German production useful as a foundation for modern, post-Fordist production, including long cycle times (5 to 6 minutes at AWE) and highly skilled and experienced workers used to conditions of flexibility and problem-solving (due largely to continuous production problems in the GDR resulting from obsolete equipment and material shortages).

At the same time, according to Lieske, the new team organization represented a radical break with the old authoritarian and hierarchical structures of the past. Teams of eight to twelve members scheduled their own work, rotated among jobs, held regular team meetings, pushed productivity constantly upward in processes of continuous improvement, and standardized and documented each task, in practices quite similar to new work organization at other "lean" plants such as the NUMMI GM-Toyota model plant in Fremont, California.

At first, team members also elected their own team leaders. Management soon decided, however, that in many cases the most competent workers were not being elected; in some cases, in fact, workers who were at odds with management were elected. As a result, management and the works council set up a parity commission to appoint team leaders. When parity proved too time-consuming, a management committee, with one or two works councillors, took over. Although management rescinded the opportunity for workers to select their leaders in open, democratic processes, the works council supported the change and in 1994 claimed to have full input into team leader selection, maintaining also that the process was successful in locating the best team leaders and had been widely accepted on the shop floor.

Both works council and management professed to have close, cooperative relations, in which the works council received full information from management in time to contribute its voice to all important decisions made at the Eisenach plant.[19] The works council appeared to view its role as both representing the workforce and co-managing the plant. Nonetheless, Opel works councillors as well as union officials at the local IG Metall headquarters complained about excessive performance pressure from middle managers, especially from the former AWE old red socks. Workers resented such pressure, in the name of lean production, from their former communist bosses. One union official suggested that such men had slipped over from a command communist to a market economy with well-studied images of brutal, early capitalism in mind—images that their authoritarian past had made them well suited to carry out in the present.

Relations between labor and management at Opel-Eisenach were tested during the strike of 1993. Hoping to undercut potential union militancy, the company joined the employer association in March and announced its intention to pay the going rate. In addition, management offered the works council a plant premium that would bring Opel workers up several percentage points above the 9 percent raise scheduled for April 1. Because this was considerably less than what workers had expected, however, the Opel workforce and works council reacted with anger to management's intention. Although the strike in Saxony and Mecklenburg-Pomerania was settled before it reached Thuringia, workers in the Eisenach area voted overwhelmingly in favor of striking (and the pressure of this and other strike votes in Brandenburg and Saxony-Anhalt helped force the May settlement). In the face of conflicting pressures for militancy and cooperation, the Opel works council tread a careful line in April and May of 1993 between a desire to support the new team-based work organization and a desire to protest against scaled-back pay raises.

Although the Opel plant was never at the top of IG Metall's strike list, had the strike spread to Thuringia (given extremely cooperative relations at the plant and the corresponding uncertainty about whether workers here could be counted on to strike), protest expressed itself here in unusual and contained ways. Workers at this Opel plant, for example, wear white shirts, so that any dirt can be quickly seen and taken as a signal that either more clean-up is necessary or something is wrong with production processes. On April 1, although Opel workers did not participate in IG Metall warning strikes and demonstrations, workers protested inadequate pay raises by wearing brightly colored clothing, guided by the homegrown slogan "Anders kleiden, weiter streiten!"—translated roughly as "Wear different clothes, continue to struggle!" Later in the campaign, workers at Eisenach did participate in two brief warning strikes, one of which they agreed to end early so as not to embarrass the plant manager during a visit by Louis Hughes, the head of GM-Europe.

Close labor-management relations at Opel-Eisenach thus survived the conflict of 1993. At the same time, the conflict provided a bridgehead for slowly increasingly unionization. From the start, although all Opel works councillors were IG Metall members, the local union had looked askance at the overly cooperative stance that appeared to privilege company–works council relations at the expense of works council–union relations. The deputy chairperson of the local IG Metall was formerly the elected head of the works council at AWE, in the period between unification and the liquidation of AWE; he knew the works councillors at Opel, many of them former AWE colleagues, and was disappointed that this large local auto plant could not be counted on to support the strike. At the same time, the local union was committed to organizing the plant. By the summer of 1994, union membership at the plant was up to about 50 percent, with the first shop steward elections held in the fall. The local union had become increasingly optimistic about prospects for building a strong union structure at the plant, aided above all by growing worker resistance to management's intense production pressure.

In the face of such pressure, even the cooperation-minded Opel-Eisenach works councillors had by 1994 become advocates for a much stronger union presence, accompanied by a stronger workforce capacity for mobilization. The works council chair, who earlier had emphasized close labor-management relations and indeed was still committed to such an approach as a foundation for Opel's success in eastern Germany, now spoke with disappointment about the passivity of his workforce, the tendency for workers here to expect the works council and/or union to deliver, without the need for workforce mobilization. Lieske spoke enviously of the twelve-day strike at VW in Mosel, which had mobilized and unionized that workforce in a way that had not yet occurred at Eisenach. At the same time, he looked forward to shop steward elections, a closer relationship with the IG Metall local, and the coming of stronger unionization to back up the efforts of the works council at the Opel plant.

Management, for its part, was quite pleased with the Eisenach experiment and continued to view it as a model for new production and work organization in the auto industry. Eisenach was clearly seen as the European NUMMI: a demonstration plant that both showed the way forward and proved that such success was possible with local workforces. GM and Opel management were doubly pleased with success at Eisenach, which had been accomplished without the benefit of NUMMI's Japanese management (from Toyota); Opel-Eisenach managers were Germans and Americans who had learned the lessons of NUMMI, CAMI (a joint venture plant in Canada), and other Japanese-run, lean plants. Opel management had thus quite explicitly used eastern Germany as a greenfield from which to influence work organization at its western plants. As early as 1990, works councillors at Opel plants in Rüsselsheim, Bochum, and Kaiserslautern began to hear in their negotiations with management about the need to make major changes to match planned (and later achieved) productivity and quality at the Eisenach plant.

As one would expect, this new pressure did not endear the Eisenach plant and its works council to established union representatives and works councillors at the western plants. Opel representatives in the West resented what they took to be a distant rather than solidaristic attitude on the part of Lieske and his colleagues, who wanted to find their own way. Lieske and colleagues, for their part, resented what they perceived as "besserwessi" ("western know-it-all") paternalism on the part of their western colleagues. Although relations remained tense into the mid-1990s, there were signs of improvement as Opel plants in the West continued their own transitions to team organization while works councillors at Eisenach sought a stronger union presence.[20]

Although the Eisenach plant's successful production figures would continue to result in increased production pressure in western plants, and corresponding re-organization, relationships at Eisenach appeared capable of incorporation within a framework of social partnership that included strong unions and em-ployer associations. At the same time, Opel-Eisenach demonstrated clearly the strong potential for advanced industrial modernization in eastern Germany.

CHAPTER FOUR

Crisis, Modernization, and the Resilience of Social Partnership

Case study evidence presented in Chapter 3 demonstrates a wide range of plant-level diversity along a number of dimensions, including characteristics of the transformation, production organization, and industrial relations. For production organization, outcomes ranged from state-of-the-art lean production at Opel-Eisenach, to innovative group work at Knorr-Bremse (Berliner Bremsenwerk), to rather traditional ("extended assembly line") production organization at ABB Kraftwerke Berlin (Bergmann-Borsig). For industrial relations, outcomes ranged from plants with influential works councils backed up by strike-hardened, mobilizable workforces (Siemens in Rostock; VW in Mosel), to highly cooperative works councils whose workforces had as yet shown little interest in mobilization (Niles in Berlin; Opel in Eisenach); from firms committed to the employer association and comprehensive collective bargaining (VW in Mosel) to nonmember, weakly unionized firms (Hella in Meerane).

Although a similar range of diversity also exists in western Germany, the diversity is considerably more pronounced in the East. Cases that would be outliers in the West are less unusual in the East; it is, in fact, difficult to find a real mainstream in the new eastern states. There are, nonetheless, observable patterns of economic development and industrial relations that emerge from the ten case studies in the metal and electronics industries.

The Findings: Partnership and Modernization

The Resilience of Social Partnership

The most important observation to emerge from the case studies is the following: In a very short period (five to six years), key elements of a potential base for long-term, stable relations of social partnership have developed in eastern Germany.

Employer associations, despite low membership relative to the West and intensive internal debate regarding strategy (as in the West in the 1990s), have established a base for future growth and negotiation. Almost all large, influential firms in the East are members, and the associations play the key role from the employer side in setting wage standards at both sector and regional levels. Most of the managers we interviewed indicated that their firms were committed members of the appropriate association. Employer solidarity, they maintained, was especially important in the difficult circumstances of the East; comprehensive collective bargaining on the part of strong employer associations was viewed as the best way to prevent cutthroat and self-defeating labor-market competition and maintain the high standards, quality, and profits for which German industry in the West is known. Since most large firms in the East today either have parent firms in the West or are largely owned by western investors, this pro-association/collective bargaining attitude represents an extension of established practice. All managers interviewed, even at nonmember firms such as Hella in Meerane, Saxony (whose parent firm belongs to Gesamtmetall in the West), fully expected the associations, in time, to occupy the same prominent positions in the East that they have occupied throughout the postwar period in the West.

There also appeared to be a solid base for the continuing development of union influence in eastern Germany. At the case study firms, union membership levels for the most part were as high or higher than at comparable western firms. In some cases, membership density was considerably higher, as at the electronics firms Siemens and El Pro. The two low-density cases were Hella (a small firm, most of which are also low-density in the West) and Opel-Eisenach (a special case, at which unionization was nonetheless on the rise). In all of these cases except Hella, the works council was dominated by members of IG Metall. At several of these companies, strike preparations (or the actual strike itself) had strengthened union influence among the workforce; even where this had not occurred (as at Niles and VW-Chemnitz), works councillors remained committed union members and promoted union membership among the rank and file. In almost every case, the works councillors, union representatives, and even managers interviewed predicted future substantial rates of unionization at their firms.[1]

These findings offer a quite different perspective when set against the many pessimistic speculations on the future of unions, employer associations, and social partnership in eastern Germany (see, for example, Mahnkopf 1991, 1993; Armingeon 1991; and Wiesenthal, Ettl, and Bialas 1992). In fact, the future does not look at all bad for unions and employer associations here, as seen from the perspective of the case-study firms. Small and medium-sized employers who do not belong to the association (such as Hella in Meerane) have not joined largely in order to keep down wage costs and save on the costs of membership fees; as the economy of the East improves and as firm earnings rise, many such firms may join the larger firms in the benefits of membership (and this was the expectation of the Hella plant manager). For employees, the strike of 1993 along with contractually phased-in wage parity and union training for works councillors have ensured a base of union support among both rank and file and works councils, at least in the metal and electronics industries.

Comprehensively organized collective bargaining remains an important mechanism for wage setting in eastern Germany. Since plant premiums are low if they even exist in the economically depressed East, regional contracts bear an even closer relation to actual pay levels for member firms than is typically the case in the West. Where employers, either association members or nonmembers, are undercutting bargained wage levels (sometimes with works council consent), contractual standards remain the benchmark for downward adjustment as well as the stated goal of works councils for the coming years when economic and employment situations have improved. If such undercutting proves temporary, as works councils, union, and firms all claim that it is, this practice could even be viewed benignly as an informal flexibility in crisis circumstances.

The most important finding of this research, therefore, is that social partnership, in circumstances of crisis and extraordinary instability, has nonetheless established a solid presence in eastern Germany in a remarkably short period of time.[2]

Modernization of Industry

A second critical finding apparent from the case studies is the existence by the mid-1990s of a solid potential base for the modernization of industry in eastern Germany. Innovations at eastern plants include group work, aspects of lean production including just-in-time parts delivery, and the latest technology. In the fight for survival, works councils everywhere collaborate closely with management in the introduction of innovation; in some cases, it is the works council that has pushed management (rather than the reverse) to invest in new methods and to remove or reeducate authoritarian-minded "old red socks" who have stood in the way of modern, participatory relations. In eastern Germany, firms found greenfield and semi-greenfield opportunities to introduce innovations more easily than in the industrially and organizationally established West. They also found skilled workforces eager to accept innovation in the drive to keep plants open and preserve jobs.[3]

Whether the modernization potential in eastern Germany develops into the dominant economic reality depends on many factors, including world and European economic conditions, German federal and regional economic policy, the settlement of outstanding property claims and the development of vocational training in the East, and the outcomes of future collective bargaining rounds. From the evidence presented here, however, a case can be made for the oft-repeated predictions on the part of eastern managers and works councillors that over the next ten to twenty years, the new federal states of the East will become the most modern part of the German economy. The modernization potential that has developed in only a few years offers hope in the face of predominantly pessimistic predictions regarding economic development in eastern Germany (Voskamp and Wittke 1991; Grabher 1992; and countless others since).

Legacies of the Past: Collective Workplace Traditions

The third key finding from case-study evidence concerns the important role played in modernization and economic development by legacies of industrial and social organization from the GDR. David Stark has shown how the inherited form of industrial organization begets contrasting, "path-dependent" processes of privatization in Poland, Czechoslovakia, Hungary, and eastern Germany (Stark 1992). Thus the Treuhand as a unique organizational form and approach to privatization has roots in the industrial structure (and concentration) of the GDR. In similar fashion, the evidence considered here demonstrates a clear relationship between older shopfloor practices and the potential for particular kinds of modern production organization. Modern shopfloor teamwork in eastern Germany, where management is astute enough to develop it, builds directly upon former traditions of collective work and improvisation (see also Jürgens 1994). In many cases, such innovation-suitable traditions arise not from the formal brigade structures but as a product of tacit opposition to (and in spite of) former authoritarian practices. As a response to the inefficiency of a state-run economy, groups of workers managed to meet their production norms by improvising and through collective effort despite persistent material shortages and obsolete equipment (Voskamp and Wittke 1991; Kern 1991). Habits bred by years of common effort and adaptation in difficult circumstances, as well as a generally collective approach to work, problem-solving, and social life, provided fertile ground in the 1990s for the introduction of modern group and teamwork. This potential has been demonstrated by innovations in production organization at several of the case-study plants, including Knorr-Bremse,

Opel-Eisenach, VW-Mosel, VW-Chemnitz, and Hella (see also Mickler et al. 1996, 171–74).

Legacies of the Past: The "Old Red Socks"

The "old red socks" in management, on the other hand, are a legacy that is more mixed in its blessing. Firms in the East have built upon this legacy for want of a viable alternative. On the negative side, former communist managers need considerable training in cost-benefit analysis, human resource management, and modern nonauthoritarian relations with employees. Works councillors at several firms complained about the inability of the inherited authoritarian bosses to work in a spirit of cooperation and trust either with the works council or with other employees. On the positive side, however, such individuals do have experience in leadership and organization, they often possess considerable shopfloor knowledge by virtue of past technical training and on-the-job experience, and most important, they are desperate to hang on to their jobs and thus will often do anything top management asks. Where top management is astute, such individuals can be sifted through, the bad ones sorted out, and the remaining core retrained and obliged to work in a facilitating role (rather than a commanding one) for shopfloor and office teams. This takes a major effort on the part of management, but it can pay off, as we have seen at Knorr-Bremse, VW-Chemnitz, and Hella. In potentially successful cases, retrained eastern managers bring (1) a powerful desire to adapt; (2) technical and managerial skills; and (3) a past practice of common effort and collaboration (on the part of the less authoritarian types from within an authoritarian system) with eastern shop and office employees. This is a legacy upon which the best firms can build in the push toward modern work organization.[4]

Recombination of Resources: Employment and Training Companies

Another important legacy can be found in the employment and training companies (ETCs) that have been spun off from several case-study firms. In these cases, a legacy of available equipment, plant, and displaced employees are combined in a government-subsidized (largely with money that the government would otherwise pay out in unemployment insurance), nonprofit company that provides jobs and training while performing necessary infrastructure tasks such as demolition and environmental cleanup. In the best cases, led by entrepreneurial engineers or skilled workers, these companies have in turn spun off small private firms that have survived to provide permanent jobs and even production innovations in the new market economy. The jury is still out on the ETCs, and whether the latter successful cases end up as more than isolated exceptions

(Knuth 1993, 1997). At the very least, the ETCs provide one to three more years of employment for displaced workers who then enter the ranks of the unemployed; at best, ETCs, especially when adequately funded (the main struggle for these bodies), afford bridges to future skills, employment, and even new firms and product or process innovation.

The Crisis of Adjustment

In addition to the above findings, each of which offers some grounds for an optimistic assessment of developments in the eastern German economy, the evidence examined also shows major problems and potential obstacles on the road to a modern social-partnership economy. Employer associations, as we have seen, are undersubscribed; unions have lost membership, largely as a result of unemployment but also as a product of disillusionment; and works councils in many cases, although working closely with management and gaining some input, are weak in the capacity to mobilize the workforce and develop independent negotiating positions. Pessimistic analysts take each of these problems as indicators of the demise of employer associations, unions, and social partnership, leading in the worst case to a permanent polarization between a prosperous West and a backward East (Jürgens, Klinzing, and Turner 1993, 241–42; Lehmbruch 1994, 130–31). An alternative interpretation, however, more in line with the evidence presented here, views each of these problems as indicators of transformation and institutional adaptation, quite possibly on the road to a modern economy regulated by strong social partners.

Other problems, however, may well prove more intractable and potentially destabilizing for social partnership in the East. For one thing, although this was not true of our case-study firms, managers and works councillors told us repeatedly of *other* firms in the area that were paying under contractual levels, with the agreement of their own works councils. Some of these firms had dropped out of the employer association (or never joined) in order to do this; in other cases, they were doing this illegally despite association membership. In the latter cases, the union was reluctant to take legal action, since the better political solution lay in developing a union-conscious works council rather than fighting a legal battle against an agreement to which the elected works councillors had consented.

There is no doubt that this problem is widespread throughout eastern Germany in the current period (and has become a growing problem in western Germany as well). Possible interpretations, however, vary. Does this phenomenon represent the beginning of the end for comprehensive collective bargaining led by strong employer associations and unions—the pessimistic and perhaps prevalent view? Or does this sub-contractual wage-setting reflect a temporary period of adaptation and informal flexibility in a period of crisis and transformation?

Considerable evidence supports the latter view: the continuing unionization of many works councils that make such agreements; the consistent claim on the part both of works councils and management that such "adjustments" are only temporary, to save jobs in desperate circumstances; and the willingness of union and employer association to look the other way. IG Metallers, in fact (off the record), view such firms as strong cases for future union mobilization, if and when management attempts to break its promise and make such adjustments permanent.

The most serious problem for the future of social partnership and modernization in eastern Germany is clearly deindustrialization and the possibility that industry in the East will never recover from its dramatic collapse of 1991–92. Deindustrialization, with its corresponding mass unemployment, has indeed been the primary source of union membership decline in eastern Germany since 1992. The cases we have looked at, on the other hand, show potentially successful and innovative firms that may well attract future investment and contribute to processes of industrial recovery. Much depends here on government economic policy as well as the capacity of the social partners to continue to negotiate and promote compromise agreements that set the framework for stability and expansion (Kern 1994; Behrens 1995).

A final problem, directly linked to the preceding one, is continuing and long-term mass unemployment. In every case study, people related wrenching stories of almost unbelievable downsizing and mass layoffs. The firms that survived sell-off by the Treuhand did so with a fraction of their previously employed workforce. It is no secret that many of the displaced will never work again. Women have been heavily discriminated against in eastern processes of downsizing and restructuring (Maier 1993); and income inequality in the East has risen significantly (Steiner and Kraus 1994).

The instability of mass unemployment and growing income polarization is thus a potentially dangerous cost of rising productivity in eastern Germany. Not only does mass unemployment result in heavy and long-term fiscal burdens on the welfare state, massive dislocation and limited job opportunities open the door for demagoguery and related neo-Nazi terrorism against foreign or domestic scapegoats.[5] Mass unemployment, in other words, whether in the East or West, threatens the stability of postwar German democracy.

The long-term danger depends in part on the speed with which economic growth takes off in the East; while evidence of modernization examined here offers grounds for hope, growth rates of the mid-1990s remained far too low. The answer also depends on the ability of the social partners, especially the unions, to channel frustration and protest in constructive directions. Here again, the strike of 1993 gives reason to take an optimistic perspective. The danger of high unemployment and social instability in unified Germany, however, should not be underestimated.

THE FINDINGS: GENERALIZABLE FOR EASTERN GERMANY?

The evidence considered so far has been from the metal and electronics industries in eastern Germany. This is the most important sector to examine, given the pattern-setting role negotiations in this sector play and have played in both western and eastern Germany. To round out the case studies and assess to what extent the findings may be generalized, however, it is necessary to look at other sectors as well.

Findings for three additional sectors are briefly sketched out below: for the chemical industry, the next largest manufacturing sector after metal and electronics; for the public sector, including public transportation and a variety of other services; and for the postal service/telecommunications, public services in the process of privatization.[6] With metal and electronics, this survey thus includes within its scope the bargaining realm of the two largest manufacturing unions (IG Metall and IG Chemie) and the two largest public sector and service unions (ÖTV and DPG).

The Chemical Industry

Developments in the chemical industry in many ways paralleled those in metal and electronics. In both cases, the dominant reality in the early 1990s was industrial collapse. As in the metal industry, the Treuhand essentially took over the eastern chemical industry to engineer privatization, liquidation, and mass layoffs. After massive downsizing of the industry, new investment made it likely that the remaining eastern plants would in time be among Germany's most modern.

As firms were privatized (usually through purchase by a western chemical company), the employer association moved in to organize membership services and collective bargaining, but as in metal, membership remained lower than in the West. The union (IG Chemie) also moved in to sign up eastern members in large numbers and set the framework for eastern pay levels in bargaining with the corresponding regional employer associations, aimed above all at achieving wage parity with the West within a few years. As in metal and electronics, union membership was at first very high and then dropped, primarily with falling employment but to some extent as a product of worker disillusionment at the inability of the union to protect jobs. Elected works councillors in eastern firms were overwhelmingly members of IG Chemie who worked closely both with company and union.

Along with these similarities, there were important differences between developments in the two industries. For one thing, the chemical industry by its very structure (in both West and East) has fewer small firms than the metal industry. For the employer associations, since in both industries most of the large, influential firms belong to the associations, this means that the problem of membership is probably less serious in the chemical industry.[7] The same thing is quite possibly true for union membership; union sources estimated eastern membership density in 1993 to be around 70 percent.

Also important is the fact that relations of social partnership in the chemical industry are considerably more explicit than in the metal industry. In the West, IG Metall has traditionally been viewed as an "activist" union, in contrast to IG Chemie, the leading "accommodationist" union of recent decades (Markovits 1986). Under the leadership of Hermann Rappe, IG Chemie was extensively centralized in the 1980s, to provide a uniform policy orientation of labor-management cooperation and social partnership, along with policy innovations such as a common pay scale for white- and blue-collar workers (to modernize the union and bring in more white-collar members).[8] Such union policies were carried into the East, where Rappe and colleagues were quicker than other unions to take aboard former eastern union officials (Fichter 1993; Kittner 1991). As IG Metall was gearing up for its 1993 conflict with Gesamtmetall, IG Chemie quietly accepted a renegotiated 9 percent pay raise in a one-year contract that extended the projected wage-parity phase-in by two years, from 1994 to 1996[9]—in a move that IG Metall denounced as cutting the ground from under the bargaining position of metalworkers. By avoiding conflict, IG Chemie maintained close relations with employers in the East, receiving perks—such as full plant access with a chauffeured company car at the plant gates—that IG Chemie officials claimed were the envy of IG Metall.

Consideration of the chemical industry brings up an important point: the precise form that social partnership takes varies from industry to industry (as well as from region to region, firm to firm, and plant to plant). In the chemical industry, in the West as now in the East, labor-management relations are considerably less conflictual and more explicitly partnership oriented than in the metal industries. The chemical industry model may indeed be what some employers in Gesamtmetall would like to see, if only they could "tame" IG Metall. "Social partnership" therefore refers to a range of behavior and relationships, more or less independent, conflictual, or collaborationist.

Important differences notwithstanding, similarities prevail in an assessment of the future of social partnership in the chemical industry in eastern Germany. If anything, the chemical industry presents an even stronger case for optimism.

Both the union and active employer associations are solidly established in this industry in eastern Germany, with collective bargaining agreements that set the terms of pay and other standards for the entire industry. And the linkage to metal industry developments is also apparent. When Gesamtmetall demanded a raise reduction to 9 percent (from 26 percent) in 1993, the social partners in the chemical industry quickly settled on this exact figure. IG Chemie justified this course of action by arguing that because earlier pay raises in the chemical industry had been higher, the 9 percent would bring chemical workers up to the same level that 26 percent would bring metalworkers. Although IG Chemie officials were critical of what they saw as IG Metall's unnecessarily adversarial stance, they did not want to be seen as undercutting IG Metall demands. And IG Chemie officials in the spring of 1993 watched the metal negotiations and conflict closely, admitting that if IG Metall was defeated, then their own future contract negotiations would surely face new pressure.

Despite differences in strategy and industry structure, the chemical industry, like metal and electronics, offers evidence both for the possibility of future modernization in the East and for the resilience of social partnership (of different kinds) in adverse circumstances.

The Public Sector

The largest public sector union, Gewerkschaft Öffentliche Dienste, Transport und Verkehr (ÖTV, which is also the second largest German union after IG Metall), is the least homogeneous union in Germany, organizing in a variety of branches, from public transportation (the largest sector), to hospitals, to public administration, to universities, extending beyond the public sector into the private sector as well. To some extent, the union is internally decentralized to match its many branches; and internal debate has become increasingly lively, as demonstrated in 1992 when the membership in western Germany voted down a leadership-negotiated contract following a fourteen-day strike.

Despite this heterogeneous and somewhat chaotic internal structure, the ÖTV moved quickly into eastern Germany, recruiting members and founding an ÖTV-East in June of 1990. In early negotiations with the federal government, the union received guarantees in the fall of 1990 that ÖTV contracts would be negotiated for public workers in the East. The latter signed up quickly in large numbers for the new ÖTV-East, and in February of 1991, eastern and western unions merged into one much larger ÖTV (with over 2 million members).

By 1991, the rate of unionization for ÖTV in the public sector was up to 60 percent in the East, exceeding levels commonly found in the West. The eastern level would drop in subsequent years, as high expectations of union performance were not met: the union could neither prevent downsizing, deliver instant wage parity, nor supply vacation homes (as the old eastern union had done). The rate would nonetheless remain higher in the East than in the West, as steward structures were built up, personnel councils (the public sector equivalent of works councils) were elected and established as important union-supported negotiating bodies, and people learned what the union could and could not provide.

Eastern contracts were tied to western levels in two ways: first, easterners received automatic pay raises when westerners received their annual negotiated raises; and second, the ÖTV and the federal government established phased-in wage parity as the basic principle guiding pay levels in the East. Pay levels were set at around 60 percent of western levels in the first parity agreement in 1992; by July of 1993, eastern pay was up to 80 percent, followed by an increase to 87 percent in 1994.

ÖTV officials and activists followed the IG Metall strike of 1993 closely, convinced as they were that an IG Metall defeat (and successful employer contract cancellation) would provoke an attack on their own phased-in wage parity agreement. Thus ÖTV, the second-largest German union, strongly supported the IG Metall campaign, including active participation in demonstrations on April 15 and 24 prior to the strike. When IG Metall successfully defended the principle of phased-in wage parity, ÖTV officials breathed a sigh of relief, knowing that their own employers (principally the federal government, with bargaining power largely centralized in the Ministry of the Interior) would probably not attempt to imitate Gesamtmetall's defection.

By 1993, formal organizational transfer of ÖTV structures from West to East was completed. The major task of the union entering the mid-1990s was now to bring eastern union activists into the substructure, building up the elected shop steward and personnel councils into bastions of proactive unionism. Western ÖTV officials on assignment to the East noted the usual problems with eastern ignorance of what a union can (and cannot) do and what the members must be ready to do (to mobilize and strike when necessary); at the same time, they pointed to steady learning on the part of easterners and spoke with praise of the many easterners who had become active in the union. Many of the latter had held union positions under the old regime but had become enthusiastic supporters of western-style unionism now that they were freed of the dysfunctional constraints characteristic of the FDGB.

Despite continuing tensions within ÖTV between eastern and western members (easterners complaining that they weren't reaching parity fast enough; westerners maintaining that their interests were taking second place to the easterners), union officials expressed satisfaction at their organizational success in the East so far. The union appeared to have consolidated itself solidly in the East (as in the West) as the major organized workforce representative and collective bargaining agent in the public sector. Although the virtual identity of union and personnel council often seen in the West had not yet come about, most elected personnel councillors in the East were union members; and union officials viewed it as a matter of time before the tensions of the dual system had been overcome in the East as well as they had in the West. There seemed little doubt that the public sector in eastern Germany would establish itself as an important bastion of unionism, with pay and other standards set in social partner–style negotiations primarily between government and union.

Telecommunications and the Postal Service

The pressures of unification for postal and telecommunications services between East and West beginning in 1990 were complicated by the federal government's drive, already in progress, to privatize the Deutsche Bundespost (the large federal agency that in West Germany had included postal services, telecommunications, and the government savings bank). Major institutional change was therefore added to the already difficult processes of institutional transfer.

For the Bundespost, with each of its three divisions (postal services, telecommunications, savings bank) scheduled for privatization by the mid-1990s, the main task was to bring modern services to the East. As in other industries, top management saw opportunities to introduce the latest technology (since most equipment in the East had to be replaced) and high-productivity work organization (often referred to in this sector, as elsewhere, by the term "lean production"). Managers and union officials in telecommunications in particular described the new technology of the eastern infrastructure as "the most modern telecommunications system in the world."

Massive investment in the early 1990s was accompanied by severe downsizing, through early retirement, attrition, buyouts, and layoffs. By 1993, the workforce in the postal service and telecommunications had been reduced by 20,000, all but 250 of these "voluntary"; although the union had negotiated employment protections, buyouts occurred in many cases under pressure and were not as voluntary as had been contractually intended.

Employees eager to retain jobs, and their elected personnel councillors equally determined to preserve jobs, accepted major reorganization and productivity improvements along with the introduction of new technology. Managers from the West who came in to serve tours of duty found it much easier in the East than in the West to pressure the workforce to raise productivity. Eastern managers also quickly learned the new high-pressure, high-productivity ways, much to the resentment of their subordinates. By 1993, productivity in the telecommunications industry, according to both union and management sources, was already higher in eastern than in western Germany.

As in other sectors, the union faced great challenges and often found itself overtaxed. The Deutsche Postgewerkschaft (DPG) established its first office in East Berlin in March of 1990, negotiated its first contract that summer, and merged DPG West and East into one all-German postal and telecommunications union in November of 1990. In the face of great new employment insecurities, membership levels in the East quickly surpassed 90 percent. For the next three years, the rate of unionization would stay around this level, considerably exceeding the 73 percent level found in the West.

In the 1991 bargaining round, pay levels in the East were set at 60 percent of western levels, with no recognition of years of service (either for pay determination or for employment security). Eastern employees responded to the latter deficiency with anger, rank-and-file pressure, and union-led warning strikes, which finally resulted in a new contract later the same year recognizing years of service under the old system. In subsequent bargaining rounds, patterned by the Minister of the Interior after negotiations with ÖTV, eastern postal and telecommunications employees reached 80 percent of western pay levels in July of 1993, raised again to 87 percent in 1994.

The union, in this sector as in most other sectors public and private, thus quickly established high membership levels and broad collective bargaining coverage in the East. The development of a committed union organization, capable of mobilization and conflict when necessary, was nonetheless a longer-term proposition. Union officials claimed that three conflicts in 1991–92, each one including warning strikes, helped to educate eastern employees to the possibility and occasional necessity of mobilization. Convinced that an IG Metall defeat in the strike of 1993 would have led to the cancellation of their own scheduled pay raises in July of that year, DPG officials also pointed to that widely observed "demonstration" strike as a powerful learning experience for their own members.

In a period of extreme job insecurity, however, building up a strong union presence in the workplace was a slow process; the first elections for shop stewards held throughout eastern Germany did not take place until the fall of 1993. In the meantime, personnel councillors, almost of all them now DPG members, had been elected throughout eastern Germany.[10] Some of these had been leaders in the BGL (*Betriebsgewerkschaftsleitung*, the plant union committee under the old regime) and were now working with their former management counterparts to follow orders from above regarding downsizing, modernization, and dramatic productivity improvements. Non-BGL leaders elected to the personnel council also tended to work cooperatively with management in the face of new imperatives for survival in a market economy. The union saw one of its primary tasks as the training and socialization of these elected personnel councillors into the role of strong union members and independent negotiating counterparts for management, leaders capable of actively promoting worker interests even when the latter clashed with company interests.[11]

In continuing downsizing in both East and West (a result of privatization and technological and organization innovation), the union faced major challenges in keeping its membership satisfied.[12] At the same time, DPG officials saw grounds for optimism in other developments as well. For one thing, the *union* was taking advantage of the transformation in the East to introduce organizational innovations long planned in the West. Instead of local unions, for example, the DPG in the East promoted plant unions, which headquarters in Frankfurt favored as a more efficient structure (eliminating, in a sense, the local union office "middleman" role). As elections for plant union leadership were held, full-time personnel councillors were often elected to these posts as well, a development that consolidated worker interest representation and to some extent undermined the separations and tensions inherent in the dual system. DPG officials saw this as a positive development, one they predicted that would increase union influence at the plant level, rationalize national union structure, and lead to innovations in union structure in the West (where some regions already functioned this way). Thus institutional transfer in this case was accompanied by potentially union-strengthening institutional reform.

In addition, in anticipation of future privatization, eastern postal and telecommunications employees were in most cases not given the status of civil servant (*Beamte*) as in the West. Because civil-servant status eliminated the right to strike, the union viewed this development in the East as another one that could potentially increase union influence. In addition, the majority of postal and telecommunications employees (and union members) in the East were women, a development that was yielding new female leadership at the regional and plant levels and on the personnel councils. Union officials predicted a spillover effect in the West, strengthening the position of women who campaigned for union office and thereby contributing to the modernization of the DPG.

The most troubling development for the DPG in eastern Germany appeared to be the future impact of privatization, with accompanying firm restructuring that would include smaller, more weakly unionized subsidiaries along with contracted-out services. The union was determined to use its existing high membership levels to get an early foothold in such spin-offs, and to develop new strategy to organize and keep such subsidiaries and other supplier and service firms organized. Despite the massive pressure accompanying unification, institutional transfer and reform, continual downsizing and organizational change, and privatization, however, the DPG seemed on the whole well placed to maintain a central position of influence, high membership levels, and comprehensive collective bargaining coverage.

Social Partnership: Resilience
and Adaptation in Eastern Germany

Evidence from other sectors supports conclusions drawn from the metal and electronics industries: relations of social partnership exist throughout the eastern economy; employer associations and unions (or government and unions in the public sector) have established significant collective bargaining coverage (although not yet as comprehensive as in the West); both employer associations and unions, despite enduring pressures and difficulties, have solid bases for present and future membership; eastern Germany appears in many ways well positioned for future economic growth and modernization in both industry and services.

Although membership density is lower for the employer associations in the East than in the West, most large and many middle-sized firms belong. The associations have established offices and a network of services (legal, collective bargaining, strike support, codetermination advice) and have taken an aggressive stance in the consolidation of broadly acceptable collective bargaining agreements. Union membership density, by contrast, is higher in most sectors in the East than in the West.[13] Unions in each of the sectors considered have established solid membership bases that include most elected works and personnel council members, who have in turn been trained by the unions. Successful labor conflicts and bargaining outcomes, above all in the pattern-setting metal industry, have helped to establish a workplace base for union influence. At the same time, the challenges of eastern economic crisis have promoted a decentralization of union activity, to the sectoral, local, and firm levels (through bargaining adjustments and industrial policy)—decentralization not at all incompatible with continuing union influence and which could even contribute to the revitalization of German unions in the West (Behrens 1995, 86–92).

In each of the sectors considered, while economic collapse, deindustrialization, and mass unemployment have taken an enormous economic and personal toll, there is important evidence of modernization. Innovations in many cases surpass standard practice in the West, including new technology (new machinery in the factories; a state-of-the-art fiber-optic network for eastern telecommunications) and production organization (semi-autonomous group work; just-in-time supplier relations). Sectoral evidence shows elements of a modern base for potential economic takeoff in the East.

The most serious problem for modernization of the economy in eastern Germany is deindustrialization. The "industrial core" has dropped to a dangerously low level, beyond which the necessary networks and infrastructure for the expansion of modern industry may no longer be available (Grabher 1992). On the other hand, the skills base is substantial in eastern Germany, contributing to significant increases in productivity. When compared to areas such as Northern

Ireland where great effort has been expended to develop industry, "underlying productivity" has risen far more rapidly in eastern Germany—given access to western capital, the transfer of an institutional framework from western Germany, and the solid human capital base in the East (Hitchens, Wagner, and Birnie 1993). Direct causes for rising productivity include new work organization, retraining, increased intensity of work, and new plants and technology (Wagner, Hitchens, and Birnie 1994). Although it is far from a foregone conclusion, the potential is clearly present in eastern Germany for rapid growth and modernization.

Explaining Resilience

Three factors stand out, from close examination of the case studies and other evidence, as most persuasive in explaining the consolidation and resilience of social partnership relations in eastern Germany. First, the transfer of institutions—employer associations, industrial unions, comprehensive collective bargaining arrangements, elected works councils, and legally mandated codetermination—from West to East has provided an important framework or superstructure for a new social partnership in the East.[14] In the absence of this dense and flexible institutional apparatus, it is difficult to imagine the rapid consolidation of cohesive and encompassing interest groups that could engage in meaningful bargaining relationships (and indeed no such consolidation has occurred in other eastern European countries where such extensive institutional transfer is not the case). Time and again in the case and sector studies, we have seen works councils, unions, employer associations, and individual employers using newly established collective bargaining or codetermination channels to promote their interests and negotiate settlements that all actors can accept.

Second, this institutional apparatus has taken root in the remnants of the old system; the institutions, in other words, have proven compatible (in many instances although certainly not all), with appropriate adaptations, to existing circumstances and historical legacy. The combination of inherited skills and a tradition of informal, common workplace effort, for example, has provided a base both for modern production innovations such as group work and for works council and union solidarity and activism.

Finally, within the framework set by institutional transfer and historical legacy, actors have made choices and adaptations that have promoted the consolidation of social partnership. At the plant and firm level, employees and elected works councillors decided overwhelmingly to join unions, and in many cases to give active support to union-led campaigns when called upon to do so; and this is true despite ongoing tensions and distance between eastern works councils and unions in the transferred dual system. At the industry level, metal and electronics workers quite surprisingly chose to back a risky strike that significantly consolidated the position of pattern-setting IG Metall in eastern Germany. Large employers, for their part, have so far chosen to belong to appropriate employer associations and to give their backing to comprehensive collective bargaining. At the same time, the militancy of small and medium-sized employers, many of them not members of the associations, has pushed employer associations to take a more aggressive stance in collective bargaining. This latter choice (one among a menu of possibilities) has in turn resulted in (1) contractual adjustments and innovations, including the lengthening of the time period for phased-in wage parity, that made labor more affordable in the East; and (2) a solidaristic labor response that considerably strengthened the position of unions in the East.

Each of these choices has been shaped by the framework of institutional transfer and adaptation. Very different choices were possible, and indeed were made elsewhere (in eastern and central Europe) where similar institutional frameworks do not exist.

Relations of social partnership, in other words, were consolidated in eastern Germany in the early to mid-1990s because of appropriate institutions (transferred in from the West), the flexible adaptation of these institutions to existing circumstances and historical legacies, and the choices, themselves shaped by the combination of new institutions, existing circumstances, and legacies, that individuals and organizations have made to work with and within these given channels. The evidence points to each of these as necessary conditions for the consolidation and adaptation of social partnership in eastern Germany.

CHAPTER FIVE

Renewed Conflict in the West, 1993–1994

Having failed in the spring of 1993 to defeat IG Metall and substantially change power relations between employers and unions in eastern Germany, Gesamtmetall tried again later the same year, this time in western Germany. In the fall of 1993, the employer association for the metal and electronics industries announced the cancellation of contracts covering wages, salaries, and vacation pay, to take effect upon the expiration of the contracts in early 1994. Once again, employers anticipated a victory of breakthrough proportions.[1] With unemployment high and traditional job security undermined by waves of firm downsizing and with investment threatening to flee Germany for new cheap-labor locations in central and eastern Europe, employers rightly perceived their own high bargaining power. IG Metall, thrown on the defensive again, braced itself for another major battle. The ensuing conflict and its outcome provided the second watershed event in post-unification industrial relations.

1993–1994: METAL BARGAINING IN THE WEST

Employer Offensive

Collective bargaining throughout West Germany's history was typically initiated when the union announced its intention to seek improvements by formally canceling an existing contract, effective the date of its expiration. Bargaining would then precede the expiration date, leading to the signing of a new contract or to a strike, which the union would be free to initiate only after expiration of the "peace obligation" (allowing time for a bargained settlement as well as mediation). The burden in this arrangement lies generally with the union, the proactive partner seeking change (such as pay increases or reductions in working time) in established working conditions (Berghahn and Karsten 1987, 103).

At the end of September 1993, Gesamtmetall, for the first time ever in western Germany, took the offensive by announcing the cancellation of contracts covering pay and vacation bonuses and declaring its intention to negotiate levels of compensation downward. Only once before had Gesamtmetall canceled a contract, in late 1992 for the metal industries of eastern Germany. As we have seen, that previous cancellation occurred in the middle of a contract period, in response to unexpectedly adverse economic circumstances faced by employers in the East. After a passionate and successful strike by eastern metalworkers, the settlement in May 1993 included a formal statement by Gesamtmetall that cancellation had been an extraordinary event and should not constitute a precedent for collective bargaining in unified Germany. Four months after making that statement, however, Gesamtmetall announced cancellation of the western contracts in a fashion that *was* accepted as legal by all involved: cancellation not in the middle of a contract period but upon expiration. Although unquestioned in its legality, the fact that the employers had taken the offensive in collective bargaining was widely viewed as a dramatic and provocative step, the western counterpart to the earlier eastern drive to eliminate phased-in wage parity.

What pushed the employers to such bold action? The answer, similar to what we have seen in parallel eastern events, is threefold: the perceived *need* to lower costs; the internal *politics* of Gesamtmetall, especially the escalating demands of small and middle-sized firms for greater flexibility and lower costs; and the *opportunity* for a successful offensive afforded by rising unemployment, job insecurity, and the credible threat of disinvestment in Germany.

By 1993, German firms were widely perceived as facing substantial cost disadvantages relative to competitors from other nations. As reported in the *Financial Times*:

> Since the mid-1980s, industry has been hit by above-average increases in wage and non-wage costs and an appreciating D-mark. The Federation of German Industry's research institute calculates that west Germany's unit labour costs in 1992 were 23 per cent higher than a weighted average of other industrial countries, compared with a position 14 per cent below the average in 1985. According to the OECD, Germany's share of world exports has fallen more since 1987 than that of any other of the group of seven leading industrial countries. Germany needs lower labour costs.[2]

More and more employers seemed to believe that the unions, especially IG Metall, had made too many bargaining gains in the 1980s, with economic growth and union strength driving both rising real wages and a declining workweek. By the late 1980s and early 1990s, there was widespread talk of renewed militancy within employer ranks, especially on the part of small and medium-sized firms. As president of Gesamtmetall, Hans-Joachim Gottschol, himself a representative of the *Mittelstand,* had shown a willingness to take a hard line, as evidenced both in his public statements and in the contract cancellation that had provoked the strike in eastern Germany. As in the East, there was widespread concern that small and middle-sized employers would abandon an employer association that had let costs rise too fast. The contract cancellation in the West, announced in September of 1993, was widely seen as "a grassroots insurrection of smaller companies in the industry."[3]

Finally, as earlier in the year in the East, the temptation to go for a major victory over labor must have proven irresistible. Unemployment had risen steadily in 1993, to exceed 4 million in January 1994 for the first time since the Great Depression. At 8.8 percent unemployment, there were 2.7 million out of work in western Germany; at 17 percent, there were 1.3 million in eastern Germany.[4] Employment in the metal and electronics industries represented by Gesamtmetall and IG Metall was dropping at a rate of 30,000 jobs per month.[5] Severe economic recession combined with the new availability of skilled and very low-cost labor nearby in central and eastern Europe to put heavy pressure on the German labor market. As Hans-Peter Stihl, president of the German Chambers of Commerce, put it: "Either German unions will accept substantial reductions in incomes and wages or we will lose more jobs. We also have the possibility of moving more jobs abroad."[6]

Labor market pressure and new employer determination to cut costs resulted in innovative and widely noticed firm-level agreements at important western firms in the period leading up to the 1994 metal industry bargaining round. At both Opel and Mercedes, for example, 1993 agreements between the company and works council traded-off pay and benefit concessions for new investment and job guarantees.[7] At the electrical engineering firm Robert Bosch, a cost-cutting, income-reducing agreement was reached in October after eight months of negotiations.[8] IBM Deutschland reached an agreement with the white-collar union DAG (not a member of the DGB) to increase working hours from thirty-six to thirty-eight hours without a corresponding increase in pay.[9] In the most widely noted firm-level settlement, Volkswagen (not a member of Gesamtmetall) reached an agreement with its general works council in November (to take effect January 1, 1994) to reduce the working hours of all employees by 20 percent, with an accompanying 10 percent drop in pay and a company promise to save 30,000 jobs that would otherwise have been lost.[10] The VW agreement in particular was widely praised in union and large-employer circles and viewed as a possible model for the introduction of greater firm-level flexibility within comprehensive collective bargaining frameworks.

Industry-Wide Mobilization

In public statements in the fall of 1993, Gesamtmetall highlighted the trend toward greater flexibility and cost reduction, emphasized the danger of disinvestment in Germany due to high costs, and demanded both a 10 percent reduction in labor costs along with new working hours flexibility in a "corridor" between thirty and forty hours, to be determined at the firm level. The union denounced the employer offensive and its radical demands, asked for a 5.5–6 percent pay raise (in a year in which inflation was expected to be around 3 percent), and demanded guarantees of employment security in exchange for any new agreements on plant-level flexibility. Public posturing continued through the fall and winter with little evidence of movement on either side.

In January of 1994, Gesamtmetall was heartened (and IG Metall disappointed) when labor and management in the chemical industry settled on a new contract that included both a working hours corridor for firm-level flexibility and a sub-inflation pay raise.[11] While IG Metall and some large firms continued to hold up the VW agreement as a reasonable compromise between the employer need to cut costs and the employee need for income and employment security, small and medium-sized employers criticized the settlement at Volkswagen as too expensive. Driven by the militancy of its small and medium-sized members, Gesamtmetall showed little willingness to compromise, threatened lockouts in response to a union strike, and actively prepared for a protracted labor conflict.

Once again, the rhetoric of battle filled the air. In this dominant and pattern-setting industry, employers spoke of the need to decentralize bargaining, cut costs substantially, open up the rigid central bargaining system, and knock the powerful IG Metall down off its perch. The union spoke of the need to defend jobs, living standards, the social partnership, and trade unionism in the face of an all-out employer offensive. Although IG Metall signaled its willingness to accept reasonable wage restraint and Gesamtmetall indicated flexibility on a demand for the elimination of holiday pay, the two sides remained far apart. When formal talks collapsed on February 11, 1994, a major strike looked likely; expectations were widespread that a strike in 1994 would be the biggest in western Germany since the 1984 strike/lockout in the metal industries that had resulted in first movement toward the 35-hour workweek. Once again, in a situation of high unemployment, widespread layoffs, deep economic recession, and high firm inventories, many predicted a defeat for IG Metall, one that would decentralize the collective bargaining system, substantially weaken union influence in unified Germany, and thereby undermine the foundations of social partnership. Given employer determination and economic reality, many union supporters (along with some union leaders, off the record) feared the worst, an employer-provoked strike that the union could not win.

IG Metall, meanwhile, called out its members for warning strikes three times in February. On February 2–3, an estimated 270,000 metalworkers participated in warning strikes and rallies across western Germany in actions directed against the pay cuts demanded by employers. In the north around Hamburg and Bremen, for example, 65,000 workers from 200 different firms stopped work for four hours or more, many of them joining spirited, banner-waving marches and demonstrations.[12] After a second wave of warning strikes on February 11, 300,000 metalworkers, blue- and white-collar, joined warning strikes and rallies on February 25, in the biggest single day of action.

The warning strikes demonstrated convincingly the level of workforce passion and solidarity that IG Metall had hoped to arouse. Even in the most adverse circumstances—high unemployment, severe recession, unprecedented job insecurity, strike-weakening legislation[13]—employees appeared ready to strike. With a passion paralleling that seen in eastern Germany a year earlier, western workers expressed widespread anger at the consessionary demands of the employers as the union and its members prepared for a long strike.[14]

With talks still suspended and no settlement in sight, IG Metall announced Lower Saxony as the target area for the first strike votes in early March. Observers had expected the union to target one of its stronger bases of industrial concentration, such as Baden-Württemburg (where the 1984 strike had begun) or North Rhine-Westphalia (including the industrial Ruhr district). The surprising choice of Lower Saxony reflected three decisions on the part of IG Metall (each sending a specific message to the employers). First, Lower Saxony, less heavily industrialized than other regions with a correspondingly lower number of metalworkers, represented a potential de-escalation of the momentum building toward a major labor conflict.[15] Second, because Volkswagen, based in Wolfsburg, dominates the industrial landscape of the area, the union signaled its focus on the VW model—work sharing through general hours reduction in return for employment guarantees—as a basis for negotiation. And third, the choice of Lower Saxony undermined the threatened employer lockout strategy in a rather sophisticated manner: by targeting specific firms without supplier relationships to VW for the first round of strikes, the union left Gesamtmetall with little choice but to include VW suppliers in its threatened lockouts. Fearing permanent loss of their supplier status at a time when VW was putting great pressure on suppliers, these firms could be expected to exert pressure within Gesamtmetall against the planned lockout strategy. In addition, lockouts at VW suppliers could have quickly spread the shutdown effects to Volkswagen itself, where employees were not subject to paragraph 116 restrictions (since VW does not belong to the employer association and had already settled with IG Metall) and were thus eligible for unemployment benefits from the state. A lockout strategy that closed VW plants in Lower Saxony would therefore have mobilized a massive labor contingent (the highly unionized VW workforce) in support of the strike at little cost to IG Metall.

With great fanfare, the results of the strike vote in Lower Saxony were announced on March 3. Of 41,000 members eligible to vote, 97 percent participated, and 92 percent of them voted to strike.[16] The results exceeded IG Metall expectations. The union announced Monday morning, March 7, as the strike deadline, targeting twenty-two companies, including 11,000 employees in the first round. President Gottschol of Gesamtmetall immediately called for talks with his IG Metall counterpart Klaus Zwickel to prevent the coming strike. On March 4, regional union and employer negotiators, with Gottschol, Zwickel, and other executive board members from both sides either present or in the background, began once again to bargain seriously. This session lasted continuously for fourteen hours until an innovative settlement was announced on the morning of March 5.

The union bargaining commission (*Tarifkommission*) for Lower Saxony approved the settlement unanimously, suspended the strike threat, and scheduled a second strike vote (to approve or reject the proposed settlement) for March 9–11.[17] Needing only 25 percent to approve the agreement (since a strike requires a 75 percent vote), the union secured a vote of 68 percent from the IG Metallers of Lower Saxony in support of the settlement.

Meanwhile, executive boards of IG Metall and Gesamtmetall had approved the settlement and sent it out to all regions for pattern bargaining. On both sides, ratification occurred quickly. Although union opponents denounced the low wage raise, which meant a loss of real income for workers, the settlement was approved in most areas by large majorities. The strike/lockout threats were over; the largest threatened labor conflict in the West in ten years had been headed off at the last moment.

Settlement: Wage Restraint, Flexibility, Employment Guarantees

The negotiated settlement was a compromise that both sides could portray to their members as a victory on key points. Most importantly, the employers secured a level of wage restraint that would ensure significant cost reductions; and employees, for the first time, received provisions for employment security, to be negotiated at the plant level, in regional contracts.

The pay settlement was in effect a "null" round. From January to May 1994 the workers received no pay raise at all; from June to December, the pay raise was 2 percent, but this was offset by a small reduction in both Christmas bonus and holiday pay. With a net wage freeze for the year, employees would lose real income against the estimated 3 percent inflation level. Gesamtmetall announced this result to its members as a major breakthrough in the cost of doing business in Germany;[18] IG Metall took credit both for having blocked employer demands for a 10–15 percent pay cut and for having made a reasonable contribution to improving the competitiveness of German industry.[19]

Both sides also referred to the VW model in including new provisions on hours reduction and employment security. The union defended the basic 36-

hour workweek (to be reduced as scheduled to 35 hours in 1995), while firms achieved the right to reduce the workweek to 30 hours, with works council agreement. If the hours of all employees of a plant were reduced, the employees would receive no pay compensation for the lost hours but would receive full employment security at least through the end of 1995.[20] If only particular groups of employees had reduced hours, they would not be guaranteed employment security but instead would get negotiated pay compensation of at least 35 percent.[21] Finally, acceding to an important IG Metall demand, the employers agreed to hire for at least six months all apprentices completing their training.

While portraying this "null pay round" as a necessary compromise, the union claimed victory in turning back all of the key consessionary demands of the employers, especially the call for a large pay cut, and in securing for the first time an employment security framework in a regional/national agreement. Gesamtmetall, meanwhile, lauded the null pay round as an important contribution to the preservation of "Germany as a production site," noting both the modest improvements in labor flexibility as well as the stiff resistance of IG Metall that prevented further breakthroughs.[22]

PATTERN BARGAINING

The Resilience of Social Partnership

As both sides acknowledged, the agreement was clearly a compromise. At the very least, both sides gained from the avoidance of a major strike/lockout. At best, each side could reasonably present the settlement to its members as a measured success under adverse circumstances. In the employers' camp, the null pay round was widely praised and appeared to satisfy for the time being the outspoken small and medium-sized firms that had pushed for a hard line in bargaining. There was no sign of employer flight from Gesamtmetall in the wake of this settlement. On the union side, the agreement was widely ratified, both by regional bargaining commissions and the rank and file.

In an era marked by the widespread decentralization of bargaining in most countries, the center had held remarkably well in Germany. Although the agreement in the metal industries opened up new possibilities for firm-level negotiations on pay and working hours between works council and management, the framework conditions for such negotiation were uniform throughout all regions of western Germany. And looking beyond the pattern-setting metal industry, bargaining outcomes throughout German industry remained as closely linked as ever. The chemical industry bargaining settlement of January 1994, a virtual null pay round itself, set the pay pattern for the metalworking industry, although IG

Metall added stronger provisions for employment security.[23] The metal agreement in turn established a pay pattern followed closely in the major public sector bargaining settlement agreed to a few days later on March 11, covering 3.5 million public employees.[24]

The bargaining outcomes of 1994 appeared quite promising for the future of German industry and industrial relations. An editorial in the *Financial Times* referred to the March metalworking agreement as "an accord which unambiguously favours competitiveness while preserving Germany's consensus-based social partnership."[25] And as argued in a *Süddeutsche Zeitung* editorial:

> The bargaining partners in the metal industry, who have long played a key role in the regulation of working conditions that extends far beyond their own sector, have once again established a milestone in the collective bargaining landscape. . . . In one of the most difficult crisis situations of the postwar period, the social partners have succeeded in finding a good compromise, one that corresponds to economic reality and thereby demonstrates that free collective bargaining is not an instrument suitable only for good weather.[26]

Vitality of the Employer Associations and Unions

In the wake of 1994 settlements in the chemical and metal industries and the public sector, pattern bargaining remained firmly established in western Germany. In addition, pattern bargaining demonstrated a new flexibility in its capacity to offer firm-level variation, approved and regulated by the social partners. All wage settlements were fixed below inflation, at 2 percent or less, even in thriving sectors such as construction and banking where larger gains may have been possible.[27] Wage restraint, pattern bargaining, and new flexibility worked together in 1994 in the interests both of competitiveness for German firms and the preservation of social partnership.

Not only did employer associations and unions in different sectors follow economy-wide patterns, important new instances of cross-sector collaboration occurred as well. For white-collar employees, ÖTV (the large public sector union within the DGB) and DAG (an exclusively white-collar union outside the DGB, traditionally a rival of the ÖTV in the public sector) announced a new intention to work together.[28] The leaders of the two unions called for the development of common bargaining positions, an end to adversarial competitive organizing, and new contacts and cooperation at all levels of the two organizations. At the same time, in response to the coming privatization of telecommunications, two powerful DGB unions, IG Metall and Deutsche Postgewerkschaft (DPG), reached an agreement to demarcate clearly noncompetitive union membership lines, to support each other's negotiations and labor conflicts, and to put forward common positions within works councils at the plant level.[29]

After the successful IG Metall strike of spring 1993 in eastern Germany and the western metal industry compromise of 1994 (each followed by similar agreements in other sectors), the patterned linkage between collective bargaining agreements in eastern and western Germany appeared solid. The ÖTV contract of 1994, for example, brought bargaining for East and West together for the first time, pegging eastern pay levels at 87 percent of western levels by 1995. To prevent layoffs in the East, the contract opened up the new possibility of reductions in working hours to 32 hours per week, with the terms of pay compensation to be negotiated between district union offices and public employers. A new provision also allowed for part-time work for parents of young children, for up to five years.[30]

As pattern bargaining consolidated itself across unified Germany in the mid-1990s, the possibility arose that innovations such as those described above in the eastern public sector could in the future set useful precedents for contracts in the West. Influences now appeared to be moving both ways between East and West. In the metal and electronic industries, for example, we have seen how the eastern strike victory of 1993 was supported by warning strikes in the West; this victory in turn provided important lift to the solidarity of western metalworkers in their successful campaign of February–March 1994. And after the latter settlement, both Gesamtmetall and IG Metall officials in the East pointed to the new hours-reduction/employment-security framework as a pattern for their own future bargaining.[31]

In 1994, a planned restructuring and downsizing of the umbrella DGB began to take shape. With the death of DGB president Heinz-Werner Meyer, IG Metall candidate Dieter Schulte was elected to succeed him and to guide the federation into a new era in which the leading role of the large member unions would be reinforced. Such changes were in some cases strongly opposed by DGB staff, smaller unions (which relied on the DGB for services such as training), and advocates of progressive issues such as union democracy and a stronger organizational role for women (for which DGB staff had provided active support). The primary effect of consolidation and downsizing at the DGB, however, would be to recognize and reflect the long existing postwar reality: that power in the German labor movement resides in the member unions, especially in the larger pattern-setting unions such as IG Metall, ÖTV, and IG Chemie. To the extent that much-needed reforms such as union democracy, increased participation of women, and strategies for new production organization are to realized, the major locus for debate and change will continue to be within the member unions, rather than through the organizational channels of the DGB.

More important than the reconstitution of the DGB itself was the prospect of merger among various member unions, to consolidate the federation into a smaller number of larger unions (Silvia 1993, 33–35). By the mid-1990s, merger processes were well under way, as smaller unions signed on with larger unions to strengthen bargaining power. Both the consolidation of large, powerful industrial unions and the continuing relatively weak position of the umbrella federation are entirely consistent with the central role of comprehensive collective bargaining and codetermination as the sector and firm-based centerpieces of social partnership in unified Germany.

Critical to the survival of social partnership, of course, is the ability of both employer associations and unions to retain existing and recruit new membership. Low membership levels in Gesamtmetall in the new states of eastern Germany were an important reason for the hard-line bargaining position of the employer association in the winter and spring of 1993. Through the mid-1990s, membership levels in the East remained low relative to the West, a source of concern for employer associations and unions alike.

In the West, there had been much talk ever since the late 1980s about the flight of small and medium-sized (and possibly even some large) firms from the employer associations. As we have seen, discontent among medium-sized firms was a major catalyst for the employer offensive in the metal industry bargaining round of 1993–94. Yet a 1993 survey of 232 firms in the metal industry of the state of Hesse (in the center of western Germany, including Frankfurt) showed clearly that "employer flight" was a myth. On the contrary, 84 percent of the firms expressed a positive opinion of the work of the employer association (called Hessen Metall in this area). Firms cited numerous important and valuable services provided by the association, including collective bargaining as well as the representation of individual firms in dealings with the Federal Labor Bureau, the union, the political arena, and economic regulatory agencies.[32]

Union membership in unified Germany rose sharply, both in absolute numbers and in membership density, in 1990–91, as new eastern members joined western (now all-German) unions in large numbers. As we have seen, eastern membership subsequently dropped off severely in 1992–93 under the impact of deindustrialization and economic collapse. While the drop was primarily due to the loss of jobs, disappointed expectations also contributed to a more gradual drop in membership density, so that by 1994, levels were headed down toward the more "realistic" levels of the West.[33] Under the impact of rising unemployment, union membership totals also dropped significantly in western Germany in 1991–95, from 7.6 to 7.0 million (Fichter 1997).

Falling membership was a major union concern in the mid-1990s. Overall union membership density, nonetheless, bolstered by new recruitment in the East, remained in unified Germany in the 1990s close to the relatively stable levels observed in western Germany in the 1970s and 1980s (variously cited through the mid-1990s as somewhere in the 30–35 percent range, depending upon the method of calculation).[34]

Most troubling for the unions was persistent weakness in recruiting new legions of professional, technical, and other white-collar workers to add to the continuing high-density base among blue-collar workers. What had already been a widely noted problem in the 1970s and 1980s (Armingeon 1989, 6–8) became an even more serious problem in the 1990s, as the employment structure continued to shift in favor of white-collar employees. The future of the German labor movement in the mid-1990s hinged significantly on the development of new strategies to organize and address the needs of the new white-collar employees (including large numbers of technically and professionally trained young men and women).[35]

Although prospects here appeared limited, signs of hope could nonetheless be discerned. Most unions were making the recruitment of white-collar employees a major priority (at least for study and strategy development). IG Chemie, for example, had reached a breakthrough agreement with the employer association to eliminate separate salary grades for blue- and white-collar workers, as a way to bring into the union the white-collar employee of the future. IG Metall led an important strike victory at the American computer firm DEC (Digital Equipment GmbH) in Germany in 1993, in the course of which union membership rose dramatically from under 10 percent to over 30 percent (Rossmann 1994; Wever 1995). Finally, the percentage of organized white-collar employees remained considerably higher in eastern than in western Germany (note, for example, the Siemens and El Pro case studies in Chapter 3), offering hope for a spillover effect as unions learned from their extensive representational work with white-collar employees in the East.

UNIFIED GERMANY AT MID-DECADE

By 1994, after watershed metal industry settlements in both East and West, the new Germany stood unified on the basis of social partnership negotiation and regulation. The battles of 1993 and 1994 consolidated the framework of industrial relations and labor-management negotiation for unified Germany. In a broad sense, social partnership, with all the concept entails—strong unions and employer associations, comprehensive collective bargaining, codetermination, and regularized conflict and negotiation throughout the political economy—had been tested and confirmed as a central element of the institutional framework for unified Germany.

What remained to be achieved was important, especially in the East: continuing adaptations of the institutions to local circumstances, in local workplaces and in networks of individuals and associations, the deepening of roots as local actors made the institutions their own. All of this would take time, great effort, and continuing institutional reform and change. East-West tensions and cultural differences would persist, for a generation or more. The pain and suffering of an overburdened society, the dislocation and injustice, would last for years. It is fair to say, however, that by 1994 Germany was unified, in a broad sense and in important ways, irrevocably and with remarkable success in a very short period of time.

Did this mean that all problems were solved? Of course not. By the mid-1990s, several critical problems stood clearly in focus. The ability to meet these challenges would test, and to a large extent determine, the future viability of social partnership regulation, in a global economy marked by growing pressures for deregulation (Albert 1993).

Unified Germany as a Production Site? The Growing Debate

High Costs

One positive product of social-partner negotiations throughout the postwar period has been rising wages, benefits, and other social standards. In the 1980s and 1990s (especially in the months preceding important bargaining rounds), rising wages accompanied by declining work hours and improved social benefits resulted in escalating government and employer criticism of the cost of doing business in Germany. In this view, rising labor costs threaten the future vitality of *Industriestandort Deutschland* (Germany as a production site), which in turn endangers hard-earned German living standards and social harmony.[36]

As the German economy fell into deep recession in 1993, the *Standort* debate escalated. As in the United States, major companies announced planned layoffs numbering in the tens of thousands; unemployment rose toward 4 million in unified Germany, a level unheard of since the 1930s. A government report issued in September 1993 warned of the danger to the competitiveness of German firms posed by high labor costs and long vacations.[37] Comparative data indeed showed troublesome recent trends for German productivity growth and unit labor costs in relation to other industrial societies.[38] While union research reports downplayed the problems and accused employers and the conservative government of exaggeration for political purposes, employers loudly trumpeted the comparisons, using them (as we have seen above) as justification for major bargaining offensives aimed at labor cost reduction in 1993 and 1994 (and on through the 1990s).

Evidence presented and analyzed by independent sources does not appear to support the claim that Germany in the mid-1990s was in fact in the throes of a major labor-cost-induced crisis of competitiveness. The Deutsches Institut für Wirtschaftsforschung (DIW), for example, an independent (although "labor-friendly") research institute based in Berlin, issued a report in July 1993 showing the relatively slow growth of unit labor costs in the Federal Republic, when compared to the average for industrial societies over the preceding twenty-five-year period.[39] To the extent that relative costs had risen in Germany, this was largely a product of an appreciating deutschmark. DIW's findings emphasized Germany's competitive strengths, such as its highly skilled workforce and enormous investments in machinery in the early 1990s and concluded that the German economy was well poised in the 1990s for both productivity growth and good economic performance.

Another independent source, the International Institute of Management Development, rates countries on a scale of international competitiveness based on eight factors, including infrastructure, technology, finance, and labor. Although Germany had fallen relative to the United States, Denmark, and Switzerland since 1992–93, Germany still ranked fifth in 1993 on a "world competitiveness scoreboard" of twenty-two industrial societies (with Japan at the top).[40]

As concluded in an independent, employer-oriented industrial relations newsletter based in London in 1994:

> The "hysteria" surrounding the debate on Germany as a location has at times suggested that the country is on the verge of an industrial apocalypse. Arguably, this has little to do with the realities of Germany's economic performance, which despite recent problems—largely associated with economic recession and unification—continues to be outstanding by international standards, and more to do with the fact that interest groups have sought to manipulate the debate in pursuit of their own short-term ends, particularly in the collective bargaining arena.[41]

When the wage restraint (falling real wages) and new hours flexibility of the 1994 bargaining rounds were added to the above reports (all of which preceded those bargaining rounds), Germany and its social partnership appeared well poised to cope at least with the labor-cost challenges of the mid-1990s. This issue, however, would resurface throughout the decade, in labor battles such as the metal bargaining rounds of 1995 and 1996–97, as German industry continued to seek cost reduction in an increasingly competitive global economy. The key issues for the social partners would be shaped by escalating debates within the employer camp: was social partnership an expensive relic of an earlier sheltered era, now to be swept away through conflict, deregulation, and growing disinvestment in domestic German industry, or could the social partners find viable consensual solutions? While the evidence presented in this book supports the latter conclusion, the debates, cost adjustments, and danger of a breakup of social partnership through protracted open conflict were sure to persist into the new millennium.[42]

FIGHTING FOR PARTNERSHIP

The Reorganization of Production

At least as serious as cost problems for the competitiveness of German industry were problems with economic restructuring and the reorganization of production. We have examined the seriousness of these challenges in the East
(Chapters 2 through 4). In the West, these problems included a relative weakness
in high technology innovation in areas such as microelectronics and biotechnol-
ogy as well as existing rigidities in German production organization that interfered with attempts to import "lean production" processes or at least match the
productivity levels of new process innovation.

The problems are well described by authors such as Gary Herrigel, Horst
Kern, and Charles Sabel (Kern and Sabel 1990; Kern 1994; Herrigel 1997). Despite the steady if unspectacular economic rebound beginning in 1994 and continuing at least through 1997, it was clear that long-term changes were necessary
to adapt German industry to the requirements of modern production organization. In addition to expanding research, development, production, and market-
ing in advanced industries, German industry, to meet the new challenges,
needed to loosen up functional divisions, hierarchical relations, traditional skill
categories, and established supplier relations.

In some cases, the social partners could take direct credit for flexible bargaining agreements that kept production in Germany. In a widely noted case, for example, Mercedes-Benz decided to locate new car production at the Rastatt plant
in Germany, after a lengthy study of alternative sites in Britain, the Czech Republic, and elsewhere. Key to the decision was a package of cost-cutting reforms
and flexibility measures negotiated between management and the works council
at Rastatt, which had the effect of keeping 3,000 well-paying jobs in Germany.[43]
In 1994, the company announced that the 1992 "productivity gap" of 35 percent
between Mercedes and comparable Japanese firms would drop to 15 percent by
the end of 1994.[44]

Bargaining innovations in both East and West aimed at contributing to such
adaptation. Horst Kern, for example, has written about two such innovations. In
Saxony, in order to preserve the critical "industrial core" at a time of rapid deindustrialization, and at the same time save jobs, IG Metall, in negotiations with
the government of Saxony, the Treuhand, and Gesamtmetall, established a regional industrial policy project called Atlas. The purpose of this undertaking
was to establish a "Holding" (in contemporary German terminology) that would
identify Treuhand firms capable of restructuring and survival and offer them in-
jections of capital and other support for approved restructuring plans to help
them attract private investment (Kern 1994, 38–45). Although Atlas's small scale
limited its contribution to regional development, similar projects were established throughout eastern Germany and together they offered an important test-

ing ground for the capacity of unions, employer associations, and state governments to play a broader role in industrial development (and thereby to expand the scope and role of the social partnership).[45]

The second example cited by Kern is the new role played by IG Metall in Baden-Württemberg, one of its old bastions in the West, in negotiating the terms of new supplier and firm network relations in an evolving post-Fordist regional economy (Kern 1994, 45–52). Here again the union, along with employer associations and the state government, was carving out an innovative role for itself in the development of new production organization.

In addition to the industrial policy examples cited by Kern, case studies in both eastern and western Germany in the 1990s show a growing engagement of works councils and unions in promoting and negotiating the terms of new production and work organization at the firm level.[46]

Arrayed against innovation by unions, works councils, employer associations, and particular employers are (1) the tendency of employer offensives to focus on cost-cutting to the exclusion of fundamental innovations in production; (2) the tendency of unions to limit their efforts to the defense of wages, working hours, employment security, and other new or old rights in lieu of promoting basic innovations in work organization; and (3) the persistence of traditional hierarchical and functional divisions in firms and unions alike (Kern 1994; Herrigel 1997). To the extent that such conservative forces dominate, the reform and reinvigoration of production in Germany may be limited, with potentially dangerous long-term effects on both future economic growth and social partnership.

One of the common defining features of modern production organization, in contrast to traditional mass production, is the need for proactive participation by the employees and their representatives.[47] Both unions and employers in Germany have officially advocated such a new direction.[48] In a period of rapid technological and organizational change, however, enhanced input requires a shoring up of the dual system, especially of the capacity of works councils and unions to receive timely information and participate in ongoing decisions (Altmann and Düll 1990). For this to occur, works councils and unions must push forward the proactive frontiers, and managers must accept the new voice and input that is offered. To what extent these changes take place as a broad pattern in the coming years will likely play a major role in determining the long-term success of modern production organization in Germany. With conservative forces still strong in both employer and union camps, the compatibility of social partnership with the transformation of production organization remains an open question, dependent on the choices made by major actors and the outcomes of their future conflict and negotiation. At the very least, the institutions of social partnership do not appear to stand in the way; and they do appear to offer a framework in which the continuing German pattern of "negotiated adjustment"

(Thelen 1991) and "incremental change" (Katzenstein 1989) makes necessary innovations in production organization both possible and likely.

Unemployment Crisis

Since 1984, IG Metall had promoted as an important bargaining demand the reduction of the workweek (from 40 hours in 1984 to 35 hours in 1995); a major goal of this bargaining focus was to create new jobs. The "VW Model" of 1993 (to reduce the workweek to 28.8 hours with only partial pay compensation), negotiated between VW and IG Metall, likewise aimed at saving jobs.[49] Despite these and other bargaining innovations, unemployment in unified Germany climbed through the 1990s, reaching historic highs for the postwar period (12.2 percent of the workforce, 4.66 million unemployed by February of 1997, with no end in sight).[50] The unemployment crisis intensified the ongoing debate: can this problem be solved in the context of social partnership negotiation, or is more radical U.S.-style deregulation required?

In the 1980s, it became commonplace for German critics to characterize West Germany as a "two-thirds society" (Windolf and Hohn 1984; Hohn 1988). This designation referred to exclusion of roughly a third of the potential workforce from good permanent jobs and full participation (although as in eastern Germany in the 1990s the welfare-state safety net did ensure basic needs and decent living standards). Disproportionately represented among the excluded third were women, foreign workers, the unskilled, younger entrants, and eased-out older workers, thus raising important issues of social justice.

Shorter workweek campaigns and work-sharing agreements were supposed to reduce unemployment and ameliorate inequities. Chancellor Kohl's 1996 promise to cut unemployment in half by the year 2000 through tax and spending reforms aimed at the same goal. The skyrocketing of unemployment through 1997, however, has undercut the efforts made so far and pushed "progress" in the opposite direction.

In addition to issues of social exclusion and injustice, high unemployment imposes an enormous cost on government and society, draining resources that could otherwise be put into new investment and economic modernization. And so for the late 1990s and beyond, perhaps the single most burning social and economic question for unified Germany is whether unemployment can be substantially reduced within the parameters of the German model. Can social partners come up with substantial and innovative *bargained* solutions? Will reduced costs, economic restructuring, and modernization in the East spur growth to levels that can create new jobs? Some say yes.[51] Others considered the unemployment crisis unresolvable without a full-scale dismantling of social partnership institutions and practices.[52]

The problem with the latter solution concerns the side effects: deregulation-led lower unemployment in the United States and the United Kingdom in the 1980s and 1990s has been accompanied by growing income polarization, with an expansion of poverty-level wages and incomes, creating what in many ways looked more like a "one-third" than a "two-thirds" society. It is not at all clear how either the unemployment problem in Germany (and much of continental Europe) or the polarization problem in the United States are to be solved. It is quite clear, however, that the resolution, or at least amelioration, of the unemployment crisis in Germany will test to the limit the capacity of social partnership to negotiate major reforms and innovations. And it is also clear that failure in this crucial area will greatly strengthen the hand of would-be deregulators, increasing the likelihood of the future breakup of social partnership in Germany.

CHAPTER SIX

Permanent Crisis?
Social Partnership in the European
and Global Economy, 1995–1997

Once again, in 1996, refrains of profound "crisis in the German model" filled the air. By now, the little boy had cried wolf so many times that many no longer listened. Still, this time the crescendo rose to such a fevered pitch that it was hard to ignore. On April 25, 1996, for example, the *Financial Times* ran an article titled "German workplace consensus 'has failed.' "[1] Two days later, the *Economist* wrote that "Germany's consensual traditions will wriggle for a long time before they expire" (April 27, 1996, p. 55). On June 10, 1996, the *New York Times* ran an op-ed piece by the chief economist of the Dresdner Bank titled "The End of Germany's Economic Model."[2] Consider, for example, the following:

> The German model of consensus in industrial relations has failed. . . . In an interview, Mr. Hans-Olaf Henkel, president of the Federation of German Industry (BDI), said the German trade union movement was facing terminal decline, and suggested that Germany would move increasingly towards an Anglo-Saxon style emphasis on individual self-reliance.
>
> Mr. Henkel said public sympathy for an alliance for jobs—proposed by the unions as a trade-off between pay restraint and job creation—"corresponds to the desire among Germans to generate jobs by means of round-table discussions, by putting arms around each others' shoulders, by signing papers, instead of swallowing bitter medicine. The public is being conned into believing that employment can be generated through alliances and fiddling with symptoms . . . the employers will have no choice but to do what they did in the last few years. We will vote with our feet, and go abroad."[3]

None of us has a crystal ball. I expect, however, that the doomsayers were wrong once again. On the other hand, they have told us all this so many times that by the law of averages perhaps they are finally right. Unemployment was persistently high (over 10 percent from late 1995, rising to over 12 percent in early 1997), while growth stayed sluggish in the fading rebound from the earlier recession. IG Metall's widely acclaimed "Alliance for Jobs" initiative (negotiations between employers, unions, and government aimed at reducing unemployment through a package of trade-offs, including wage restraint, reduction of overtime, and job creation) was dead by the spring of 1996. Chancellor Kohl announced unilateral cutbacks in social benefits, loudly opposed by the unions, while employers once again announced their intention to cut labor costs, even at the expense of social peace. Unions geared up for warning strikes and demonstrations and talked boldly of bringing a French-style strike wave to placid Deutschland.[4] By late 1996, a major labor-management battle had erupted over the reduction of sick pay.

How should we understand this new crisis? The first point to emphasize is that this was *not* primarily a crisis of German unification. If the evidence and arguments presented in this book are credible, then the crisis of unification has been substantially weathered. Germany has been peacefully, if painfully, unified under the aegis of broad relations of social partnership, now encompassing labor-management relations in both eastern and western Germany.

This is, by contrast, a second and distinct crisis, a crisis of social partnership in *unified* Germany in the face of increasing European and global economic integration. This crisis is all the more severe because it comes on top of the still unsettled problems and legacies of unification. Although it is important to recognize that unification has fundamentally succeeded despite all continuing difficulties, that victory will be short-lived if unified Germany cannot now cope with the challenges of the European and global economies.

The second point to emphasize is that social partnership does in no way mean the absence of conflict. As we have seen for the eastern strike of 1993 (and earlier episodes such as the prolonged and large-scale 1984 strike for the shorter workweek), intense conflict, followed by conflict resolution, is not only compatible with but may be necessary for the preservation, reinvigoration, and appropriate reform of social partnership relations.[5]

The current crisis will bring social partnership to an end only if it cuts the ground from under comprehensive collective bargaining and firm-level codetermination. If these processes and institutions endure, however, social partnership can well absorb (and may even be invigorated by) an escalation of conflict. As yet, there is little evidence that either comprehensive collective bargaining or codetermination are headed for history's dustbin. Despite a great deal of talk and some well-publicized cases, for example, there continues to be no evidence of massive flight from the employer associations. And where employers have left, they have often been forced by the union to adhere to the terms of existing regional collective bargaining contracts.

And third, social partnership also does not mean the absence of major problems. Periodic economic crises and periods of high unemployment have occurred throughout the history of capitalism, under widely varying forms of market organization. The situation in Germany in the mid-to-late 1990s is particularly acute in this regard: high unemployment and low manufacturing profitability in a context in which restrictive fiscal and monetary policies, in the run-up to European economic and monetary union (EMU), appear necessary (Carlin and Soskice 1997). The relevant question here is whether social partnership negotiation can contribute to solutions for these problems.

In the previous chapter, we considered some of the challenges to social partnership in unified Germany, such as rising unemployment and the introduction of "lean production" techniques. Here we consider briefly the challenges of global economic integration and in particular the effects of Germany's growing immersion in the single European market.[6] In western Europe, the potential problem is the supersession of high German labor and social standards by the European Union's much weaker and less enforceable "social dimension." For eastern and central Europe, the threat is massive disinvestment and job loss in Germany in favor of flexible and skilled but much less expensive workforces in the new market economies of the former Soviet bloc.

"Bookends" for this discussion are brief accounts of the 1995 metal industry bargaining round and strike, and the 1996–97 metal bargaining round and sick-pay battle, each of which occurred in the context of the escalating "second crisis" of European integration and economic globalization.[7]

1995: THE STRIKE IN BAVARIA

After the moderate 1994 settlement, resulting in real wage losses for their members, IG Metall sought better pay gains in the post-recession economy of 1995. As conflict within Gesamtmetall continued over questions of cost, flexibility, and militancy, the employer association presented a hard front, refusing even to place a wage offer on the table until the union made advance concessions. The result was a spirited eleven-day strike by over 20,000 workers, targeted at Bavaria (like Lower Saxony in 1994 a region hardly known for labor militancy). Bavarian metalworkers, backed by warning strikes all across Germany, demonstrated great resolve and solidarity; employers, on the other hand, continued to fight among themselves, muffed their halting attempts at strategy, came across as bumblers in press accounts, and caved in to what was perceived on all sides as a solid union victory.

The two-year settlement provided wage increases of approximately 3.8 percent per year, with the final scheduled one-hour reduction to the 35-hour workweek to proceed on October 1, 1995, as previously agreed. The employers gained no significant concessions. Bavarian metalworkers, who had voted 88 percent in favor of striking, cast a record 92 percent vote in favor of the settlement. Gesamtmetall, under great pressure to settle from Bavarian employers disgusted with the lame performance of their association, ratified the agreement, which then served as the pattern for metal industry settlements across Germany—and in other subsequent sector settlements as well.[8]

While the settlement generally pleased IG Metall members and leaders, criticism escalated within Gesamtmetall, resulting in a major leadership turnover by the end of the year. As one reporter put it: "The highly generous accord has left companies aghast and baying for their negotiators' blood."[9] Although the IG Metall victory reconsolidated union strength, disarray in the employers' camp caused new uncertainty and instability. By early 1996, *Handelsblatt* was running a regular series of articles on firms operating with new flexibility outside employer associations and comprehensive collective bargaining agreements. Cause for concern? For proponents of social partnership, yes indeed. The demise of comprehensive collective bargaining? Far from it, as we will see in the metal bargaining round and sick-pay battle of 1996–97.

European Economic Integration

In an era of deepening pessimism, Wolfgang Streeck (1991, 1997) has grappled in great depth with the profoundly unsettling implications of accelerated European integration for labor even where it is most strongly organized. As capital in the single European market moves beyond the bounds of national regulation, supranational actors and institutions such as the European Commission fail to provide adequate new social regulation at the European level. At the very least, employers wield increasingly credible relocation threats. The bargaining power of German unions, for example, rooted as it is in national institutions, faces the threat of long-term decline in a gradual devaluation of national institutions (Mosley 1990; Streeck 1991). Where labor is already in decline (France, the United Kingdom, and elsewhere), unions have even less of a chance in the developing single market.

Streeck is surely right in his analysis of the dangers facing organized labor in the single market. Many European union officials, at the European Trade Union Confederation (ETUC) in Brussels as well as at national unions throughout Europe, share Streeck's general concerns in a less analytical but nonetheless fully developed way, based on their own day-to-day practice and observations. For many of these unionists, such understandings are precisely what drives their cross-national union work. Although such efforts may bear fruit in the future, they are often thwarted in the present by institutional constraints and market realities. Nonetheless, Streeck's pessimism needs tempering by the possibility that actors, still in the early stages now, will continue to develop cross-national strategies to cope with the dangers inherent in an emerging "neopluralist social Europe" (Lange 1992b, 256). Most importantly, cross-national regulation in the new European (and global) economy requires the building of a cross-national labor movement (Hyman 1995; Turner 1996).

The central problem here for organized labor, and for nationally based forms of market regulation such as social partnership, is that as firms become more international, they become more difficult to regulate (S. Jacoby 1995). Enhanced international mobility, as in the case of the single European market and the opening up of central and eastern Europe, allows firms to escape national constraints. Newly mobile capital can engage in "regime shopping" (Streeck 1991), playing national production sites and workforces off against each other in search of the lowest wages or loosest regulation. The effect can both seriously weaken the bargaining power of nationally based unions and undermine the effectiveness of national laws, practices, and broad regulatory arrangements, such as the structures and agreements that social partnership offers in Germany.

Proponents of a European "social dimension" have therefore sought to supplement national regulations with European-wide social and labor standards (Teague 1989a, 1989b; Springer 1992; Leibfried and Pierson 1995). With roots in the social activism of the 1960s and 1970s (Turner 1993, 51–54), this movement grew with the European Community "relaunch" of the 1980s that took shape in the drive toward a single European market (then commonly known as "Europe 1992"). Although the drive toward "social Europe" has produced a Social Charter (1989), an action program of European-level directives (1990–94), a social protocol in the Maastricht Treaty (signed in 1991, ratified in 1993), and legislation that took effect in 1996 to mandate the creation of European works councils at multinational firms, regulation of markets and firm behavior at the European level remains only a shadow of national regulation. The great danger that Mosley (1990), Silvia (1991), Streeck (1991, 1997), Altvater and Mahnkopf (1993), and others cite is that national regulation is being replaced by a much less developed and weaker form of international regulation—one that allows firms greater latitude in decisions on labor and social standards. National regulation is thus being replaced by "supranational neo-voluntarism" (Streeck and Vitols 1996).

The analyses of recent years cited above emphasize the single European market taking shape among the fifteen member states of western Europe (the European Union) and the dangers for social and labor-market regulation especially in northern Europe where such standards tend to be highest. The danger is greatly magnified, however, by the fall of the Iron Curtain and the opening up of central and eastern Europe. Firms in northern Europe, for example, can now threaten to relocate production not only to faraway Spain, Portugal, or Greece but to neighboring Poland and the Czech Republic as well. In the latter countries (as well as in Hungary, Slovakia, and the small Baltic states), firms can find highly skilled workforces willing to work for a fraction of typical wages in northern Europe.

For German unions and the social partnership form of labor-market regulation, new opportunities are thus presented for firms either to escape regulation altogether (leading to the decline of production and employment in Germany) or to use the credible threat of relocation to undermine the bargaining power of the German unions, from IG Metall on down. At least in the long run, analysts such as Streeck who see such international dangers for social partnership as greater than the dangers of German unification may well be right—especially given the evidence presented in previous chapters indicating the resilience of social partnership in the face of unification.

The Evidence: Continuing Salience of National Institutions

Evidence available through 1997, however, does not support the pessimistic thesis. A central argument made by Streeck (and others) is that European integration substantially weakens the bargaining power of German unions. Although declining membership in unions and employer associations alike had become cause for concern by the mid-1990s (Fichter 1997; Silvia 1997), union bargaining power had clearly not weakened relative to that of the employers. The dramatic 1993 IG Metall strike victory in the East, the system-reinforcing compromise of 1994 in the West, the 1995 rout in Bavaria, and the sick-pay battle victory of 1996–97 all provided strong and consistent evidence for the continuing bargaining power of IG Metall (and other German unions, which largely followed the metal industry patterns). The problem appeared not to be union bargaining power but rather strategic disarray and deepening internal conflict within the employers' camp (Silvia 1997).

The evidence also shows little convergence of national institutions within Europe. Anthony Ferner and Richard Hyman, for example, in a comprehensive volume on industrial relations in the new Europe, found "persistent national diversity in the face of cross-national pressures for convergence" (Ferner and Hyman 1992, xvii); continuing diversity is explained largely as a product of the persistence of institutions (ibid., xxxiii).[10] This conclusion is reinforced on a global scale in a wide variety of recent studies.[11]

National institutions continue to be salient within Europe in part simply because institutions tend generally to be "sticky": as products of historical development and past political battles, institutions are difficult to change. In addition, however, there are quite specific reasons why national institutions (industrial relations, for example) continue to play a predominant role within the European Union.

For one thing, the chief decision-making body of the EU, the Council of Ministers, is explicitly intergovernmental. Made up of one representative of each member nation (each possessing a veto in critical policy areas), the Council defends national interests, policy, and structures against excessive encroachment from supranational European authorities. A guiding principle within the European Union in the preservation of national sovereignty is known as "subsidiarity": the notion that decisions should be made at the lowest possible level (nationally or even subnationally whenever possible). Although much has been made of the danger of this approach for efforts to strengthen European-level social regulation, subsidiarity cuts both ways. National actors, including governments, employer associations, and labor unions, have used the principle of subsidiarity to defend national rules and practices.[12] At the European level, such pressure has been recognized in the campaign for a directive on "posted workers," requiring firms that bring employees across borders within the EU to pay prevailing wages in the country where the work is performed.[13] This is an important regulation in a broader effort in countries such as Germany to prevent the undercutting of accepted (either bargained or legislated) national standards.

In any case, momentum toward European integration has slowed considerably since the heady "relaunch" days of the mid-to-late 1980s. The opening up of central and eastern Europe, greatly complicating the drive toward integration in western Europe, along with deep economic recession in the early 1990s and rising popular opposition (reflected in the traumas of the Maastricht Treaty ratification in 1992–93) combined to knock the EU train off its fast track. Government officials, and not only nationalist anti-Europe demagogues, have responded to popular fears of the risks of integration—from German fear of losing the beloved deutschmark to French fears of Bundesbank domination of monetary policy and employment levels—with a new wariness at yielding national sovereignty. Economic and monetary union (EMU), for example, an extension of "1992" scheduled for 1999 that would establish a common currency and central bank, appeared unlikely to meet the target dates without considerable hedging, extensive social unrest, and the exclusion of several countries.[14]

For Germany, it is highly implausible that social partnership would have proven so resilient, and even transferable from West to East, had European integration begun seriously to undermine the foundations of national industrial relations. Having to choose between cross-national unionism and the fight for a European social dimension on the one hand and a focus on spreading social partnership to eastern Germany, German unions have clearly chosen the latter as top priority. While this choice of strategy may have detracted from efforts to promote new European-level regulation, the effort to spread western-style unionism and social partnership to eastern Germany has succeeded surprisingly well—indicating a thus far quite successful defense of national institutions in an unusually challenging situation.

A question for future research concerns the degree to which industrial relations practices in Germany will change as a result of European integration. As we have seen in Chapters 4 and 5, the employer drive toward cost reductions and greater flexibility in working hours, largely accommodated by the unions, is changing established practices within the system. These changes are clearly driven in part by the pressures of intensified international and European market competition. So far, however, despite dire predictions and much hand-wringing, such changes have not added up to a substantial transformation of social partnership or a serious weakening of German unions.[15]

National Unions: Pinned Down on the Home Front

The Brussels truism that labor has always supported European integration[16] is not true. Labor has been no more unanimously pro-Europe than it ever was "proletarian internationalist." In West Germany and Benelux, socialist and Christian-democratic labor federations (separate in Belgium and the Netherlands and rolled into one in West Germany) supported the European Community from the start as part of pro-growth strategies in export-oriented economies. But the CGT (Confédération Générale du Travail), France's largest labor federation, has been anti-EC since the 1950s, while the British TUC (Trades Union Congress) carried a similar position through most of the 1980s. Popular support for the relaunch no doubt benefited from the serious decline of the CGT in France in the 1980s as well as the conversion of the TUC following Labour's third drubbing by Thatcher in 1987.

By 1992, Europe's umbrella labor confederation (the European Trade Union Confederation, or ETUC) had in fact become so unreservedly pro-integration (pro-single market, pro-Maastricht, pro-EMU) that it could be criticized as having converted to monetarism. As the European Monetary System pulled apart and recession deepened in 1992–93, throwing hundreds of thousands out of work across Europe, and as Maastricht wobbled in the face of popular opposition, the ETUC's vulnerability became magnified. Rather than jumping on a populist anti-EU bandwagon, however, ETUC shifted quickly to an emphasis on macro policies at the EU level, promoting expansionary fiscal policies to create jobs, revive economic growth, and thereby make EMU (along with Maastricht's budgetary and monetary discipline) possible in the long run. The ETUC's argument, with the backing of its national members, continued to be that it is better to stay aboard a moving integration project to influence policy than to take potshots from the sidelines for temporary domestic gain.

Beneath the surface of European labor unity, however, one finds a variety of alliances as well as a pattern of national union preoccupation with domestic concerns. Often these concerns and alliances stand in the way of a full and energetic commitment to cross-national union collaboration.

On the French side of the critical Franco-German alliance (still the heart of EU politics), the central problem remains plural unionism and the particular shape that inter-union adversarial relations take in France. The view from Brussels, union officials typically claim, is that seriously declining union membership density (well under 10 percent in France by the mid-1990s) is not as great a problem as one might think. In fact, only union activists and those seeking a career in the union join up in France (since there is neither a dues checkoff nor positive incentives to join). A more accurate reflection of rank-and-file support, therefore, is the fact that the various unions combined continue to receive over 70 percent of the votes in works committee elections, a figure that is not far from the total union votes in German works councils elections.[17] Adversarial relations among the three main federations, however, weaken union influence in ways that range from their ability to make positive use of legislated French plant-level works committees for other than recreational activities to the ability to formulate joint European strategies.[18]

But the biggest obstacle to cross-national unionism in the EU in the mid-1990s, according to numerous participants in Brussels and elsewhere, was the weak presence of the German unions, the strongest in Europe. While German unions are unreservedly committed on paper both to European integration and to cross-national union cooperation, German union Euro-activism is not nearly what it could or should be (according to both German and non-German Euro-unionists, speaking for the most part off the record). Some say that German union commitment in practice to European activism was always minimal in relation to the need; in this view, the nascent Europe discussion of the late 1980s within German unions was related to a broader debate for internal and strategic reform that encompassed issues of union democracy, the place of women and national minorities, and strategic redirection to organize a new generation of professional, technical, and service workers. Because German unification so concentrated union efforts on one problem—organizing the East—these debates were stifled (much to the relief of threatened traditionalists) and a possible major new Euro-commitment never got off the ground.

An alternative view posits that an already substantial German union commitment to Euro-organizing withered under the impact of German unification. The shift was personified by a change in leadership at the DGB from Ernst

Breit, who was both interested and involved in European issues, to Heinz-Werner Meyer, who focused to the virtual exclusion of all else on the problems raised by unification. Both views, however, lead to the same conclusion: that German unions in the 1990s were preoccupied with unification to the detriment of expanded cross-national union collaboration in Europe.

There are, to be sure, different positions among the German unions. IG Chemie, for example, in an industry operating very much in global markets, sees international collective bargaining on the horizon in the chemical industry and wants to prepare for it. IG Medien (printers and journalists), on the other hand, operating in a still nationally based industry, shows little interest in cross-national union collaboration. IG Metall contains both viewpoints and has yet to work out a consistent approach. Once again one sees the crucial role of IG Metall not only as an actor itself in possible future European union collaboration but for the overall stance taken by German unions in European arenas.[19]

German unions were clearly disillusioned with the watered-down, nonbinding Social Charter, the lack of subsequent progress on the social dimension, and the heavy emphasis on subsidiarity that throws national labor movements back on their own resources.[20] At the same time, populations across western Europe, including the Germans, became increasingly disillusioned with the European project as unemployment mounted in the early 1990s. In Germany, western workers were angry about the real costs of unifying their own country (for which they were paying a 7.5 percent "solidarity" income tax surcharge); they hardly wanted to hear about European integration, for which they could reasonably expect that they would also have to pay. Unions cannot make a major commitment to cross-national unionism at a time when their own membership would likely oppose such efforts (and especially the costs of an enhanced commitment).

It is not hard to comprehend the dilemma facing German unions, torn between European and German integration, and the choices that they have made. The problem for German unions is that they have needed simultaneously to build, transfer, or transform institutions in two distinct situations in which market boundaries have been radically changed: in the single European market and in eastern Germany (and by extension all of Germany). It would take an extraordinary effort to deal with either of these; German unions after 1990 chose to concentrate their energies on the immediate and obvious choice: the incorporation of eastern German workers into a once-stable industrial relations system. In the face of such problems of immediate life-threatening scope for German labor's influence and position in society, problems associated with EU integration looked distant by comparison.

If German unification, as a result of extraordinary costs and accompanying inflationary pressures resulting in high interest rates in 1991–93, helped to rob the entire EU project of its momentum, then the preoccupation of German organized labor with a related set of problems deprived the ETUC and other cross-national actors of the energies of their most powerful participant.

Should this situation change, perhaps as a result of the stabilization of union influence in unified Germany, there now exists a nascent institutional framework, ranging from the ETUC and European-level social dialogue to the establishment of European works councils at 1500 multinational firms (as required in the new EU directive), in which German unions could play a greatly expanded role (Turner 1996; Lecher 1997). And despite the very real limitations on progress so far, in either the social dimension or the building of cross-national unionism, important advances have been made. It is much too early to write off prospects for a European labor movement, and corresponding possibilities of cross-national regulation, for the twenty-first century.

CENTRAL AND EASTERN EUROPE: THE THREAT OF LOW-COST LABOR

Austria, Finland, and Sweden joined the European Union effective January 1, 1995. Poland, the Czech Republic, Slovakia, Hungary, Romania, and Bulgaria (among others) have all signed associate status agreements intended to lead to full membership in the EU. Formal members or not, however, these countries offer skilled labor and educated workforces at a fraction of the cost of labor in western Europe, and in particular in Germany.[21] Manufacturing locations in the Czech Republic and Poland, for example, are right next door to markets in Germany and other parts of western and eastern Europe. Since 1990, German union representatives and works councillors have increasingly heard a refrain from employers to the following effect: "Give us concessions—wage restraint, new flexibility—or we will move the plant (or at least future investment) to Poland or Czechia, where labor costs are one-tenth of levels in western Germany."

German capitalists have long had the option of investing abroad instead of in their expensive labor markets at home. The expansion of such investment, however,—into southern Europe, Latin America, and elsewhere—has been gradual and not necessarily associated with falling investment levels at home. Investments abroad, in fact, can and have increased simultaneously with investment at home, as foreign plants require parts, machinery, and other capital goods from the home country. This could also turn out to be the case for contemporary German investment in central and eastern Europe (Deutschmann 1995). The opportunities in these regions, however, are qualitatively different from the investment opportunities that German capital has had in the past: central Europe is literally right next door to Germany; the central European workforce is well educated, skilled, and eager to be hired; and the cost of employing it is extremely low by German standards. As infrastructure and markets continue to develop, these sites become highly desirable production locations, and not only for products at the low end.

The contemporary debate about *Standort Deutschland* thus assumes the very real possibility of wholesale relocation of production from Germany to the East—to an extent that has never been contemplated in earlier discussions of the pros and cons of foreign investment by German firms. In contemporary, post–Cold War circumstances, the danger of "social dumping" (the relocation of production to cheap-labor countries) to the East would seem to dwarf the earlier threat of such southward dumping within the EU (Erickson and Kuruvilla 1995).

The issue has entered the public arena in a prominent way. Chancellor Helmut Kohl, for example, has called for a rethinking of the conditions for production in Germany:

> Just a few kilometres east of Berlin and Munich, serious new competitors are growing up, with great cost advantages and increasingly impressive products. Yet we allow ourselves the luxury of being a country with ever younger pensioners (average retirement age 59) and ever older students (average matriculation age 30). . . . With ever shorter working hours, rising wage costs, and ever longer holidays, our competitiveness is in danger. . . . The simple fact is that a successful industrial nation cannot allow itself to be organized like a collective leisure park.[22]

Since these memorable words were spoken, German firms have engaged in major cost-cutting efforts, including workforce downsizing, while unions have settled for wage restraint in bargaining agreements. There is widespread recognition of the "production location" problem.

Nonetheless, or perhaps in part because of adjustments made, the German economy, led by rising exports, boomed strongly again in 1994 before easing into slow but steady growth in 1995–96. In 1996, the continuing export boom fueled a large German trade surplus. These are hardly the sort of trends one would expect to observe if investment and production were leaving Germany en masse. At the same time, however, the problems were very real, including unemployment levels that by 1997 appeared stuck at 11 percent or more, a phenomenon that did reflect employer reluctance to create new jobs through added investment.

As always, there are two sides to the "social dumping" story; and as in the past (during the economic crises of the 1970s and again during the acceleration of European economic integration in the late 1980s), the dangers to the German economy and its social partnership may have been overstated. For one thing, the labor cost situation looks less serious when high productivity in Germany is also considered. Unit labor costs in Germany have in fact fared quite well in recent decades in relation to other countries. From 1981 to 1993, for example, the growth of unit labor costs in Germany ranked in the bottom third for OECD member countries; and while costs rose 28 percent during this period, profits per unit of sale rose 63 percent.[23] Despite all the rhetoric and threats of disinvestment, as well as the very real economic problems, Germany remained in the mid-1990s an essentially prosperous economy and society. Although costs were considerably lower in central and eastern Europe, these areas also contained much more uncertainty for investors in ongoing and protracted processes of economic, political, and social transformation.

In comparison to German investment and production in countries such as Britain and Spain, eastward investment remained small. For the first six months of 1994, for example, German investment in Britain was DM 2.79 billion, in Spain DM 2.55 billion, and in the Czech Republic DM 347 million.[24] While German investment in central and eastern Europe was growing, and by 1994 accounted for 10 percent of total German foreign investment,[25] the amounts were still much smaller than necessary to stimulate rapid economic development.[26]

Where German investment in eastern and central Europe is largest (in Hungary, the Czech Republic, Slovakia, and Poland), trade has also expanded rapidly. But these countries typically run large trade deficits with Germany. Hungary, for example, reported a trade deficit with Germany for 1994 of DM 700–800 million.[27] While German imports from central Europe were growing (with some of the increase no doubt resulting from the products of German-owned plants shipped back to the home country), German exports (goods produced *within* Germany) to these countries were increasing even faster.

There is as yet little evidence of net job, investment, or production loss, or other harmful effects on the German economy resulting from rising German investment to the East. Just as the "southward dumping" bogeyman failed to materialize during the EU integration debate, the "social dumping" bogeyman has yet to materialize for Germany in relation to production in central and eastern Europe. Outward investment has traditionally exceeded foreign direct investment in Germany. Although the difference rose substantially between 1983 and 1993 (and beyond), gross fixed capital formation also fared quite well over the same period, indicating continuing strong total investment in Germany.[28]

Hopes for continued rising production levels in eastern Germany, in fact, hinged largely on the expansion of eastern markets. Investment in the Czech Republic, as an example, was viewed primarily not as a displacement of investment in Germany but rather as a gateway to the vast markets of Russia and other former Soviet republics. To the extent that German capital helps develop eastern markets, the long-term effect of such investment may well be net production and job growth for Germany. According to the Economics Ministry: "One should avoid reading too much into the reduction of unprofitable workplaces that is taking place in Germany. Investment in the reform states creates increased demand particularly for German products . . . and contributes to securing Germany's international competitive ability."[29]

The new availability of inexpensive, skilled labor close at hand exerts a pressure for reform that may on the whole have positive effects for German labor and industry:

> "Social dumping"—the feared transfer of capital from countries with high standards of labour protection to those where labour is least protected—has not materialised in Europe. . . . But economic integration means that developments in one European labour market are now influencing others. The threat of locating new plants abroad has recently persuaded German workers at Bosch and Daimler-Benz to make concessions. . . . The result is a gradual trend towards greater flexibility across Europe, whereby continental countries are adopting some aspects of British-style deregulation without abandoning European social partnership.[30]

Taking this perspective one step further, Christoph Deutschmann (1995) argues that expanded supplier networks in eastern and central Europe will in fact boost the competitiveness of German industry in relation to contemporary Japanese and American firms. In this view, the predominant cost advantage of Japanese "lean production" lies in low-cost and flexible supplier networks, from which manufacturing firms can source much of their parts. German firms stand at a competitive disadvantage, however, because comprehensive collective bargaining keeps wages uniformly high and relatively egalitarian, effectively prohibiting such low-cost supplier opportunities at home. The opening of eastern and central Europe, however, now makes it possible for German firms to develop the low-cost supplier networks necessary for competitiveness in today's global economy right next door. The growth in competitiveness for German firms may well offset any negative investment or employment effects in the domestic German economy.[31]

While it is probably too early to calculate accurately the net effects of rising German investment in central and eastern Europe for domestic jobs, production, economic growth, and relative bargaining power, the dangers may well be as exaggerated here as they have been in the past for other areas of concern such as southern Europe.

Europe: Opportunities for German Social Partnership?

Dangers are often easier to identify than opportunities, especially in circumstances of rapid change. But social partnership, in various forms, is in fact now quite widespread throughout Europe. The European Commission, in its policy efforts, promotes social partnership among its own member states as well as for prospective members such as the countries of central and eastern Europe.[32] The coming buildup of cross-national European works councils may well afford important new channels for cross-national union collaboration (Turner 1996). And just as we cannot rule out the possibility of an increasingly European labor movement that could reinforce national-level social partnership, nor can we discount the possibility that a medium-term, low-cost production area in central and eastern Europe could contribute importantly to the modernization of Europe as a whole (Deutschmann 1995). If such a development occurs, the influence of newly opened up and growing central and eastern Europe on western Europe could in the end mirror, for both modernization and social partnership, the potentially positive effects on unified Germany of its own newly incorporated eastern states.

1996–97: THE BATTLE FOR SICK PAY

Final evidence for the resilience of social partnership and the continuing strength of German unions came in a highly publicized battle over sick pay in the fall of 1996, finally resolved in metal industry contracts of January 1997.

In September of 1996, the Kohl government passed a "savings package" (*Sparpaket*) that included a reduction in the amount employers are required to pay absent employees who are sick—from 100 to 80 percent of normal pay. Unions claimed that their bargaining agreements (providing 100 percent sick pay) took precedence over the new legislation. Although existing contracts ran through the end of the year, Gesamtmetall, still trying to redeem itself after the Bavarian rout of 1995, urged its members to reduce sick pay (*Lohnfortzahlung*) unilaterally beginning October 1. A number of high-profile firms, most notably Daimler-Benz, announced they would do so. IG Metall responded with militant rhetoric and highly successful warning strikes. Workers responded with angry passion and great solidarity: union officials called these warning strikes "ecological," because workers were so angry there was no need to print leaflets; it was only necessary to restrain them until the scheduled beginning of planned job actions.[33] After massive production losses due to plant walkouts (and the threat of many more), Daimler-Benz and other firms quickly backed down, agreeing to continue paying 100 percent sick pay and to resolve the issue in the upcoming bargaining round. IG Metall claimed to have signed up 10,000 new members in the fall sick-pay battle.

In November, IG Metall and Gesamtmetall reached an early pilot settlement in Lower Saxony, a two-year agreement that included wage moderation (1.5 percent raises in 1997, 2.5 percent in 1998), 100 percent sick pay (for the first six weeks of illness), and no other major contract changes. Despite employer grumbling, the pilot agreement had spread throughout Germany, in the metal industry and beyond, by January of 1997. Resolution of the sick-pay issue was widely viewed as a union victory, and the two-year metal industry contracts offered extended stabilization of conflict.

In a December 1996 interview, BDA President Dieter Hundt suggested that the unsuccessful sick-pay battle would in fact *strengthen* employer associations, since employers could now see clearly what happens (i.e. defeat) when they take on a union individually. He also worried—in direct contradiction to the fears of Streeck (1991) and others concerning the weakening of union bargaining power— that because firms in a global economy cannot afford the great losses incurred in strikes, employers in Germany were no longer an equal bargaining partner for the unions.[34]

Another battle, another compromise. The intensity of conflict in the fall of 1996 led many, on both sides, to predict at the time that social partnership would now break apart, leading to a prolonged period of open conflict. Moderate, pattern-setting two-year settlements in the metal industry once again belied the dire predictions. Despite enormous problems yet to solve, such as high unemployment, by the mid-to-late 1990s it was fair to say that western institutions and practices had weathered both the crisis of German unification and the effects of major changes in the European and global economies. As *The Economist* put it in an extensive survey of unified Germany: "Western upholstery has been frayed, but the furniture is unchanged."[35]

CHAPTER SEVEN

Institutional Change in Turbulent Markets

Enough evidence is in. In the most adverse of circumstances and despite a steady drumbeat of pessimistic prediction, social partnership in Germany has adapted surprisingly well to the traumas of unification. Successful adaptation and reform have taken place not only in response to the unparalleled challenges of unification but in a demanding context of European integration and intensified global trade competition as well.

To be sure, the costs have been high. To incorporate the new eastern states, the German federal government has run up unprecedented budget deficits. Literally millions of people, in particular older workers and women in eastern Germany, have been excluded from employment in the new order. Germany today includes countless stories of personal unhappiness and in some cases devastation, despite the extensive safety net stretching across East and West. Westerners resent the costs of unification, reflected in higher taxes, stagnant income, and reduced take-home pay, and often unfairly blame the Easterners themselves. Easterners resent the takeover of their economy and the sometimes heavy-handed arrogance of incoming Westerners. Such resentments have combined with persistently high unemployment in both eastern and western Germany to provide a fertile recruiting ground for small, violent bands of neo-Nazi thugs. Unification and the collapse of existing institutions in the East have forced western employer associations and unions to expand rapidly in a fight for survival that has brought new tensions and conflict both within and between employer and labor organizations. Unified Germany of the mid-to-late 1990s presents to the world and to its own residents a much more problematic and uncertain picture than did West Germany in the mid-1980s.

Enormous difficulties notwithstanding, the institutions and major actors of the German political economy have responded on the whole remarkably well.[1]

Most importantly, the ultimately disastrous instability of Weimar Germany echoes only faintly in modern Germany, even under the extraordinary pressure of unification and the continuing crisis of high unemployment. Democracy has proven stable in unified Germany: unshakable in the West where it is forty years entrenched; firmly established as a form of governance in the East after only a few years.[2] Although the burning of hostels and the homes of foreign workers, in some cases with murderous results, has presented a hideous face to the world, neo-Nazi revival has found only marginal support within a largely peace-loving and democratic society. The violent actions of small bands of skinheads have been protested by hundreds of thousands of silent, candle-bearing demonstrators. The once-feared and rising right-wing Republican party (*Republikaner*) all but vanished in the 1994 Bundestag elections. From all indications, democracy is as solidly grounded in unified Germany as it is in the much older democracies of Britain and France (Schmidt 1992; Merkl 1994; Lane 1995; Radice 1995).

Although still in the building process, western employer associations and unions have established solid foundations in the new states of eastern Germany—and in so doing, they have to some extent become "eastern." As we have seen, unions and employer associations have built stable membership cores and together have established comprehensive collective bargaining throughout eastern Germany (Bispinck 1995). When called upon to participate in the legal strike activities that accompany modern negotiating rounds, eastern workers have responded in overwhelming numbers with great solidarity, achieving favorable results in difficult circumstances. Employer associations and unions have been included in major government-led rounds of negotiation (in 1992–93, 1995, and 1996) aimed at finding solutions to unified Germany's economic and social problems. Relations of social partnership between labor and capital, in other words, often in new ways, continue to be the order of the day in modern Germany.[3]

The consolidation of social partnership in unified Germany is, to be sure, a mixed blessing for unions and employer associations, because they now have to take responsibility for and find solutions to the growing economic problems of the late 1990s. The coming of EMU, in Germany and throughout Europe, has driven increasingly restrictive fiscal and monetary policies. Although still the export powerhouse of Europe, Germany finds itself now caught in a bind between high labor and social standards (a good thing, let us emphasize) and low firm profitability , in a context in which expansionary fiscal policy appears excluded (Carlin and Soskice 1997). Solutions require compromise and painful concessions on all sides. The social partners, in negotiations with each other and with government, now have no choice but to tackle these problems in comprehensive and politically risky ways; and this is true whether Kohl stays in office or German voters opt for the SPD, and quite possibly the new experience of a federal level "red-green" coalition.

If social partnership has successfully weathered the challenges of German unification, it is nonetheless unclear whether this means that "social capitalism" is resilient and likely to do well in contemporary world markets, or whether any reasonably functional dominant system would have had similar success in parallel circumstances. Unfortunately, we have no appropriate contemporary test cases upon which to build a comparative analysis. We can only speculate. It seems likely, for example, that Japan's "cartel capitalism," had it been faced with the need for territorial expansion, would if anything have had to intensify its organized state-business relations in the search for solutions to difficult new economic and social problems. And it seems equally likely that U.S.-style "liberal capitalism," by contrast to both the German and Japanese cases, would have used such an opening as a greenfield for further deregulation, entrepreneurial initiative, and marginalization of organized labor.

It may be, therefore, that as a general rule a dominant system will seek to reproduce itself, doing what it knows best in order to ward off collapse. If this is true, we still do not know how successful either Japan or the United States would have been in similar circumstances (although I think it is likely, given past responses to serious challenges, that either would have been fairly successful). The evidence presented in this book does demonstrate, however, that German social capitalism (with its social market economy and social partnership regulation) has successfully expanded into the new territory and adapted remarkably well (although with great difficulty in the most trying of circumstances) to the extraordinary challenges of unification.

A NEW "GERMAN QUESTION"

> Germany's current search for solutions holds out the intriguing possibility that an economy doesn't have to undergo brutal, American-style mass layoffs and dislocations to be successful. Perhaps with the milder mixture of reforms that government, unions and industry are talking about, this country can resume its competitive position without letting its high pay and benefits standards be dragged down by global competition.[4]

A widely studied and debated question of the postwar period asks why Germany led the world into two world wars and produced the horrors of Nazism and the Holocaust (cf. Blackbourn and Eley 1984, Calleo 1978, and Dahrendorf 1967). German unification in the 1990s has understandably raised old fears on the part of modern Germany's neighbors and former victims. The eminent social scientist Reinhard Bendix, for example, himself a refugee from Nazi Germany, argued in 1990 that in fact two specters had haunted Europe in the nineteenth and twentieth centuries (as opposed to the one specter identified by Marx and Engels in the memorable opening words of the *Communist Manifesto*): the specter of communism and the specter of Germany.[5] Historically speaking, Bendix was right, and his argument was meant to remind people about the possible dangers of German unification in 1990. Several years later, however, the dangers appear to be well contained. On the contrary, we are faced with a new and very different German question for the end of the twentieth century: How is it that Germany, the country that gave us such earlier horrors, now appears to offer the best prospects (at least among the large industrial societies) for a relatively benevolent and socially conscious form of capitalism in the modern world economy?[6]

The historical alternatives to capitalism as a framework for the economic organization of society certainly seem exhausted in the present period. The collapse of the Soviet Union and the communist regimes of central and eastern Europe are the landmark events of our era. Even in China, still politically communist, the economic vitality of recent years is linked to the introduction of market reforms. If capitalist markets are everywhere economically dominant, then the method by which society regulates the market economy becomes the important comparative question. Does regulation include nondemocratic, authoritarian political structures to control society while opening markets, as in China and other newly industrializing countries such as Singapore? Do business cartels and the state play a central role in regulation, as in Japan? Is the dominant trend toward increasingly deregulated markets within the context of a democratic society, as in the United States, Canada, Britain, and to a certain extent within the European Union?[7] Are capitalist markets in the contemporary global economy still compatible with socially oriented and consensually bargained regulation as in Germany's social market economy?[8]

For European social democrats, an appealing version of the market economy (and viewed by some as the forerunner of a gradual transition to democratic socialism) was the successful postwar "democratic corporatism" found most notably in Sweden, Norway, and Austria.[9] The decline of the Swedish model since the late 1980s, however, has put such dreams to rest. As it turns out in the 1990s, a softer version of social democracy, a less complete and perhaps more market-oriented version of democratic corporatism, such as modern Germany's social market economy, may be the version of social democracy with the best prospects for long-term viability.[10]

To put it bluntly, can unified Germany, the same country that once brought us Hitler and the horrors of Auschwitz, now perhaps offer the best prospects for social democracy in the contemporary era? If so, how is this possible?

The first and perhaps most important answer is the following: *people can and do change*. Institutions, political and economic frameworks, and behavior also can and do change. Although people are resistant to change and institutions are sticky, future outcomes simply cannot be confidently extrapolated from past or present behavior or from institutional configurations. Institutions may be fairly good predictors of behavior in periods of economic and social stability; but such stability can come unraveled remarkably fast under new external or internal pressure. In addition, actors can make surprising choices, and institutions can and do change as a result of both external pressure, actor choice, and adaptation to new circumstances.

Under the combined influence of allied occupation forces and domestic reform efforts, German institutions, although building on existing foundations, changed dramatically in both West and East Germany in the early postwar period. In the East, the new institutions ultimately failed, in large measure because of their inability to spur economic innovation and growth at western levels. In the West, the evolving social market institutions of the Federal Republic succeeded because they were flexible, inclusive, and versatile: able to accommodate at once economic growth, export success on world markets, high wages, strong social protections, and incremental innovation (Katzenstein 1989; Streeck 1992; Crouch 1993). The key to successful and inclusive flexibility lay in regularized and comprehensive processes of negotiation among strongly organized interest groups throughout the political economy.

EXPLAINING RESILIENCE: INSTITUTIONS AND ACTORS

Social partnership, the evidence here indicates, succeeded after 1990 in unified Germany because it incorporated the major interests into flexible bargaining processes in which both the needs of the economy and the firm on the one hand and employees and their organizations on the other hand were considered. The key to flexible, inclusive bargaining and market-oriented outcomes in unified Germany lies in the dual system: comprehensive collective bargaining at the industry level to establish basic pay and other standards; firm and plant-level codetermination to adapt broader agreements to the specific interests and power relations of specific firms, plants, and groups of employees (Thelen 1991; Crouch 1993). There remains, to be sure, much work to be done in the new states to adapt the institutions to local circumstances and make them fully "eastern"; but basic social partnership relations and regulation were intact by the mid-1990s.

While the demanding world markets of the 1980s pulled the rug out from under more solidly institutionalized and ideological social democracy in Sweden (undermining, for example, the viability of basic union principles such as wage solidarity), Germany's more limited and slightly less egalitarian form of social democracy proved adaptable (cf. Swenson 1991; Pontusson 1992, 1995; and Thelen 1993; Locke and Thelen 1995). Even after seven years of conservative rule, including a government push toward deregulation, the West German model was going strong in 1989 (see, for example, Katzenstein 1989) when the East suddenly and unexpectedly opened up. And even under the enormous strain of unification, social partnership has held up surprisingly well: adapting to the new circumstances, allowing workable compromise if not consensual solutions.[11]

The central argument presented in this book is that social partnership endures in unified Germany because (1) the institutions of interest representation and bargaining are at once inclusive and flexible; and (2) the major actors of social partnership—employer associations and firms on the one hand, unions and workers on the other hand—*enabled by the institutions* (Schmid 1994), have deliberately extended the framework into eastern Germany, effectively organizing and defending their interests when necessary. Both institutional structure and actor choice are essential to the explanation.

Evidence presented here—from firm-level case studies, participant observation of the eastern metalworkers' strike of 1993, and analysis of the development of industrial relations in unified Germany—demonstrates the central role that institutions have played in enabling favorable outcomes for social partnership. The rapid push eastward of employer associations and unions, with their accustomed practices of comprehensive collective bargaining, cast an early framework for the social partnership regulation of labor markets in eastern Germany. Both employer associations and unions found an immediate and significant role in the new eastern states within the context of western-style institutions of collective bargaining, given life in the new territory by the participation (both enthusiastic and critical) of eastern workers and managers and their active efforts to adapt the new institutions to local circumstances.

At the firm and plant levels, we have seen how codetermination law and its accompanying institutional framework—most importantly, elected works councils on the employee side and personnel departments on the management side, both with formal rights and obligations to share information and decision making—have made it possible for the social partners to gain a solid foothold within the firm.[12] Unions have trained the works councillors and used these bodies, as in the West, to recruit members and establish a strong presence in the workforce.

Employer associations have trained eastern managers in codetermination law and appropriate works council relations, providing valuable services as an incentive for eastern firms to join. And eastern managers and works councillors themselves have used the practices of codetermination to build close relationships in the common battle to preserve eastern firms and jobs within a collapsed economy. The dual system's "particularly sophisticated form of articulation" (Crouch 1993, 213) has not only survived unification but has been transferred in its essential elements from West to East.

In the absence of these institutions, it is easy to imagine alternative scenarios for eastern labor-management relations in the new market economy: either cooperative relations through management domination at the firm level (in conditions of high unemployment that markedly strengthen management bargaining power), or highly adversarial relations as each side battles for position in the absence of a facilitating institutional framework.[13] The empirical evidence (case studies, strike outcome, union membership, comprehensive collective bargaining coverage) suggests a close causal relationship between institutions transferred in from the West and the central, successful roles played in the eastern German economy by the social partners, labor and capital.[14]

Major actors have made controversial and sometimes surprising decisions that have had an important impact on observed outcomes. But the institutional framework has had a significant influence on the possibilities open to actors as well as on definitions of their own interest. Workers at Siemens in Rostock and VW in Mosel, for example, mobilized for strike action in 1993 under the leadership of eastern works councillors with secure positions of leadership and within a comprehensive collective bargaining framework made possible by the transfer of industrial relations from western Germany. Large employers at first saw western-style comprehensive collective bargaining as the best framework for stabilizing labor-market uncertainty in the East; by 1993, as approaching wage parity for eastern workers began to look too expensive, employer associations fought to revise pay schedules, eliminate phased-in wage parity, and introduce "opening clauses" for troubled firms, without nonetheless attempting (Swedish-style) to dismantle the bargaining system.

The emphasis on institutional influence is not meant to downplay the fact that actors made sometimes surprising and even courageous decisions, without which outcomes would likely have been quite different. Employer militancy in 1993 in eastern Germany and again in 1994 in the West, for example, was quite unprecedented in the postwar period. In the first instance, as we have seen, Gesamtmetall unilaterally abrogated a three-year contract to demand pay concessions. In the second instance, Gesamtmetall for the first time in western Germany took the initiative in a bargaining round, canceling provisions scheduled to expire and calling for major concessions in wages, holiday bonuses, and working hours. Employer militancy in both East and West was a product of internal employer association politics, in particular the increasing dissatisfaction of small and medium-sized firms with the terms of existing agreements (Silvia 1997).[15] In each case, the employer decision to pursue a new, hard-line strategy was hammered out only after extensive internal debate. Although in neither case did employers achieve the bargaining breakthrough for which they had campaigned, in both cases major pay concessions, a result of the militant employer position, contributed importantly to cost reduction and the viability of industry production and profits in Germany.

The most surprising actor choice in eastern industrial relations after 1989 was the decision on the part of thousands of metalworkers to vote for and support strike action in the spring of 1993, in circumstances of mass unemployment, ongoing and massive downsizing, economic collapse, and widespread job insecurity. This outcome was predicted in advance neither by the employers nor by the union; it came as a great surprise and shock to employers and even to many of the participants themselves. It was not at all clear, and cannot simply be "read" off the institutions, that eastern workers in large numbers would actually use the channels in the risky and courageous way in which they did. At the same time, the institutional channels for such action were available in eastern Germany for the first time in sixty years, offering a framework that encouraged activism and made victory possible.

The error of the pessimists (Mahnkopf 1991, 1993; Armingeon 1991; McFalls 1995; and many others) lay not in the analysis of possibilities open in a period of great uncertainty and change but in the failure to recognize the potential of major actors, given supporting institutions, to make surprising, high-risk decisions. The pessimistic scenario *was* in fact present as a real danger. What the pessimists failed to comprehend, however, was the inclusive flexibility of social partnership institutions, which encouraged successful mobilization on the part of workers and unions. German unions, in particular, have played an important socialization role, acting in this way as a barrier to the rise of an extremist Right in both eastern and western Germany in a potentially dangerous period of turbulence (Kinzer 1994).[16] Although collective actors are always, to some extent at least, free agents, capable of deciding for themselves in processes of internal debate, capable of following or providing leadership, capable of both stupid blunders and heroic action, the institutional context in which they operate has a powerful influence in shaping options and decisions.[17]

ALTERNATIVE EXPLANATIONS

What would disprove the institutional arguments made here? Given the reality of at least formal institutional transfer from West to East (the primary independent variable), the most decisive refutation would come from indications of the subsequent decline and collapse of social partnership. Instead of the enduring, adaptable social partnership relations identified in this analysis, we would (and might in the future) witness very different indicators, such as: a collapse in union membership density in the East (as of 1996 still higher in eastern than in western Germany); a seriously declining percentage of eastern works councillors who are union members (the ratio after the 1994 elections was higher in the East than in the West); a serious decline in comprehensive collective bargaining coverage in the East (where despite firm undercutting and the weakness of employer associations the majority of employees in 1996 remained covered by the terms of collective bargaining agreements); a breakup of or split within employer associations (that could pull the rug from under comprehensive collective bargaining); a prolonged escalation of conflict (for example enough to push Germany from the ranks of the low-strike-rate countries into the medium- or high-strike-rate category); a major perceived union *defeat* in a collective bargaining conflict in eastern Germany; a breakdown of democracy (as predicted, for example, by McFalls 1995—with many possible indicators ranging from regime instability, to party fragmentation, to the rise to prominence of an anti-system party of the Right or Left); or any of the above happening also in western Germany, which could indicate a seriously destabilizing effect on the West of unification with the East.

Could the union victories of the 1990s (and the persistence of comprehensive collective bargaining) be costly Pyrrhic victories in a long-term union collapse? Time will tell—but I don't think so. One thing employers have learned in the 1990s is this: in the German institutional context, repeated attacks have if anything strengthened German unions. The obvious conclusion is that solutions to cost problems, unemployment, and all the rest lie in innovative social partnership negotiations.

The institutional explanation could also be disproved, or at seriously questioned, if another causal argument fit the evidence, offering an equally plausible explanation for the same outcome (stable, adaptable relations of social partnership). Possible alternative explanations include the following (as outlined in Chapter 1):[18]

Economic efficiency arguments would either fail to predict the rapid rise of wage levels through comprehensive collective bargaining in the East (to well beyond "market levels"), or would view this as a distortion that should cripple the eastern economy—which in turn would destabilize the regulating framework of social partnership relations. After the initial collapse, however, the eastern economy appears poised for future growth (although "takeoff" remains so far illusory), within a framework that includes high wages and higher rates of union membership in the East than in the West, and in which comprehensive collective bargaining agreements provide the benchmark.[19]

Personal preference or *rational choice* arguments could hardly have predicted the courageous and risky strike action of eastern metalworkers in the spring of 1993, in the absence of empowering institutions (transferred from West to East). The major *personal interest* for each eastern employee, in a period of mass unemployment, lay clearly in staying employed—an interest that was superseded by the collective interest (to defend collective bargaining gains) that took shape and became viable only in the newly established institutional context. Related *pluralist interest group* explanations also afford little insight in a period in which the major interest group structures (unions and employer associations) were transferred into eastern Germany from the West.

Perspectives based on *culture, identity,* and *collective understandings* are useful in explaining the eastern propensity for group work and collective action. The "political constructionism" derived from such perspectives helps explain both how institutional transfer could succeed and the continuing institutional change necessary for adaptation to eastern circumstances. This is an important contribution without which it is impossible to understand either the politics of successful institutional transfer or the ongoing processes of reform and adaptation. But the overwhelming lesson that emerges from the data (case studies, metal industry strike, the overall picture) is that identities *do* change, quite rapidly in some cases, especially when a new institutional framework defines new interests and possibilities. Decades of socialization in a radically different political culture could hardly explain the constructive role played by so many rehired eastern managers and newly elected eastern works councillors in the shift to a market economy framed by new relations of social partnership.

Finally, *economic and social structure* in eastern Germany, itself in massive turmoil and flux after 1989—as the percentages, for example, both of manufacturing employees and women in the workforce dropped dramatically over an extremely brief period—while helping to explain the difficulties of institutional transfer, affords little explanatory leverage into the successful transfer and adaptations of modern relations of social partnership.

Other possible explanations—such as those that emphasize *power relations, political coalitions,* or *social movements*—can only be understood in the context of the radically new institutional context. While protest movements generated the domestic political power necessary to bring down the old regime, such groupings dissipated quickly in the new environment. To the extent that such groupings (or their "legacies") reformed, they did so largely within channels of the new order—in collective bargaining, in the 1993 strike, in firm-level groups of newly elected works councillors, in local politics—in bodies and promoting interests defined by the new order.

Each of the above alternative explanations offer insights into the *problems* for institutional transfer, and the instabilities and shortcomings that persist. None of them, however, can explain the dominant outcome: the emergence, adaptability, and relative stability of new relations of social partnership between labor and management in eastern Germany.

New institutions provide the analytical glue and the shaping causal force for the dominant outcomes observed in this study for eastern Germany. As indicated above (and throughout), however, the process of transformation has two over-lapping and necessary steps: first, the transfer of institutions such as comprehensive collective bargaining and codetermination from West to East; and second, the processes of negotiation, conflict, adaptation, and reform that enable the new institutions and practices to take root in the new soil. So conceived, the institutional analysis offered here contributes to a synthesis, elegantly suggested by Richard Locke and Kathleen Thelen (1995), between contrasting perspectives of historical institutionalism and political constructionism. The key to such a synthesis, I would suggest, is the recognition that institutions are not only constraining (as much of the institutional literature implies) but enabling as well.

EXPLAINING INSTITUTIONAL CHANGE

Here we reach the limits of a predictive model. If actor choice is open to a range of alternatives, even within narrowly constrained institutional circumstances in which certain choices are more likely than others, then actors can indeed change institutions. Institutional change, therefore, depends on both the given institutional framework (or remnants, in the case of institutional collapse) and actor choice to modify or contest the institutions. Because institutions tend by nature to be entrenched, institutional change, while requiring strategic action by key players, probably also depends on dynamic external influences and change. In the contemporary world, the most important external change is the dynamism of markets: regional integration, intensified global competition, the coming of freer markets to previously planned economies.

Much excellent social science research of recent years has highlighted the importance of institutions as a causal variable explaining economic, political, and social outcomes.[20] Institutions themselves, however, do change, either gradually over time or sometimes quite suddenly. On the frontiers of research in the study of political economy and related fields such as industrial relations, therefore, is the question of how and why institutions change (Thelen and Steinmo 1992, 13–26).

The research presented in this book points toward three major sources of institutional change. The first and most important source of change is *market dynamism*.[21] Changing world markets clearly have major impacts on national, regional, and local institutions everywhere. In the German case, currency union, the collapse of the eastern economy, formal political and economic unification, and the coming of a western-style market economy to eastern Germany had major impacts on existing institutions. In the East, the new market economy drove the rapid transformation of existing economic institutions, from public policy, to firm structure, to industrial relations. The old institutions had little chance or capacity to adapt to the new market circumstances; change was sudden and thorough, a clear, market-driven instance of what Schumpeter (1962) termed "creative destruction." Dynamic markets constitute an *external* (or environmental, to use the language of organizational behavior and industrial relations) source of institutional change.

The second source of change is the *politics of conflict and negotiation*, as for example when institutions must be adapted to new circumstances. Employer associations and unions in western Germany made the choice, rapidly and to some extent in unison, to expand their organizations into the East. In both cases, major resources were devoted to this effort and as a result a solid organizational presence was established as early as 1991. The social partners further chose, in the spring of 1991 for the pattern-setting metal industry, to negotiate comprehensive collective bargaining agreements, as in western Germany, for entire eastern industries. Surprisingly to many, the social partners quickly agreed on the principle of phased-in wage parity for eastern workers, to bring them up to western standards within a few years. When Gesamtmetall chose two years later to abrogate that agreement and abolish phased-in parity, IG Metall and its new eastern membership decided to fight, engaging in dramatic and successful strike action that restored the parity principle.

The above choices, made possible by and reinforcing a successful transfer of western institutions of social partnership and industrial relations to eastern Germany, resulted in wholesale institutional change: the coming of a wholly new industrial relations system to eastern Germany.

Institutional transfer, although an important aspect of what occurred in this case, is obviously not the whole story. As we have seen, the institutions transferred into eastern Germany have to some extent been changed in the process, akin to what David Stark (1996) calls "recombination" (see also Lehmbruch 1994). The transfer of union organization and comprehensive collective bargaining to eastern Germany, for example, made possible the successful metalworkers' strike of 1993. But the risky decision to use the new channels to wage a high-stakes strike effort was made by thousands of eastern metalworkers, surprising employers (and most other observers) in their determination and solidarity. This mobilization in turn transformed IG Metall from a western organization pushing its way into the East toward a rank-and-file organization of eastern workers. Whereas Gesamtmetall and IG Metall in a sense imposed the collective bargaining agreement of 1991 on its eastern members, the 1993 agreement was very much a participatory one in which both firms and employees played an active role. As we have seen in the case studies in Chapter 3, relationships between employers and employees (a deeper understanding both of conflicting and common interests, often accompanied by a new mutual respect) and between works councils and the union (in the best cases a much strengthened relationship of mutual support) were changed as a result. In the process, the new institutions of social partnership in eastern Germany were transformed from an externally imposed, bureaucratic structure resting on shaky foundations toward a locally supported framework for the pursuit of eastern interests (Behrens 1995). Actors thus breathed new life into the imported institutional structure, greatly expanding its vitality and potential for interest representation.

Institutions thus influence the pursuit of interests, yet actor choices in the pursuit of such interests can in turn transform institutions.[22] Another example is the spread of group work at innovative firms in eastern Germany. Here, the collective traditions of the eastern workforce bumped up against the individualism of western organization. When offered the choice, eastern workers have opted for modern group work, reorganizing the workplace in productivity-enhancing ways that now serve as models for work reorganization in the West (as, for example, at Opel in Eisenach, Knorr-Bremse in Berlin, and VW in Mosel).

Institutions are thus not only enabling as well as constraining, they are also politically constructed and therefore to some extent *malleable*, subject to adaptation, reform, and change by actors in political processes of innovation and negotiation.

The third source of institutional change lies in processes of *institutional expansion*. When institutions expand into new environments, those institutions are in large or small ways changed through processes of adaptation. Thus it is not only eastern Germany that is transformed but incoming western institutions as well (Lehmbruch 1994; Behrens 1995). This mutual process of influence and change, even in the one-sided process of German unification, points to a broader conclusion: institutional expansion, transfer, or adaptation to new circumstances leads to institutional change. Such a process of change, although painful, may result in institutional reinvigoration or even reinvention; if it does not, the alternative outcome may well be institutional stagnation and decline.

For proponents of social partnership, therefore, the story does not necessarily have a happy ending. As an important component of market regulation in the new Germany, social partnership now finds itself saddled with the imperative to solve enormous problems and meet high expectations. Widespread, inevitable dissatisfaction in the East, which in 1993 IG Metall was able to channel into a winning strike effort, could just as easily in the future take shape as dissatisfaction with the accomplishments of both unions and employer associations, and the framework agreements they have negotiated. If the major economic and social problems facing unified Germany (see, for example, Carlin and Soskice 1997) are not solved by existing actors operating within the current institutional framework, the expansion of social partnership to eastern Germany could be the beginning of its end.

Institutional expansion, in other words, requires institutional change in order to solve new problems. Such change can be a source of institutional reinvigoration: dissatisfied eastern members, for example, with higher percentages of white-collar employees and women (as in telecommunications and the public sector), push for organizational reform within unions; a decentralization of bargaining and industrial policy in the East promotes a broader decentralization of responsibility and influence within unions (Behrens 1995). If, on the other hand, change and reinvigoration are resisted or fail, expansion can lead to organizational decline. Although the extension of modern relations of social partnership into eastern Germany is no longer in question, the future success of this mode of market regulation remains uncertain. The institutions of social partnership will either continue to find new life, reinvigoration, and reform in the new Germany or, overtaxed and unable to make the necessary changes, they will stagnate and decline.[23]

Implications for Theory and Practice

Markets are powerful and efficient mechanisms that stimulate productivity and innovation through competition. But markets are also impersonal and can destroy individuals, families, and communities. Progressive movements since the nineteenth century have consisted to a large measure of efforts, more or less successful, to regulate the market. Chartists, Owenites, trade unions, consumer cooperative movements, and labor and social-democratic parties have all been fired more or less explicitly by a general vision of social democracy, in which society regains control over the great productive energy of the market for the common good (Polanyi 1957).

The work of Marx and Engels provided theoretical inspiration to some extent both to communism and to social democracy, the former finding historical manifestation above all in the Soviet Union, central and eastern Europe (including East Germany), and China, the latter finding its strongest historical manifestation in northern Europe, and especially in Scandinavian countries such as Sweden. Both the demise of communism in the Soviet bloc and the simultaneous decline of the Swedish model of democratic corporatism can be viewed as products of the power of market dynamism. Markets, in the end, have thus undone precisely the forces and institutional frameworks that have sought to suppress (in the communist cases) or even to regulate strongly (in the Swedish case) those same markets.[24]

Markets, nonetheless, remain both liberating and devastating in their effects, as contemporary eastern Germans now well know. The paradoxical calling of modern social democracy and progressive social movements, therefore, remains similar in one sense to what it was a hundred years ago: to unleash yet at the same time harness markets in the interests of society. This is the complex, historic task toward which a new generation of "moderate" social democrats, in different ways, appears to be groping (including Tony Blair in Britain, Gerhard Schröder in Germany, Lionel Jospin in France, and Massimo d'Alema in Italy).[25]

In eastern Germany since 1989, we have witnessed in extreme forms both the negative and the positive effects of a market economy. Thus the critical question for reformers, in Germany and elsewhere: what kinds of institutions and policies can harness market forces, unleashing and channeling market power (to promote rising productivity and innovation) while at the same time protecting employees and citizens and giving them a voice in the direction and shape of change? Social capitalism in Germany, now proven resilient in the most trying of circumstances, offers one viable model from which to learn and upon which to build.[26]

Although extreme pressures such as the unification of eastern and western Germany are uncommon, there can be little assurance of prolonged institutional stability in the dynamic markets of the contemporary global economy. Institutions, we know, have a major influence on relative actor power, definitions of self-interest, and economic and political outcomes (Hall 1986; Steinmo, Thelen, and Longstreth 1992). Yet institutions themselves must adapt to changes in context and required tasks. They may fail to do so, leading to stagnation and decline, as, for example, they did in the Warsaw Pact countries of the 1980s. The external pressure of market dynamism, however, does generate internal pressure for reform and open up possibilities for actors promoting innovation. We know that actors can, to some extent, change the policies, functioning, and even structure of institutions from within (e.g., Selznick 1949). The argument here is that the possibilities for such change and the leverage available to actors rise in a period of rapid market change, when new adaptations become necessary.

Changing world markets, requiring production reorganization and innovation, have strengthened the hand of employers throughout the world economy. Increased employer leverage and initiative have been driving forces for deregulation and de-unionization in the United States and Great Britain as well as for the breakup of central bargaining and the decline of the once preeminent social-democratic model in Sweden (Swenson 1991; Thelen 1993). Employers have also taken the offensive in the new Germany.[27] Yet here, in contrast to the other cases, unions have held the line; the existing model of organized social capitalism has so far been maintained.

As we have seen, German resilience resides both in institutions that provide a flexible framework in which unions and employer associations can each pursue and defend their interests, and critical actor choices to work within, stretch, and modify the institutions. Central to institutional flexibility and successful actor strategy here is the synergistic, coordinated combination of rights and power used by organized employers and workers at two distinct levels: at the firm/plant level in processes of codetermination, and at the sectoral and national levels in comprehensive collective bargaining and even occasional but important instances of peak discussion and negotiation (such as Solidarity Pact negotiations of 1992–93).

For the German case, it is crucial both that appropriate institutional channels of interest representation exist and that the actors have expanded their use of such channels in innovative ways to promote both incremental and, since 1989, more radical innovation (Katzenstein 1989; Thelen 1991, 1993; Wever 1995). German institutions, for example, have proven more stable than Swedish institutions because they are better suited to the requirements of new markets, to successful "diversified quality production" (Streeck 1987, 1992; Pontusson 1995). The problem in Sweden was that bargaining was too centralized, allowing not enough firm- and plant-level flexibility in wages and other issues. The German model, by contrast, *has* allowed such flexibility, which unions and employers have exploited in innovative ways in important areas such as production reorganization and work sharing.[28] And only if such innovation, and accompanying institutional reform, continues will social partnership adapt well to the uncertain market circumstances of the future (Kern and Sabel 1990; Kern 1994; Herrigel 1997).

The success of social capitalism in Germany in the 1990s, in other words, is a product of institutions and actor strategies that have ensured representation and negotiation of labor and management interests at both the shopfloor and national levels—and levels in between such as the firm and region. Especially important to the development of employee representation has been the emergence of a growing role for the rank and file. Since the Humanization of Work initiatives of the 1970s, unions have promoted new forms of employee participation at the workplace. Beginning in the mid-1980s, IG Metall made the campaign for group work a central component of its efforts at the works council level (Turner 1991, 111–17). Companies have included team forms of organization in their drive to implement elements of "lean production" (Roth 1996; Streeck 1996). In eastern Germany, workers have responded enthusiastically to the opportunity to adopt new group forms of work organization, offering a potential magnet, and in some cases a model, for the modernization of industry in Germany. And finally, eastern metalworkers mobilized the successful strike action of 1993 with great passion and solidarity, serving both as an inspiration to other eastern and western workers and as prominent defenders of social partnership at a critical juncture.

Thus it is not enough to say that the primary social partners—employer associations and unions—are the critical actors in the German political economy.[29] Within the employer associations, as we have seen, conflict among firms, and especially between dominant large firms and more pressured and militant small and medium-sized firms, has been important in shaping policy and conflict within (and beyond) the social partnership (Silvia 1997). And within unions and company workforces, the role of rank-and-file activism, expressed in strike actions, new work organization, and vibrant shop steward groupings that bubble up into works council activism, has also been crucial in shaping policy and conflict. Workers and small employers, operating from within their own family and community networks of support—"society"—are thus key actors in the formulation of choice, in the conflict and negotiation that lead to bargained outcomes in Germany. In contemporary unsettled circumstances, this has been particularly true for the processes of institutional transfer and transformation. No analysis of German unification, social partnership adaptation, or organizational change that operates only at a superstructural level (from the DGB and BDA to the firm, union, or works council) can be complete. Where this has not already been done in the social sciences, it is high time indeed to "bring the people back in."[30]

The emphasis in this study has been on the importance of unions, works councils, and workers themselves as key players in the crisis of German unification and social partnership adaptation. This is not to say that employers are unimportant: as we have seen, employer association strategies, intraorganizational conflict between larger and smaller firms, and management in eastern firms (including the "old red socks") have been crucial in contemporary developments. Much recent research in comparative political economy highlights the often neglected, pivotal role played by employers and employer associations in the building or dismantling of bargaining relationships that underpin a given framework of political economy (Swenson 1989, 1991; Soskice 1990; Kochan, Katz, and McKersie 1994; Wever 1995). While it is clear, for example, that Swedish employers played a major role in both the rise and decline of the Swedish model (Swenson 1991; Pontusson and Swenson 1992), the implication does not necessarily follow that employers are *the* decisive actor in democratic corporatist or social partnership arrangements.

Employers and their associations are by definition important in a capitalist economy. But the difference between varieties of capitalism is to a large extent also a product of the relative capacity of workers and their unions to organize. If Swedish employer centralization in the 1930s caused union centralization rather than vice versa as previously assumed (Swenson 1991), employer organization in the first place was itself largely a response to working-class militancy and mobilization.[31] Postwar cartel capitalism in Japan consolidated itself in part through the defeat of independent unionism in the 1950s and 1960s, and the substitution of more company-friendly enterprise unionism (Cusumano 1985, 135). The resurgence of liberal capitalism in the United States since the 1970s was made possible by labor's inability to reverse its own decline (Milkman 1991).[32]

In a similar fashion, social partnership in Germany is only possible because labor is well organized and able to defend its institutional underpinnings in comprehensive collective bargaining and firm-level codetermination.[33] Although German employers like their profitable system in Germany (Wever 1995), it stretches the imagination to believe that many if not most of them, if given the choice, would not prefer something more deregulated. Famous "social partnership" firms such as Volkswagen and BMW have shown that they can be just as union-busting as native employers in non-German production sites. In processes of German unification, social partnership has survived above all because unions have organized the East and eastern workers have proven willing to back union action to defend their gains. In eastern Germany, in fact, it is the employer associations, less densely organized than in the West, that form the weak link in the consolidation of social partnership—a weakness to some extent reproducing itself in the mid-to-late 1990s in the West.

I see little evidence to indicate that employers in Germany could have defeated the unions and broken up the social partnership had they chosen to do so. On the contrary, when metal employers were most militant—in bargaining campaigns of 1993 in the East and 1994, 1995, and 1996–97 in the West—their leaders were clearly caught off guard by the overwhelmingly solidaristic response from workers, works councils, and unions. The implication (or hypothesis) I infer from this evidence is the following: Precisely because employers are in the driver's seat as the owners of the means of production in a capitalist economy, prospects for labor-friendly social partnership reside above all in the capacity of employees and their unions to organize and mobilize.[34]

Innovative recent research highlighting the importance of employer organization in social democracy (Swenson 1991; Thelen 1994) also brings out the importance of cross-class alliances and intra-class divisions. In the German case, it is certainly true, for example, that the chemical industry social partnership is less conflictual (and some would say more employer dominated) than metal industry relations emphasized in this study. It is also true that "cross-class alliances," emerging as a product of negotiation and conflict in both the metal and chemical industries, have set patterns that are widely followed (and sometimes follow each other) throughout the German labor market. At the same time, however, the evidence presented here does not point to the conclusion that intra-class conflict is necessarily decisive. On the contrary, social partnership works because each social partner, within metal, the chemical industry and elsewhere, is well organized, capable of conflict and negotiation, closely linked to its "class allies" through pattern bargaining and federation membership, and sits clearly across the table from the other social partner. To a significant extent, the German case of social partnership paradoxically demonstrates the continuing viability of organized classes facing off (at various levels and in new ways, perhaps) to negotiate the terms of employment and market regulation.

It is far too early, in other words, to downplay or write off altogether the role of organized labor in the contemporary global economy. Social partnership, one element of a soft or flexible version of social democracy, has so far proven viable and resilient, even in the extreme circumstances of German unification, only because labor has maintained its organizational capacity and institutional underpinnings in the face of major employer challenges.

Persistent union strength in Germany (and in other EU countries such as Sweden, Denmark, Finland, Austria, and Italy) also means that viable solutions to contemporary problems such as high unemployment are unlikely to be found without labor movement collaboration. Having tried and failed to inflict a substantial defeat on IG Metall several times in the 1990s, it seemed that German employers would sooner or later have to accept the obvious: that labor needs to be aboard any major reforms in economic and social policy. For this reason alone, since labor will support neither massive social cutbacks nor declining living standards, EMU-driven budget austerity interferes with the negotiation of viable solutions to persistently high unemployment. Faced with a choice between attacking union influence and loosening the straitjacket of EMU monetary policy (driven ironically by the German Bundesbank), European governments and societies may have no choice but to loosen or substantially modify EMU. This would not necessarily be a disaster (as shrill press reports often imply), and could well be a positive development for the resolution of contemporary social problems.

If German unions lose their strong organizational capacity, as they conceivably could in challenging future circumstances that include European integration and continuing globalization of trade and capital, social partnership could become history. The persistence of both organizational capacity and institutional underpinnings depends not only on employer interests and strategies but on tactical and strategic decisions, including internal reform efforts, made by unions, works councils, and employees themselves in changing circumstances. To a significant extent, as we have seen, institutions such as comprehensive collective bargaining and codetermination shape choice. For German unions, however, the range of choice in present circumstances extends beyond the conventional decisions to the necessity for continuing internal and institutional reform and adaptation.[35]

Institutions are important, but they can be changed—as a result of both external and internal pressure. This is a heartening conclusion for those of us, dissatisfied with present inequities, who seek to expand the scope of citizen participation and employee representation in the ever-changing market economy.

From Rostock to Bonn

In the midst of a deepening sense of political crisis for unified Germany in 1996, two mid-year events signaled the continuing force behind established relations and practices of social partnership. In June, the German labor movement—led by the DGB and its member unions—remarkably united across East and West, organized the largest demonstration seen in Germany since the second world war. Three hundred and fifty thousand demonstrators from throughout unified Germany converged on the old capital city of Bonn to protest government cutbacks in social standards. They arrived on special trains in large contingents from Dortmund, Bremen, Hamburg, Rostock, Berlin, Dresden, Leipzig, Munich, Frankfurt—from everywhere in unified Germany. In Bonn, they celebrated together their numbers, their unity, the excellent "Stimmung" (mood), the sense of power and social mission. This mobilization of union strength demonstrated powerful backing for labor's commitment to defend the social partnership and its prominent union role. Chancellor Kohl, for his part, quickly announced important compromises in his social spending plan, conceding to the demonstrators both their very real power and his own desire to preserve the basis of social consensus.

A few weeks later, in July, formal wage parity with the West arrived at last for eastern metalworkers, whose enhanced paychecks reflected once again the unexpected and passionate solidarity of 1993.

I have argued that in the unfolding of such important events, institutions play a central role. But the heroes of this story, I would now like to reemphasize, are people, not institutions. Above all, they are eastern Germans, still in the midst of almost unimaginable upheaval and profound transformation. Not all easterners, to be sure: not the violent thugs who attack foreign-born scapegoats; not the clowns who laugh off the pain and drink their troubles away with strong German beer; not the plodders who keep heads down and do as they are told under communism or capitalism; not the authoritarian jerks who feed on hierarchy and bark orders in planned and market economies alike; not the quitters who endlessly whine and complain—no, the eastern heroes of this story are the activists, the risk-takers, the people who have made positive change possible.

They—and their friends and colleagues—know who they are, and they are many. They grumbled in repressive and inefficient communist workplaces yet improvised with colleagues to produce goods and services, to put food on the table, to carve out semi-autonomous space. They joined the revolution in 1989–90, speaking out at meetings, organizing new rank-and-file groupings, demonstrating, pushing for change in the workplace. They greeted incoming western unions and climbed aboard new processes of collective bargaining and codetermination, to expand opportunities for representation and minimize the damage of downsizing and economic collapse. Many of them serve today as elected works councillors and local union representatives, somewhere within the now-eastern dual system of industrial relations.

My colleagues and I met or heard about such people in every eastern workplace we visited in the course of this research. They are people of passion, quiet or loud, pushing at the bounds of the possible. The joys of liberation and the bitterness of disillusionment coexist uneasily in such people. They push within and beyond the institutions, to make progress possible. In eastern Germany today, their passion, their pain, their endless struggles continue.

Institutions shape choice. But human beings, in pursuit of their own interests, dignity, and meaning, press within and occasionally beyond the constraints of structure. In so doing, they push through where it is possible to do so, challenging and changing the status quo.

Two such eastern women, for example, elected works councillors, led the 1993 strike at Siemens in Rostock, contributing importantly to a remarkable success for IG Metall and its new eastern membership. White-collar employees, products of the revolutionary social movement of 1989–90 (as it impacted their workplace), itself transformed under their leadership into the activist labor movement of 1993—this new generation of rank-and-file activists have made modern relations of social partnership possible in eastern Germany. They offer hope for the revitalization of today's all-German labor movement. Against managerial (including "old red sock") and rank-and-file opposition, they and their colleagues mobilized a majority workplace coalition for high labor standards and strong representation, even in the face of massive downsizing. They played out their changing activist roles, from within a planned to within a market economy, with steady courage and persistent dignity.

In July of 1996, I spoke once again with one of these women. She shared her concerns about a Siemens spin-off plan that would further downsize her workforce—although she recognized that this was a problem of production reorganization similar to those faced by workers and unions all over Germany and Europe (and the world) these days. She worried that union membership density at Siemens in Rostock had fallen to 45 percent, although she also acknowledged that this was still considerably higher than comparable union density at electronics firms such as Siemens in the western part of Germany. She knew that life was terribly unfair, that jobs would be scarce, and that things would be difficult for many years to come in the new eastern Germany. But she spoke with pride and quiet passion about the strike of 1993 and the important role it played in consolidating union strength at her workplace and elsewhere in the East. And she spoke enthusiastically about the massive demonstration in Bonn the previous month and its important positive effects for labor and for all of Germany in contemporary battles for social justice.

These two women at Siemens in Rostock represent both past and ongoing struggles of eastern transformation as well as the promise of German trade unions and social partnership in the years ahead.

And among their much more modest accomplishments, they have also inspired me to write this book.

Notes

PREFACE

1. Or, as written in the November 9, 1996, issue of *The Economist*: "Did it ever seem likely that east Germany, after four decades of communist rule, would take just a handful of years to invent a brand new identity for itself, conjure up a shiny new economy, and live happily ever after? Landscapes might flourish, pigs might fly. . . ."

PROLOGUE

1. Although I cite published work where appropriate, most of the facts and analysis here in the prologue are based on interviews as well as participant observation conducted in eastern Germany in the spring of 1993.

2. The extent of economic difficulty in eastern Germany was kept out of the public eye during the fall 1990 election, unification festivities, and the headlines-grabbing Gulf War of early 1991. Only when that war began to fade from the front pages in February did the rapidly developing economic collapse in eastern Germany come to the forefront of public attention. The March 1991 agreement on phased-in wage parity between bargaining parties in the metal industry may therefore have come at the last possible moment; employer criticisms of the agreement grew from that point on. It is interesting to note, however, that the agreement was signed after, not before, the collapse was becoming apparent—indicating perhaps that the large employers and the union wanted such an agreement even under the most adverse circumstances. I am grateful to Werner Seibel who clarified for me the timing of this agreement.

3. For a useful discussion of the dissatisfaction and renewed "alienation" of eastern association members (in the employer associations as well as other interest organizations), see Wiesenthal, Ettl, and Bialas 1992.

4. For the employer perspective, see, for example, *Handelsblatt*, April 6, 1993, p. 3. For the union view, see *Der Gewerkschafter*, March 1993. For a debate between the two viewpoints just prior to the first warning strikes, see *Tagesspiegel*, March 23, 1993, p. 21.

5. *Handelsblatt*, April 5, 1993, p. 1.

6. *The Economist*, April 24, 1993, pp. 71–72.

7. In late March and early April, I spent three weeks based at the Wissenschaftszentrum in Berlin, conducting research at workplaces and union and employer offices in eastern Germany. Because I became personally immersed in these events, this section is written from the methodological perspective of a participant-observer. There is a rich tradition of such methodology in the social sciences; see Beynon 1974; Burawoy 1979, 1985; Whyte 1994; and

Belanger, Edwards, and Haiven 1994 for prominent examples in industrial relations and sociology.

8. Gesamtmetall president Gottschol even renounced use of the lock-out, another sign that the employers felt no need to prepare for a sustained labor conflict (*Süddeutsche Zeitung*, April 8, 1993, p. 2).

9. For press accounts of the April 2 warning strikes in Rostock, see "20,000 auf der Strasse," *Ostsee Zeitung*, April 3, 1993, pp. 1–2; "Werftarbeiter im Warnstreik," *Frankfurter Rundschau*, April 3, 1993, pp. 1, 3; and "Warnstreik am Werftdreieck," *Hansestadt Rostock*, April 3, 1993, p. 13.

10. See also Mahnkopf 1991, 276–79, and Röbenack and Hartung 1992. As *Der Spiegel* put it on the eve of the strike: "In the workplace, employees are profoundly insecure; fear of losing their jobs is paralyzing their willingness to strike" (*Der Spiegel*, March 29, 1993, p. 122; author's translation).

11. For an account of the early abortive settlement, see *Der Spiegel*, May 10, 1993, pp. 114–17.

12. Press accounts ranged from the shrill "mass suicide" perspective expressed in *Handelsblatt* and *The Economist* to a more balanced view expressed in newspapers such as *Süddeutsche Zeitung*. In the latter, editorials expressed disbelief that a last-minute settlement would not be reached. See, for example, Dagmar Deckstein, "Streik im Osten: Ein hohes Risiko," *Süddeutsche Zeitung*, April 29, 1993, p. 4.

13. See, for example, Andreas Oldag, "Metallerstreik in Ostdeutschland," *Süddeutsche Zeitung*, May 6, 1993, p. 3.

14. Reported by IG Metall in its newsletter "Metall Nachrichten für den Bezirk Küste," May 13, 1993.

15. Dagmar Deckstein, "Ein fast genialer Kompromiß," *Süddeutsche Zeitung*, May 15, 1993, p. 4.

16. As reported by Incomes Data Services: "Under the settlement, the employers recognised that breaching the original agreement was an 'unavoidable emergency measure solely occasioned by the unique situation in the five new *Länder*. . . . Terminating collective agreements is not an appropriate means for resolving collective disputes' " (*IDS European Report*, June 1993, p. 5).

17. The amount has been estimated to be as high as DM 6 billion (Silvia 1993, 13; *Süddeutsche Zeitung*, May 21, 1993, p. 1).

18. Works councils are elected at the firm level; the union is organized at the firm (shop stewards), local (Verwaltungsstelle), regional (Bezirk), and national levels. For English-language descriptions of the structures and practices of industrial relations in modern Germany, see Adams and Rummel 1977, Streeck 1984a, Katzenstein 1987, and Berghahn and Karsten 1987.

19. The lower figure for the Berlin area reflects a market converging rapidly around West Berlin levels, with both higher living costs and greater pressure on employees to work at western standards. The last of the eastern regions to settle, Berlin-Brandenburg produced a strong union critique against the Saxon settlement, arguing for quicker wage parity in an area where social differences were most painfully visible (Bispinck 1993b, 477; *Süddeutsche Zeitung*, May 19, 1993, p. 2).

20. This explanation begs the question of whether employers wanted only to improve their bargaining position within the social partnership or whether they were seeking more fundamental deregulation. Because views were split within the employers' camp (with large firms typically leaning toward the former position and small to medium-sized firms more likely to support the latter), I don't think the leaders of Gesamtmetall themselves really knew which outcome they preferred.

21. The last previous major IG Metall strike, the six-week 1984 strike for the shorter work-week in West Germany, had a similar beneficial effect for union influence in the plants, at a time of growing "plant egoism" on the part of works councils (cf. Hohn 1988 and Thelen 1991).

22. See, for example, Marc Fisher, "Many in East Germany Redirect Their Anger," *International Herald Tribune*, March 27–28, 1993, p. 6. See also the editorial "Politisches Warnsignal," in *Süddeutsche Zeitung*, May 18, 1993, p. 4; "Wir stehen unter Druck," *Der Spiegel*, April 26,

pp. 124–25; and Ferdinand Protzman, "Strike in Eastern Germany: Economics and Anger," *New York Times*, May 5, 1993, p. A3.

23. The "nominal" distinction is important here. Because other benefits, pay groupings, and company pay premiums remained lower in the East, eastern workers would not reach *full* wage parity for many years beyond the date (1996 for metalworkers) of nominal wage parity.

24. In a perceptive analysis, Horst Kern (1994, 38–45) argues that what IG Metall gained above all from the eastern strike was credibility: a demonstration of the capacity to mobilize its membership that would greatly strengthen the political and economic role of the unions in the new German states.

25. Note the long history in the United States and elsewhere of great labor victories followed by prolonged periods of union decline. I am indebted both to Nick Salvatore and Jonas Pontusson, each of whom separately impressed upon me this point—all the more important given widespread employer undercutting of agreed wage levels in the East in the years after 1993 (discussed further in Chapter 4). And see Behrens 1995, 14–48, for an analysis of the special circumstances—drastic employer contract cancellation and the extraordinary pent-up anger of eastern workers—that contributed to IG Metall's eastern victory, circumstances that may not exist in future union campaigns.

CHAPTER 1. SOCIAL PARTNERSHIP AT THE CROSSROADS

1. See, for example, Fukuyama 1989 and Jowitt's penetrating critique (Jowitt 1992, 306–31).

2. For recent affirmative answers, in addition to the one offered in this book, see Hollingsworth, Schmitter, and Streeck 1994; Boyer 1995; and Berger's introduction to Berger and Dore 1996. For parallel analyses that highlight persistent and fundamental cross-national variation in industrial relations, see Adams 1991; Bamber and Lansbury 1993; Poole 1993; Bean 1994; S. Jacoby 1995; Keenoy 1995; and Locke, Kochan, and Piore 1995.

3. See, for example, Womack, Jones, and Roos 1990; Ostry 1996; and Dore 1996.

4. Social democracy, as traditionally understood, is not the same thing as social partnership or the social market economy. In the social-democratic corporatist democracies of the postwar period, however, social partnership relations between strongly organized employers and unions are a central component of the system of regulation (cf. Schmitter and Lehmbruch 1979, Katzenstein 1985, and Wilensky and Turner 1987); and these countries are organized very much around "social markets" (market economies with strong social protections and powerful social-partnership-oriented interest groups). While it is beyond the scope of this book to analyze fully the various aspects of social democracy in the modern world economy, the focus on social partnership does offer one important indicator of the prospects for social democracy.

5. Marc Levinson, "It's Hip to Be Union," *Newsweek*, July 8, 1996, pp. 44–45.

6. For example, as reported by Wolfgang Münchau in the *Financial Times*, April 25, 1996, p. 3: "In an interview, Mr. Hans-Olaf Henkel, president of the Federation of German Industry (BDI), said the German trade union movement was facing terminal decline, and suggested that Germany would move increasingly toward an Anglo-Saxon style emphasis on individual self-reliance."

7. For examples of the variety of uses of a framework similar to this one, see Zysman 1983; Hall 1986; Powell and DiMaggio 1991; and Steinmo, Thelen, and Longstreth 1992; and on unions and industrial relations in Europe, see Ferner and Hyman 1992.

8. Thus Powell and DiMaggio 1991, p. 11: "Institutions do not just constrain options: they establish the very criteria by which people discover their preferences."

9. Thus Thomas Koelbe (1995), in a perceptive review of the literature on "new institutionalism," identifies three broad theoretical groupings centered around structure, culture, and action.

Using these categories, the perspectives I list sort out as follows: economic efficiency and political or personal preference fit under "action"; culture, identity, and collective understanding fit under "culture"; and economic and social structure as well as the institutional perspective presented here belong with "structure."

10. The work of Charles Sabel (1982, 1993), for example, explores the interaction between collective identities and changing production organization; Wolfgang Streeck (1992), by contrast, crosses boundaries within the "structure" category, emphasizing the interaction between institutions, production organization, and economic performance. Drawing on a rich tradition of industrial relations literature, Roy J. Adams (1995) emphasizes the causal force of institutions, yet calls for human agency (in acts of political choice and will) to change the institutions in fundamental ways.

11. Note the increasingly popular "punctuated equilibrium" model, adapted from the natural sciences, which posits periods of relative stability (when institutions may be good predictors of outcomes) alternating with periods of crisis and institutional change (cf. Krasner 1984; Gourevitch 1986; Thelen and Steinmo 1992, 15).

12. This is not a circular argument. Institutions are on one side of the equation (as independent variables); behavior is on the other side.

13. Note that the emphasis on the flexibility and enabling quality of institutions contrasts with the emphasis on constraints found in much of the institutional literature. Thus Wolfgang Streeck (1992) emphasizes the constraints of German institutions of industrial relations, and the positive effects of such constraints—such as the "external rigidity" that forces employers to move up-market and to train and retrain their employees.

14. See also, for example, Locke and Jacoby 1997.

15. See Thelen 1993 for a perceptive comparative analysis of the decline of the Swedish model and the relative resilience of the German model.

16. The generation now coming of age and entering the workforce in Japan, in fact, is popularly known as "the new human race," indicating among other things its preference for individual consumption and independent experience over company loyalty.

17. But see Weiss 1991 for the argument that German unification is a unique case, from which no broader conclusions regarding the transferability of legal systems or institutions can be drawn. Kirsten Wever (1995), however, points out significant possibilities for mutual learning between Germany and the United States; while Locke and Thelen (1995) suggest parallels in the contemporary challenges faced by U.S. and German labor.

18. Hirschman 1993. See also Kopstein 1995 on the everyday acts of worker resistance that undermined the GDR and Huelshoff and Hanhardt 1994 on the courage of eastern demonstrators whose "politics of the street" launched both the collapse of the GDR and subsequent German unification.

CHAPTER 2. WORLDS APART, THROWN TOGETHER

1. See, for example, Streeck 1989 and Katzenstein 1989, 3–29 and 307–53.

2. On the successful German political economy and its long-term competitive success, see also Katzenstein 1989, Streeck 1992, Hart 1992, Thurow 1992, and Albert 1993. For contrasting viewpoints that emphasize German "overregulation," see, for example, Donges 1991 and Gitlitz 1994.

3. To do this, a social partner could request the Minister of Labor to call upon that wonderfully concise German word *Allgemeinverbindlichkeitserklärung* (AVE), or "Declaration of Universal Applicability." For an AVE to apply, bargaining coverage must exceed 50 percent in a given region. Because most firms throughout West Germany belong to employer associations that negotiated collective bargaining contracts on behalf of the membership, the AVE was (and is today) infrequently used. The fact that it could be used, however, is probably a strong

incentive for individual firms to belong to employer associations: why not get the benefits of membership since one usually has to pay the negotiated wage and benefit levels anyway?

4. See Golden 1993 for a comparative analysis that links the combination of wage restraint and good economic performance to coordinated collective bargaining in Germany.

5. See Streeck 1984a and Berghahn and Karsten 1987 for a full discussion of the three different models of supervisory board participation.

6. Works council elections take place by law every four years. In the elections of 1990, for example, 75 percent of works council positions were won by union members (Niedenhoff 1990, 10–11), a typical outcome. Especially at large firms, these councillors are not only union members but union activists who have earned their positions on union-endorsed works council slates through previous contributions to local union activities, including serving as workplace shop stewards.

7. See Kotthoff 1994 for an in-depth study of works councils, showing the general deepening (from 1975 to 1990) of works council input and relations with management as well as the close linkage and strong mutual dependence of works councils and unions.

8. In contrast to Webber, Smyser (1993) argues that Kohl's *Wende* successfully stimulated West German economic growth through lower tax rates on business and other moderate deregulatory measures. Both agree, however, that government policies neither undermined the social partnership nor weakened union influence as in Britain and the United States.

9. For an update on German attempts to introduce lean production, which as it turns out must be significantly altered to fit the German institutional context, see Streeck 1996.

10. The 35-hour week was to be phased in by 1995 while the union accepted further flexibility in the scheduling of hours. .

11. Albert Hirschman nicely shows how the exit and voice options, which often work at cross-purposes, actually reinforced each other in the collapse of the German Democratic Republic. This happened because the exit option (leaving the country) and the voice option (the Leipzig demonstrations) both became broad public activities (Hirschman 1993). See also Torpey 1992, who argues that mass exodus both made internal opposition for the reform of socialism viable in the early stages (1989) and later marginalized such reform opposition as unification picked up steam in 1990. And Jeffrey Kopstein (1995) argues persuasively that it was "everyday acts of resistance" by East German workers over many years that set up the dramatic collapse of 1989–90.

12. See H. A. Turner (1992, 234) for a recounting of this story—including the interpretation that the opening of the Wall was at first based on a miscommunication that once implemented could no longer be rescinded.

13. On contrasting privatization strategies in eastern and central Europe, for example, see Stark 1992. For variations in labor-management relations, especially tripartism and "transformative corporatism," see Iankova 1997.

14. See the excellent collection in Liebert and Merkel 1991 for an early discussion of these questions from various points of view.

15. Thus Baethge and Wolf (1995, 253–54) refer to this "reckless unification process" as a "truly outlandish spectacle."

16. Note subsequent confessions such as this one by then West German Interior Minister Wolfgang Schäuble: "It would definitely have been better to leave some of the East German laws in effect for a transition period, and to introduce the West German legal and bureaucratic system step by step" (Kinzer 1994, 30).

17. Ken Jowitt characterizes this takeover of East Germany by West Germany not as colonization but as a necessary "adoption," which, in his view, should be forthcoming by western Europe for much more of central and eastern Europe than only the former German Democratic Republic (Jowitt 1992, 304–5).

18. For a first-rate analysis of the politics of institutional transfer in unified Germany, see W. Jacoby 1995.

19. In other words, not only were institutions transferred but elites as well. See Wiesenthal, Ettl, and Bialas 1992 and König 1993 for data and analysis on "elite transfer" from West to East in unified Germany.

20. See Ettl and Wiesenthal 1994 for a balanced discussion of the strengths and weaknesses of institutional transfer: both the capacity of the institutions to absorb stress and uncertainty and the institutional rigidity that interferes with necessary reform—resulting in ongoing processes of learning and adaptation.

21. For a consultant's perspective (from the German offices of McKinsey and Co.), comparing German unification to a corporate merger that to be successful requires not only imposing the parent firm's structure but working flexibly and intelligently with inherited culture and structures as well, see Henzler 1992.

22. This was particularly true since the DGB and its member unions had established "fraternal" relations with their counterpart organizations in East Germany—in line with West Germany's *Ostpolitik*, first promoted by the Social Democrats under Willy Brandt in the 1960s and 1970s, which opened up contacts and trade between East and West Germany (H. A. Turner 1992, 146–61).

23. Although in retrospect, union expansion to the East looks rapid indeed, the decision of IG Metall and other unions to start anew and to screen carefully did mean that workplaces were already in turmoil, often with newly elected caucuses or works councils in place, by the time the western unions arrived (Behrens 1995, 1–13).

24. On early employer association membership problems, see Wiesenthal, Ettl, and Bialas 1992, 24–25.

25. Economists who decry "union-imposed" high wages in the East are thus wrong to target the unions for their criticism (as did, for example, Dornbusch and Wolf 1992, 238). There was no major show of strength or pressure from one side or the other in the 1991 negotiations; Gesamtmetall gave full support to the parity strategy and viewed this outcome at the time as a victory for responsible social partnership. West German employer associations were explicit in their desire to transfer the West German collective bargaining structure to the East (Bispinck 1993a, 312).

26. For a contrasting opinion that emphasized the need for wage restraint in *both* East and West, see Büchtemann and Schupp 1992. Thus high unemployment levels in the East throughout the 1990s can be viewed in part as an undeniable cost of social partnership negotiation, in which the interests of the eastern unemployed were sacrificed to the interests of western firms and employees and eastern jobholders. It is also clear, however, that other important factors drove unemployment in the East, including currency union (which caused economic collapse), the collapse of markets in central and eastern Europe, and the uncertainty bred for investors by property restitution policies.

27. On the wide inequality and divergence of actual East-West pay differentials from parity-oriented contractual agreements, see *European Industrial Relations Review*, September 1993, p. 27. For a discussion of this issue by various analysts, see *WSI Mitteilungen* 44(8), August 1991.

28. For a thorough critique, especially of currency union, that calls for more hard-headed economic policies on the part of the German government, see Heilemann and Jochimsen 1994.

29. For a scathing critique of Treuhand policy and its destruction of existing economic networks and innovation potential, see Grabher 1992. For an alternative perspective that sees the Treuhand as having little room for discretion, given key macroeconomic decisions such as currency union that were beyond the Treuhand's influence, see Seibel 1994.

30. *Der Spiegel*, June 15, 1992, pp. 100–103.

31. The Welfare Survey of 1993 found that the initial optimism following unification had disappeared in both East and West by mid-1993 (*Employment Observatory*, November 1993, pp. 10–12).

32. "Underlying productivity performance," as measured by Hitchens, Wagner, and Birnie 1993, indicates productivity change excluding the impact of the sudden decline in orders brought on by currency union.

33. In a study that compares eastern and western German convergence with Britain's efforts to promote development in Northern Ireland, Hitchens, Wagner, and Birnie (1993) provide persuasive, empirical evidence for much stronger and faster convergence prospects in the German case. This is the difference, they argue, between the application of capital investment to a low-skills area and a similar application to a high-skills area.

34. In German, *Beschäftigungs- und qualifizierungs- gesellschaften*, or BQGs. See *European Industrial Relations Review*, December 1991, p. 15; Jürgens, Klinzing, and Turner 1993, 240–41; Knuth 1993; and Wiedemeyer, Beywl, and Helmstadter 1993.

CHAPTER 3. TRANSFORMATION IN THE EAST

1. Integrated, state-owned conglomerates dominated the East German economy. They were known as *Kombinate*, or *Volkseigene Betriebe* (VEB).

2. Case study presentations are based on plant visits, interviews, and documents collected between 1990 and 1995. I visited Hella in Meerane and VW-Chemnitz first in 1994; I visited the other eight firms at least three times each between 1990 and 1995. In-depth interviews were conducted with works councillors, managers, and union representatives; interviews ranged in length from one to four hours. Some of the plant visits and interviews in Berlin and Rostock I conducted alone, others were conducted together with Larissa Klinzing of Humboldt University; for the cases in Saxony, Ulrich Jürgens of the Wissenschaftszentrum Berlin and I made research trips together to those plants in 1991, 1992, and again in 1994. Eisenach I visited alone in 1993 and again with Uli Jürgens in 1994. Additional interviews were also conducted at several of the plants by research associates Owen Darbishire and Aline Hoffmann.

Early case studies also included firms that went out of business (such as Stern Radio). Because the sample presented here includes neither the many failures nor the struggling start-ups, I do not claim that it provides a complete picture of the eastern economy; it does show, however, processes of transformation at pattern-setting core plants. For similar findings based on plant research, see Kädtler and Kottwitz 1994 and Ermischer and Preusche 1995. Because such case studies provide only part of the picture, this evidence is supplemented in Chapter 4 with findings from other sectors as well as a consideration of general data and the overall picture.

3. Figures supplied by the company in April of 1994.

4. Strike votes are tabulated by region rather than plant or firm; this figure is therefore based on "informed speculation."

5. See, for example, Roger Thurow, "Volkswagen Brings Hope to a Community in Eastern Germany," *Wall Street Journal*, December 10, 1991, p. 1. The pledged VW investment in Saxony was reputed to be the single largest private investment in eastern Germany—approximately $2.9 billion, backed by an additional $1 billion in subsidies from federal and state government and Treuhand sources. VW purchased the old Trabant plant at Mosel from the Treuhand, which had taken over VEB Sachsenring (itself a part of the Kombinat IFA, which included the entire East German auto industry). VW then set up its independent subsidiarity VW-Sachsen next to the Treuhand's SAB (Sächsische Automobilbau). The latter was to subsidize production, hiring, and training at Mosel until the new plant was completed in 1994. At that time, SAB was to be absorbed into VW-Sachsen, and the Treuhand would be out of the picture. In the meantime, the continuing Treuhand role at Mosel represented a major government subsidy for the new VW production site.

6. Of the 7,000 workers formerly employed at the Trabi plant in Mosel, some took early retirement, others found new jobs in the West, and still others remained for a year or more on paid "short time" status, found job creation or training positions at local employment companies, and/or finally faced unemployment. Many of the unemployed hoped to get rehired at Mosel, as the workforce expanded in the future.

7. NUMMI is actually a GM/Toyota joint venture, run by Toyota management (Turner 1991, 53–62), while Saturn is more of a homegrown GM-UAW project. The Mosel experiment is therefore probably more akin to Saturn than to NUMMI, although these distinctions were lost on our interlocutors at Mosel back in 1991.

8. This is not as difficult as it might sound, since most former Trabi workers had completed apprenticeships and were classified as skilled workers.

9. German law at the time did not allow women to work nights. This provision was challenged by a European court and subsequently removed from German law.

10. Since 1992, only Golfs had been produced at Mosel in the refurbished old plant known as Mosel 1. At the adjacent new plant, Mosel 2, only the body shop was in full operation in 1994; full production capacity for Mosel 2 as well as full workforce hiring awaited a new model assignment to replace the Golf at Mosel in 1996 or 1997.

11. As a Wolfsburg works councillor put it in an interview in 1994: "We can't let the children eat the mother!"

12. In his role as head of the works council, Riemann could play no part in the strike, since works councils have no right to strike. As an IG Metall member, however, Riemann could and did play an active role and was widely perceived as a strike leader.

13. Eight of these were full-time. Under the Works Constitution Act, based on workforce size, the Mosel works council was entitled to four full-time members. The other four served full-time as a result of a plant-level agreement with management. It is common practice at companies where the union and works council are strong to negotiate upward the number of full-time works councillors, with salaries paid for by the company.

14. Works councillors estimated that about half of the current team leaders would be re-elected by their teams.

15. In 1994, IG Metall Verwaltungsstelle Zwickau reported 40,000 members (down from a post-unification peak of 62,000), with 22,000 of these employed and paying full dues.

16. See, for example, Timothy Aeppel, "Opel Designs Car Plant on Japanese Lines: Eastern German Facility Seen as Test for Europe," *Wall Street Journal,* January 21, 1992, p. A16; "General Motors in Germany: The Lean Machine," *The Economist,* September 26, 1992, pp. 78–80; "GM's German Lessons: Will the Eisenach plant's lean production transfer to the U.S.?" *Business Week,* December 20, 1993, pp. 67–68.

17. "The Opel Production System," booklet issued by Adam Opel AG Public Relations, 1993 edition, p. 3.

18. Harald Lieske, "Vom Kollektiv zum Team: Neue Strukturen in Eisenach," public talk, Opel Eisenach, October 1992, p. 6 (author's translation).

19. Strategic decisions, however, were made to a large extent at Opel headquarters in Rüsselsheim, GM-Europe headquarters in Zurich, or at General Motors in Detroit, for which the Eisenach works council had much less (if any) input.

20. See Mickler et al. 1996 for case studies of Eisenach and other eastern auto plants in the transformation years of 1990–94. This persuasive analysis indicates that new "lean" plants in the East have become highly modern and efficient but also include overly restrictive and controlling elements of "management-by-stress" teamwork—elements that need to be carefully regulated by works councillors and unions when the lessons of the East are transferred to the West.

CHAPTER 4. CRISIS, MODERNIZATION, AND THE RESILIENCE OF SOCIAL PARTNERSHIP

1. This is not to say that unions do not have much work to do in deepening their influence with works councils in the East, as clearly indicated in much excellent plant-level research (Kädtler and Kottwitz 1994, 1997; Hinz 1996).

2. See Hegewisch, Brewster, and Koubek 1996 for a comparative analysis based on large, post–Cold War surveys in eastern Germany and the Czech Republic. Findings included greater legitimacy for both personnel management and employee representation in eastern Germany, due above all to the transfer of institutions from the West.

3. Ursula Mensa-Petermann (1996) argues that while very close works council–management relations in eastern Germany may pose serious problems for unions and the dual system of industrial relations, such close relations may also prove a catalyst for economic modernization (cf. Kädtler and Kottwitz 1994 and Hinz 1996).

4. See Lungwitz and Preusche 1994 and Edwards and Lawrence 1996 for additional case-study evidence of the hard work and adaptability of many eastern managers. See Heering and Schröder 1995 on the basis provided by eastern traditions of workplace collaboration for modern labor-management cooperation and relations of social partnership.

5. Mass unemployment and other problems of unification have also made it possible for reformed communists in the Party of Democratic Socialism (PDS—the former SED) to consolidate and emerge in the 1990s as an important electoral force in eastern Germany. Whatever one's view of the PDS, it has played by the rules of the democratic polity and thus appears to pose no threat to the stability of democracy in unified Germany (electoral campaign rhetoric notwithstanding).

6. Sector sketches are based on in-depth interviews, conducted in 1993 and 1994, with several well-placed actors in each sector; trade and union publications; and secondary literature.

7. This observation is based on the comments of two IG Chemie union officials and one employer association economist.

8. See Silvia 1993, 40–42, for a useful discussion of developments in IG Chemie.

9. See, for example, Peter Thelen, " 'Wir mußten der neuen Lage Rechnung tragen,' " *Handelsblatt*, March 26, 1993, p. 4.

10. In the Postdienst (Postal Service), for example, 90.5 percent of western personnel councillors and 96.8 percent of eastern personnel councillors elected in 1992 were DPG members (according to union sources).

11. In addition, privatization and new technology were also creating an imperative for the DPG, in both East and West, to focus not only on union-council relations but also on *inter*-council coordination (Darbishire 1995).

12. Of 235,000 total employees in 1994, Deutsche Telekomm, for example, planned a reduction of 30,000 by 1998. After a series of warning strikes in 1994, the DPG won two-year pay and job guarantees for postal staff throughout unified Germany, including 90,000 positions in eastern Germany (*Industrial Relations in Europe*, July 1994, p. 5).

13. With union membership density in the East at 50 percent in 1991 and 45 percent in 1994, the rate remained considerably higher than comparable levels in the West (Kittner 1995, 93). Fichter (1997) cautions, however, that a continuation of losses beyond 1997 could eventually result in lower membership density in the East than in the West. Unions still have much work to do in the East, above all in building up plant structures and influence (Behrens 1995; Hinz 1996).

14. As reported in the European Commission's *Employment Observatory: East Germany*, December 1994, p. 1: "Five years after the fall of the Berlin Wall, the major institutional reconstruction measures—centering on the transition from the centrally planned to the social market economy—have been accomplished."

Chapter 5. Renewed Conflict in the West

1. After the dramatic defeat/compromise in the East, one might well ask why the employers thought they could win in the West. An employer association official answered that question

for me in this way: "Well, yes, we were wrong about the readiness of easterners to strike. But you see, they hadn't been allowed to strike for sixty years, and they just wanted to have that experience! In retrospect, one can understand that. But things are quite different in the West" (author's translation).

2. *Financial Times*, February 15, 1994, p. 15.

3. *IDS European Report*, April 1994, p. 18.

4. Ferdinand Protzman, "Rewriting the Contract for Germany's Vaunted Workers," *New York Times*, February 13, 1994, p. F5.

5. *IDS European Report*, April 1994, p. 18.

6. Reported in Ferdinand Protzman, "Rewriting the Contract for Germany's Vaunted Workers," *New York Times*, February 13, 1994, p. F5.

7. *IDS European Report*, March 1994, pp. 20–21.

8. Ibid.; and *International Labour Review*, 1993–94, p. 554.

9. *Industrial Relations Europe*, January 1994, p. 5.

10. *Der Spiegel*, November 29, 1993, pp. 114–15; and 50/1993, pp. 93–95.

11. The pay settlement was a delayed 2 percent raise, which would average out to a net 1.5 percent raise over twelve months. The agreement on hours opened up a corridor from 35 to 40 hours, around the industry standard of 37.5 hours; employees reduced to 35 hours would receive a corresponding reduction in pay, while those increased to 40 hours would receive no overtime compensation (*Industrial Relations Europe*, January 1994, p. 5).

12. *IGM Bremen, Tarifrunde 1994*, February 4, 1994, pp. 1–2.

13. The conservative government had amended paragraph 116 of the Work Promotion Act to cut off unemployment benefits to many locked-out workers, thereby strengthening the employer position in a labor conflict. Although this legislation had passed in 1986, its effect remained untested in a major labor conflict in the pattern-setting metal sector. Everyone agreed that paragraph 116 would strengthen the employer position; just how much, and how decisive this might be in a large strike/lock-out situation remained uncertain (Silvia 1988).

14. On the anger, passion, and mobilization of western workers, see *Der Spiegel*, February 21, 1994, pp. 86–87. As Kirsten Rölke, head of IG Metall in Flensburg, put it succinctly: "Our people are tired of getting the shaft" (ibid., p. 87, author's translation).

15. Quentin Peel, "IG Metall aims low in Lower Saxony action," *Financial Times*, February 23, 1994, p. 2.

16. *The Week in Germany*, March 4, 1994, p. 5.

17. *Metall Nachrichten, IGM, Metallindustrie Neidersachsen*, March 7, 1994, pp. 1–2.

18. In a letter to the international metal employers association (WEM) dated March 7, 1994, the directors of Gesamtmetall (Dr. Kirchner and Dr. v. Wangenheim) reported on the summit talk agreement of March 4–5 in Hannover. In this four-page letter, the point most emphasized was that there would be no net pay increase in 1994.

19. See, for example, *Metall Nachrichten, IGM, für die Metall- und Elektroindustrie an der Küste*, March 1994, p. 1.

20. And if an employee were laid off after the designated period of employment security, he or she would automatically be entitled to full pay restitution for the reduced hours.

21. See the Gesamtmetall letter referred to in note 18 for the details of the agreement. See also *IDS European Report*, April 1994, pp. 18–19, and Quentin Peel, "Germany's big guns pull back," *Financial Times*, March 7, 1994, p. 2.

22. Gesamtmetall letter (see note 18), March 7, 1994, pp. 3–4.

23. See, for example, "Beschäftigungsgarantien sind bei Metall härter gestaltet als in der Chemieindustrie," *Handelsblatt*, March 8, 1994.

24. "Umrechnung des ÖTV-Abschlusses in Mark und Pfennig schwierig," *Handelsblatt*, March 14, 1994.

25. "Welcome deal in Germany," *Financial Times*, March 7, 1994, p. 17.

26. Dagmar Deckstein, "Der Kraftakt der Metaller," *Süddeutsche Zeitung*, 1994, p. 4 (author's translation).

27. Peter Thelen, "Von Differenzierung keine Spur," *Handelsblatt*, March 29, 1994.

28. "ÖTV and DAG wollen kooperieren," *Handelsblatt*, June 6, 1994, pp. 1, 3.

29. "Tarifkartell in der Telebranche," *Handelsblatt*, June 8, 1994, p. 4; for a text of the agreement, see "Vereinbarung über Zusammenarbeit zwischen der Deutschen Postgewerkschaft (DPG) und der IG Metall," *Der Gewerkschafter*, June 1994, pp. 12–13.

30. "Umrechnung des ÖTV-Abschlusses in Mark und Pfennig schwierig," *Handelsblatt*, May 14, 1994.

31. As noted in the Siemens case in Chapter 3, eastern works councils and firms by the spring of 1994 had already begun trading hours reductions for employment security, following the western precedents set at VW and in the March settlement between Gesamtmetall and IG Metall.

32. "Die Verbandsflucht: Nur eine oft kolportierte Legende," *Handelsblatt*, March 21, 1994. But see Langer 1994 for a useful discussion of the growing dissatisfaction of medium-sized firms and their increasing readiness to consider abandoning the system of comprehensive collective bargaining. Schnabel and Wagner 1996 present an analysis of employer association membership in the West (in Lower Saxony), showing that while two-thirds of employees remain covered by comprehensive collective bargaining (by virtue of employer membership in the association), newer, export-oriented firms are often not joining. And Steven Silvia (1997) shows a long-term drop in Gesamtmetall membership coverage, from 74.5 percent of employees in 1984 to 64.2 percent in 1993; he argues, however, that the drop was caused neither by unification nor globalization but by a growing divergence of interests between large and small firms, a divergence that he believes could be resolved through collective bargaining. Schroeder and Ruppert (1996a, 1996b) also document a gradual downward trend in association membership but do not believe that comprehensive collective bargaining is at risk yet.

33. Thus while job losses totaled 31 percent, total DGB membership loss in the East from 1991–95 totaled 43 percent (Fichter 1997).

34. See, for example, Jacobi, Keller, and Müller-Jentsch 1992, 232, whose figures show 36 percent total union membership density for the Federal Republic in 1970, 38 percent in 1980, and 35 percent in 1990. While Fichter (1997) shows a drop below 30 percent by 1994, his figures include only DGB unions. When other unions are included (DAG, DBB, etc.), total density remains well above 30 percent through 1995.

35. On the expectations of modern workers and the corresponding need for new union and works council approaches, see, for example, Trautwein-Kalms 1990, Möller 1994, and Rossmann 1994.

36. In other words, what is known as the "competitiveness" debate in the United States is called the "Standort" debate in Germany—and there are, of course, many other relevant factors (taxes, economic and monetary policy, exchange rates, skill levels, etc.) aside from the labor costs emphasized here.

37. "Bericht der Bundesregierung zur Zukunftssicherung des Standortes Deutschland," Bundesanzeiger Verlagsgesellschaft, Bonn, September 1993. See the report and analysis in *European Industrial Relations Review*, February 1994, pp. 13–17.

38. See, for example, Neef, Kask, and Sparks 1993. Such reports touched off a plethora of sometimes gloating articles in the American press: see Rick Atkinson, "German Workers Getting Stiff Shot of Reality," *Washington Post*, February 22, 1994, pp. A1, A12, and Gitlitz 1994.

39. "Bundesrepublik Deutschland: Strukturkrise oder konjunktureller Einbruch," DIW Wochenbericht 26–27, 1993. See report and analysis in *European Industrial Relations Review*, February 1994, p. 14.

40. "World competitiveness report 1993," International Institute for Management Development, Lausanne, Switzerland. See the report and analysis in *European Industrial Relations Review*, February 1994, pp. 15–16.

41. *European Industrial Relations Review*, February 1994, p. 17.

42. See the speech by President Roman Herzog at the BDA annual meeting in December 1996, in which he lambasted employers for daring to abandon the social consensus that had served German industry and society so well (*Der Spiegel*, December 16, 1996, pp. 22–24).

43. *Financial Times* editorial, December 20, 1993, p. 13.

44. Christopher Parkes, "Sales of Mercedes-Benz cars increase by 30%," *Financial Times*, April 27, 1994, p. 15.

45. Phyllis Dininio (1996) identifies, in this regard, a broad shift in eastern Germany from western corporatist policymaking to state and local government-led industrial policy. For more on eastern industrial policy innovations and industrial core preservation, including the active role of social partners, see, for example, Nolte, Sitte, and Wagner 1993 and Nolte 1994.

46. For eastern Germany, see Chapters 3 and 4. In western Germany, for example, I visited several plants in the summer of 1994 (including Keiper Recaro, LDW, and Mercedes in Bremen) where the works council and IG Metall were playing proactive roles in promoting new work organization, including a broad shift to semi-autonomous group work on the shop floor. See also Streeck 1996.

47. See, for example, Coriat 1990, Appelbaum and Batt 1994, Boyer 1995, Levine 1995, and Heckscher 1996.

48. See, for example, Zwickel 1992, for a discussion based on IG Metall's "Tarifreform 2000," a call for innovative bargaining that pushes codetermination down to the shopfloor and office employee, while at the same time expanding works council and union input in management decision making. See Müller-Jentsch and Sperling 1995 on the downward expansion of the dual system toward a "triple system," to include greatly expanded shopfloor participation.

49. Such initiatives use work-sharing as a form of job creation, an approach that some experts see as the best long-term solution to structural unemployment in Europe (e.g., Auer 1997).

50. Edmund L. Andrews, "German Unemployment Soars, Worsening Choices for Kohl," *New York Times*, February 7, 1997, p. D3; Peter Norman, "Germany's jobless crisis deepens," *Financial Times*, February 7, 1997, p. 1.

51. These included, for example, the Christian-Democratic President of Germany, Roman Herzog (*Der Spiegel*, December 16, 1996, pp. 22–24), and economist Wolfgang Klander (*Der Spiegel*, December 30, 1996, pp. 27–29).

52. See, for example, Wolfgang Münchau, "German workplace consensus 'has failed,'" *Financial Times*, April 25, 1996, p. 3, and Klaus Friedrich, "The End of Germany's Economic Model," *New York Times*, June 10, 1996, p. A17.

CHAPTER 6. PERMANENT CRISIS?

1. Wolfgang Münchau, "German workplace consensus 'has failed,'" *Financial Times*, April 25, 1996, p. 3.

2. Klaus Friedrich, "The End of Germany's Economic Model," *New York Times*, June 10, 1996, p. A17.

3. Münchau, "German workplace consensus," p. 3.

4. Warning strikers at a Mercedes plant in early fall of 1996, for example, carried signs that read: "Wir lernen französisch" ("We're learning French"), and "Lieber französische Verhältnisse als amerikanische Zustände" ("Better French relations than American conditions"); *Der Spiegel*, September 30, 1996, p. 122.

5. In this vein, Manfred Schmidt (1992) argues that although unification will bring no end to the German "middle way," the new pressures will generate growing distributional conflict.

6. There is a vast recent literature on European integration. On the acceleration that began with the "relaunch" of the mid-1980s, see, for example, Sandholtz and Zysman 1989, Sbragia 1992, and Treverton 1992.

7. The "watershed" metal industry battles of 1993 in the East and 1994 in the West were told in detail in the Prologue and in Chapter Five. These 1995–97 "post-watershed" battles are sketched out more concisely. For more detail, please see the cited sources.

8. Similar settlements came, for example, in the insurance industry on March 8, one day after the Bavarian settlement, and in the chemical industry on March 9 (*European Industrial Relations Review*, April 1995, pp. 7–8). For news accounts of the 1995 strike and settlement in Bavaria, see, for example, Nathaniel C. Nash, "Biggest German Union Begins Strike," *New York Times*, February 25, 1995, pp. 38–39; *Der Spiegel*, March 6, 1995, pp. 121–22; Beat Gygi, "Ein teurer Tarifabschluß in Bayern," *Neue Zürcher Zeitung*, March 8, 1995, p. 21; Michael Lindemann, "3.8% pay offer set to end IG Metall strike," *Financial Times*, March 8, 1995, p. 1; Andrew Fisher, "Unions hail IG Metall deal," *Financial Times*, March 8, 1995, p. 3; Bloomberg Business News, "Big German Metals Union Settles Strike," *New York Times*, March 8, 1995, p. D4; "Punch-drunk in Bavaria," *The Economist*, March 11, 1995, p. 64; and *Der Spiegel*, March 13, 1995, pp. 105–6.

9. Wolfgang Münchau, "Heads roll over wage deal in Germany," *Financial Times*, November 10, 1995, p. 2.

10. Carl Lankowski (1996) analyzes problems for the German social-market economy associated with progress toward a European social model, yet writes (critically) of the continuing tendency toward "national self-referentiality" (p. 38).

11. Berger's introduction to Berger and Dore 1996; S. Jacoby 1995; Zysman 1996; Boyer 1995 and other essays in Schor and You 1995; Hollingsworth, Schmitter, and Streeck 1994; and Robert Taylor, "Myth and reality of labour in the global economy," *Financial Times*, June 9, 1995, p. I.

12. And this is not a new problem. See Markovits and Allen 1984 on German labor's defense of national institutions in the face of an increasingly international economy.

13. See *Industrial Relations Europe*, November and December 1994 and subsequent issues for the recent history of this EU directive on posted workers.

14. See Heilemann and Reinecke 1995 for an argument that preoccupation with budget deficits in unified Germany has interfered with a more sensible focus on economic growth and competitiveness. Writ large, this view supports the argument that the EMU "straitjacket" was interfering throughout Europe in the mid-to-late 1990s with government efforts to stimulate growth and reduce unemployment.

15. Stefan Immerfall (1996) argues, on the contrary, that Germany's social and industrial order, with its "meso-coordinated market economy," will do quite well, with appropriate adjustments, in the context of emerging European capitalism and economic globalization.

16. The discussion in this section is based largely on interviews conducted in Brussels in 1992–95 by the author and research associates Owen Darbishire and Sally Schoen (for more detail, see Turner 1993, 1996, and 1997a).

17. *European Industrial Relations Review*, September 1993, p. 7. The non-union vote in French works committee elections rose from 18.4 percent in 1982 to 28 percent in 1992.

18. The CGT, for example, has been generally anti-EU, while the CFDT (Confédération Française Démocratique du Travail) and the FO (Force Ouvrière) have been generally pro-EU.

19. See Markovits and Otto 1991 for a discussion of initial German union initiatives toward the single European market, concluding with a prediction of growing engagement and pragmatism in such efforts.

20. If decisions regarding implementation of EU policy can be taken at the lowest possible level, then national unions are left to contend with interpretations of national governments and employers—when a firm or government decides, for example, on a watered-down interpretation of EU social policy.

21. In 1991, for example, Morgan Stanley International reported that average wage costs were $22.49 an hour in western Germany and $15.27 an hour in the United States, compared to $1.38 per hour in Hungary and $1.00 per hour in Poland (Richard W. Stevenson, "East Europe's Low Wages Luring Manufacturers from West Europe," *New York Times*, May 11, 1993).

22. Reported in Quentin Peel, "Survey of Germany," *Financial Times*, October 25, 1993.

23. Ashley Seager, "German Unions, Employers Trade Accusations," *Reuters European Business Report*, November 22, 1994.

24. As reported by the Economics Ministry of the Federal Republic (*The Week in Germany*, November 18, 1994).

25. Economics Ministry Report to the Bundestag, September 30, 1994.

26. See, for example, Frances Williams, "West urged to step up aid to eastern Europe," *Financial Times*, December 6, 1994, and Craig R. Whitney, "East Europe Still Waits for the Capitalist Push," *New York Times*, April 30, 1993.

27. *BBC Summary of World Broadcasts*, January 5, 1995.

28. Net direct investment in Germany declined from -1.59 (U.S. $ billions) in 1983 to -23.05 in 1993. This change, although suggestive, does not necessarily reflect disinvestment in Germany as long as domestic capital accumulation remains adequate. In the same time period, in fact, gross fixed capital formation rose from 343.9 (DM billions) to 566.6, rising as a percentage of GDP from 19 to 23 percent (data sources: IMF, *International Financial Statistics*, February 1995; *OECD Economic Surveys, Germany*, 1994). While German investment rose worldwide, therefore, and especially in central and eastern Europe in the early 1990s, investment at home remained strong and growing.

29. "Ministry: Germany Largest Government Investor in Eastern Europe; Ranks Second in Private Investment," *Week in Germany*, October 7, 1994.

30. David Goodhart, "Can Europe Compete? Convergence in the workforce—Labour unity," *Financial Times*, February 28, 1994.

31. And see Zysman, Doherty, and Schwartz 1996 on the positive contribution of cross-national production networks extending throughout central and eastern Europe to the future strength of the regional European economy.

32. On the significance of social partnership and tripartism, or "transformative corporatism," in eastern and central Europe, see Iankova 1997. See Gray 1994 on the appropriateness of social-market concepts for postcommunist societies.

33. Manfred Muster, IG Metall-Bremen, in a talk at Cornell University, October 7, 1996.

34. *Der Spiegel*, December 9, 1996, pp. 99–102. For other reports of the sick-pay dispute and bargaining round, see, for example, *Der Spiegel*, September 23, 1996, pp. 22–24, and October 7, 1996, pp. 22–26; *Financial Times*, October 3, 1996, p. 13, and October 10, 1996, p. 3; *Industrial Relations Europe*, December 1996, p. 5; Upchurch 1996; and Bispinck 1997.

35. "Divided Still: A Survey of Germany." *The Economist*, November 9, 1996, pp. 1–24 (insert).

CHAPTER 7. INSTITUTIONAL CHANGE IN TURBULENT MARKETS

1. See Kielmansegg 1995 for a perceptive analysis of contemporary tensions, imbalance, and East-West division, which nonetheless predicts that in the end unified Germany will look very much like the old West Germany. Fuerstenberg 1993 reaches a similar conclusion.

2. Based on Rustow's (1970) three stages of democratization, Hancock and Welsh (1994) view the "preparation" and "decision" stages as having occurred for eastern Germany in 1989–90, with successful "habituation" in progress since 1990. For a grassroots perspective on habituation, see Rueschemeyer 1993. See Bauer-Kaase 1994 on the potential crisis of democracy in unified Germany, and Birnbaum 1993 on the danger of a right-wing revival.

3. For elaborations of this argument, see Sally and Webber 1994 and Webber 1994. Webber, for example, on the basis of the 1992–93 "Solidarity Pact" negotiations, suggests a "resurgence of the German model." Martin Upchurch (1995) analyzes declining union membership in the East after the post-unification upsurge, yet emphasizes the essential stability of social partnership in eastern Germany in the mid-1990s. See Sadowski, Backes-Gellner, and Frick 1995 on the post-unification stability of the dual system of industrial relations. Manfred Schmidt (1992) also predicts no end to Germany's "middle way" but does anticipate increasing distributional conflict in the wake of German unification (a prediction that proved accurate in light of escalating battles over labor and social standards in the mid-1990s).

4. Mary Williams Walsh, "Germany's Reckoning," *Los Angeles Times*, February 25, 1996, p. D13.

5. Talk given in a lecture series at the University of California at Berkeley, spring of 1990.

6. For European labor expert Jelle Visser, among others, the key contemporary question for the future of European unions is whether the German model will survive (see Visser 1994).

7. For a perspective that highlights the threat of contemporary economic and political globalization not only for labor rights but for democracy itself, see Tilly 1995. For counterarguments that emphasize the persistence of national regulation as well as the seeds of popular resistance, see Hobsbawm 1995 and Beneria 1995.

8. For analyses of transformation in eastern and central Europe that examine the shortcomings of the market mechanism alone and the need for increased negotiation and state coordination, see Amsden, Kochanowicz, and Taylor 1994; Crawford 1995; and Iankova 1997.

9. See, for example, Katzenstein 1985 and Wilensky and Turner 1987.

10. Thelen (1993, 47) explains contrasting outcomes in Sweden and Germany by showing that what matters "is not the strength of labor and capital at the national level per se but the resiliency of the institutional arrangements that link central bargaining to local negotiations and representation." See also Lange, Wallerstein, and Golden 1995 on the relative stability of wage bargaining in Germany and Locke and Thelen 1995 on fundamental differences between Sweden and Germany—especially the greater egalitarian emphasis of the Swedish labor movement—that help account for contemporary changes in each country.

11. Conservative American commentators emphasize rigidities in the "ailing German economy" (Stelzer 1994; Gitlitz 1994), but economic analyses from unified Germany in the mid-1990s looked more promising. For example: "The Munich-based Ifo economic research institute has challenged the widespread view that German wages and business taxes are too high and driving investment abroad. In a study commissioned by the Bonn economics ministry, Ifo said a 'positive picture' emerges of Germany as an investment location after taking account of real unit labour costs and generous depreciation allowances" (*Financial Times*, July 15, 1996, p. 2).

12. As Manfred Weiss (1991) correctly argues, transfer of the legal system would have been meaningless without a broader transfer of accompanying institutions.

13. The alternative scenarios, of course, do exist in eastern Germany today. The former, what Germans refer to as *Verbetrieblichung*, is especially common in the eastern economy as firms struggle for survival (Kädtler and Kottwitz 1994; Baethge and Wolf 1995; Ettl and Heikenroth 1996). What is most telling, however, is that the diversity, adaptations, and even aberrations of this turbulent period of transformation have nonetheless left social partnership and the dual system of industrial relations, with significant union influence, largely intact.

14. This is not to deny the problematic nature of institutional transfer in unified Germany, given both the uncertainty bred by policies such as property restitution and the inadequate nature of western institutions for the mammoth tasks of restructuring in the East (Wiesenthal, Ettl, and Bialas 1992). Lehmbruch 1994 also highlights the necessity for adaptation and change for the institutions transferred from West to East.

15. See Ettl and Heikenroth 1996 for a useful discussion of the problems and internal conflicts of employer associations in eastern Germany in the mid-1990s. See also Bispinck 1995, 163.

16. Richard Hyman (1996) argues, in fact, that in their ability to mobilize protest, unions in eastern Germany have served as guarantors of the social order.

17. Carola Frege (1996) presents persuasive evidence for the claim, contrary to views expressed by Armingeon (1991), Fichter (1991), and Mahnkopf (1991), that eastern workers in the 1990s are not so different from western workers, in their union and work group identities and in their willingness to engage in collective action.

18. Categories of alternative explanation are adapted in part from the lucid discussion in Dobbin 1994.

19. Although wage levels may have played a role in eastern economic collapse and later sluggish growth, currency union clearly played a primary role, as did the uncertainties of property restitution policy. Note that the eastern economy grew strongly in 1994 and 1995, even as wages were rising toward western levels (Kittner 1995, 203–5).

20. See, for example, Katzenstein 1978, 1985; Zysman 1983; Wilensky 1983; Hall 1986; Streeck 1987, 1992; March and Olsen 1989; Soskice 1990; Hart 1992; and Steinmo, Thelen, and Longstreth 1992.

21. This parallels the argument made by Peter Gourevitch (1986), who links economic crisis to changing political institutions, coalitions, and policies.

22. Based on the failure of institutional reform in France in the 1980s, Jacques Rojot argues that institutional change will only be successful if it fits with the interests and goals of a majority of the actors (letter to the author, 1994).

23. In a formulation similar to the one offered here, Thelen and Steinmo (1992, 16–17) offer three hypotheses regarding sources of institutional change (for a useful discussion, see Koelbe 1995). All are clearly in operation in the transformation of industrial relations in eastern German political economy. First, institutional change results from changes in the broader economic, social, and policy context: here the forces at work include currency and economic union and the rapid coming of a new market economy to eastern Germany (fitting into the category called here "dynamic markets"). Second, institutions change when new actors make use of existing institutions: as, for example, when eastern workers responded militantly to IG Metall's strike appeal in 1993. Third, institutions change when established actors pursue new goals through existing institutions: when, for example, western unions and employer associations use existing institutions to spread established practices of industrial relations into new territory (eastern Germany), forcing reform upon these same institutions in order to make adaptation possible.

24. If, therefore, the formulation "politics against markets" accurately describes Scandinavian social democracy (Esping-Andersen 1985), then perhaps markets have won. A better formulation for social-democratic success in contemporary world markets might therefore be "politics *and* markets," or "the politics of market regulation."

25. See Pontusson 1992 for an argument, based on the Swedish case, that social democracy cannot go much beyond the interests of capital in a capitalist world economy. See Taylor 1993 on unions and the programmatic renewal (or modernization) of social democracy.

26. This does not mean, of course, that German institutions can be transferred beyond unified Germany (Weiss 1991). Important lessons can be used, however, in cross-national processes of "adaptive learning" (Westney 1987). See Wever 1995 for a persuasive presentation of the possibilities for mutual learning between Germany and the United States.

27. And this offensive predates unification (Windolf 1989), although unification has greatly enhanced its scale.

28. Charles Heckscher (1996) argues by contrast that American institutions of industrial relations are *not* compatible with what he calls the new market-driven "managerialism," requiring greatly expanded employee initiative and participation everywhere. Thus he calls for a "new unionism."

29. Jeffrey Hart (1992), for example, in a useful analysis of the German model in comparative perspective, refers to German state-societal relations as characterized by "strong business, strong labor, and weak government."

30. Even the transfer of a superstructure was possible only through the engagement of real people: eastern workers and managers who acquired positions in the new institutions, as well as western elites who came East.

31. In addition, it is difficult to imagine employer willingness to sign the pivotal Saltsjöbaden agreement of 1938, effectively legitimizing centralized bargaining as a key element of Swedish social democracy for the next fifty years, had not the labor-supported Social Democratic party (SAP) already been elected and reelected as the dominant governing coalition party (Korpi 1980).

32. And there are now important indications, given new leadership and activism in the U.S. labor movement, that this situation is beginning to change.

33. This is precisely what early postwar skeptics of codetermination (Neumann 1951; Kerr 1954) failed to see, in mistakenly predicting either that codetermination would weaken German unions (Neumann) or that this inappropriate system would evolve toward the U.S. model (Kerr).

34. Horst Kern (1994) takes the argument even further to suggest that given conservative German managers, it is up to the unions in unified Germany to push proactively for the modernization of industry and production organization.

35. For calls to internal reform that urge German unions, on the basis of extensive contemporary evidence, to press forward within the dual system in more inclusive, participatory, international, and environmentally compatible directions, see Armingeon 1989, Altmann and Düll 1990, Kern and Sabel 1990, Altvater and Mahnkopf 1993, J. Hoffmann et al. 1993, Markovits and Gorski 1993, R. Hoffmann et al. 1995, Wever 1995, and Fichter et al. 1996.

References

Adams, Roy J. 1991. *Comparative Industrial Relations: Contemporary Research and Theory.* London: HarperCollins.

———. 1995. *Industrial Relations under Liberal Democracy: North America in Comparative Perspective.* Columbia: University of South Carolina Press.

Adams, Roy J., and C. H. Rummel. 1977. "Workers' Participation in Management in West Germany." *Industrial Relations Journal* 8 (Spring): 4–22.

Albert, Michel. 1993. *Capitalism vs. Capitalism.* New York: Four Walls Eight Windows.

Altmann, Norbert, and Klaus Düll. 1990. "Rationalization and Participation: Implementation of New Technologies and Problems of the Works Councils in the FRG." *Economic and Industrial Democracy* 11 (February): 111–28.

Altvater, Elmar, and Birgit Mahnkopf. 1993. *Gewerkschaften vor der europäischen Herausforderung: Tarifpolitik nach Mauer and Maastricht.* Münster: Westfälisches Dampfboot.

Amsden, Alice H., Jacek Kochanowicz, and Lance Taylor. 1994. *The Market Meets Its Match: Restructuring the Economies of Eastern Europe.* Cambridge: Harvard University Press.

Appelbaum, Eileen, and Rosemary Batt. 1994. *The New American Workplace: Transforming Work Systems in the United States.* Ithaca, N.Y.: ILR Press.

Armingeon, Klaus. 1989. "Trade Unions under Changing Conditions: The West German Experience, 1950–1985." *European Sociological Review* 5 (May): 1–23.

———. 1991. "Ende einer Erfolgsstory? Gewerkschaften und Arbeitsbeziehungen im Einingungsprozeß." *Gegenwartskunde* 1:29–42.

Auer, Peter. 1997. "German Industrial Relations: Institutional Stability Pays." In Turner 1997b.

Auer, Peter, Boris Penth, and Peter Tergeist, eds. 1983. *Arbeitspolitische Reformen in Industriestaaten: Ein internationaler Vergleich.* Frankfurt: Campus Verlag.

Baethge, Martin, and Harald Wolf. 1995. "Continuity and Change in the 'German Model' of Industrial Relations." In Locke, Kochan, and Piore, 231–62.

Baglioni, Guido, and Colin Crouch, eds. 1990. *European Industrial Relations: The Challenge of Flexibility.* London: Sage.

Bamber, Greg J., and Russell D. Lansbury, eds. 1993. *International and Comparative Industrial Relations: A Study of Industrialised Market Economies.* 2d ed. London: Routledge.

Barnouin, Barbara. 1986. *The European Labour Movement and European Integration.* London: Frances Pinter.

Bauer–Kaase, Petra. 1994. "Germany in Transition: The Challenge of Coping with Unification." In Hancock and Welsh, 285–312.

Baun, Michael. 1990. "Europe 1992 and Trade Union Politics: Towards a European Industrial Relations System?" Paper presented at the Seventh Conference of Europeanists, Washington, D.C., March 23–25.

Baylis, Thomas A. 1993. "Transforming the East German Economy: Shock without Therapy." In Huelshoff, Markovits, and Reich, 77–92.

Bean, Ron. 1994. *Comparative Industrial Relations: An Introduction to Cross–National Perspectives.* London: Routledge.

Behrens, Martin. 1995. *Die Gewerkschaften in den neuen Bundesländern am Beispiel der IG Metall: Tarif–und Industriepolitik.* Düsseldorf: Hans–Böckler–Stiftung.

Belanger, Jacques, P. K. Edwards, and Larry Haiven, eds. 1994. *Workplace Industrial Relations and the Global Challenge.* Ithaca, N.Y.: ILR Press.

Beneria, Lourdes. 1995. "Response: The Dynamics of Globalization." *International Labor and Working–Class History* 47 (Spring): 45–52.

Berg, Peter. 1994. "The German Training System." In Richard Layard, Ken Mayhew, and Geoffrey Owen, eds., *Britain's Training Deficit,* 282–313. Newcastle: Avebury.

Berger, Suzanne, ed. 1981. *Organizing Interests in Western Europe.* Cambridge: Cambridge University Press.

Berger, Suzanne, and Ronald Dore, eds. 1996. *National Diversity and Global Capitalism.* Ithaca, N.Y.: Cornell University Press.

Berghahn, Volker R., and Detlev Karsten. 1987. *Industrial Relations in West Germany.* Oxford: Berg.

Beynon, Huw. 1984. *Working for Ford.* Harmondsworth, U.K.: Penguin Books.

Birnbaum, Norman. 1993. "German Paradoxes: What Rough Beast Is Reborn?" *The Nation,* April 5, 441–44.

Bispinck, Reinhard. 1991. "Auf dem Weg zur Tarifunion." *WSI Mitteilungen* 44:87–98.

———. 1993a. "Collective Bargaining in East Germany: Between Economic Constraints and Political Regulations." *Cambridge Journal of Economics* 17:309–31.

———. 1993b. "Der Tarifkonflikt um den Stufenplan in der ostdeutschen Metallindustrie." *WSI Mitteilungen* 46:469–81.

———. 1995. "Collective Bargaining Policy in a Transition Economy: Taking Stock after Five Years of Collective Bargaining in the New German Länder." In R. Hoffmann et al., 62–77.

———. 1997. "Vom 'Bündnis für Arbeit' zum Streit um die Entgeltfortzahlung." *WSI-Mitteilungen* 50: 69–89.

Blackbourn, David, and Geoff Eley. 1984. *The Peculiarities of German History.* Oxford: Oxford University Press.

Blank, Michael. 1989. "Gegenmacht im Binnenmarkt organisieren: Perspektiven gewerkschaftlicher Betriebs– und Konzernpolitik." In Franz Steinkühler, ed., *Europa '92: Industriestandort oder sozialer Lebensraum,* 230–39. Hamburg: VSA-Verlag.

Blum, Ulrich, and Jan Siegmund. 1993. "Politics and Economics of Privatizing State Enterprises: The Case of Treuhandanstalt." *Governance* 6 (July): 397–408.

Borrus, Michael, and John Zysman. 1992. "Industrial Strength and Regional Response: Japan's Impact on European Integration." In Treverton, 172–93.

Bosch, Gerhard. 1993. "Collective Bargaining in the Unified Germany." Paper presented at the Industrial Relations Research Association annual meeting, Anaheim, California, January 3–5.

Bosch, Gerhard, and Matthias Knuth. 1992. "Der Arbeitsmarkt in Ostdeutschland: Längerfristige Übergangsregeln bleiben notwendig." *Soziale Sicherheit* 41 (5): 136–46.

Boyer, Robert. 1990. "Capital Labor Relations in OECD Countries: From the Fordist 'Golden Age' to Contrasted National Trajectories." Working Paper N–9020, CEPREMAP, CNRS, Paris.

———. 1995. "Capital–Labour Relations in OECD Countries: From the Fordist Golden Age to Contrasted National Trajectories." In Schor and You, 18–69.

———, ed. 1988. *The Search for Labour Market Flexibility: The European Economies in Transition.* Oxford: Clarendon Press.

Büchtemann, Christoph F., and Jürgen Schupp. 1992. "Repercussions of Unification: Transforming East Germany." *Industrial Relations Journal* 23 (Summer): 90–106.

Burawoy, Michael. 1979. *Manufacturing Consent: Changes in the Labor Process under Monopoly Capitalism.* Chicago: University of Chicago Press.

————. 1985. *The Politics of Production: Factory Regimes under Capitalism and Socialism*. London: Verso, New Left Books.

Calleo, David. 1978. *The German Problem Reconsidered: Germany and the World Order, 1870 to the Present*. Cambridge: Cambridge University Press.

Carlin, Wendy, and David Soskice. 1997. "Shocks to the System: The German Political Economy under Stress." *National Institute Economic Review* 159 (January 1997): 57–76.

Cheney, Alan B. 1991. "Employee Involvement and Self-Management: Models for Changes in the East." Paper presented at the conference "From Socialism to Capitalism: The Role of Human Resource Management in Large Systems Change." Gummersbach, Germany, June 14–17.

Cohen, Stephen S., and John Zysman. 1987. *Manufacturing Matters: The Myth of the Post–Industrial Economy*. New York: Basic Books.

Commission on the Future of Worker-Management Relations. 1994. Report and Recommendations. United States Department of Labor, Washington, D.C.

Commons, John R. 1934. *Institutional Economics: Its Place in Political Economy*. New York: Macmillan.

Cook, Alice H. 1991. "Women and Trade Unions in East and West Germany." Paper presented at the annual meeting of the American Political Science Association, Washington, D.C., August 29–September 1.

Coriat, Benjamin. 1990. *L'Atelier et le Robot*. Mesnil–sur–l'Estrée: Christian Bourgeois.

Crawford, Beverly, ed. 1995. *Markets, States, and Democracy: The Political Economy of Post–Communist Transformation*. Boulder, Colo.: Westview Press.

Crouch, Colin. 1993. *Industrial Relations and European State Traditions*. Oxford: Clarendon Press.

Crouch, Colin, and Alessandro Pizzorno, eds. 1978. *The Resurgence of Class Conflict in Western Europe since 1969*. Vols. 1 and 2. New York: Macmillan.

Cusumano, Michael A. 1985. *The Japanese Automobile Industry: Technology and Management at Nissan and Toyota*. Cambridge: Council on East Asian Studies, Harvard University.

Cutler, Tony, Colin Haslam, John Williams, and Karel Williams. 1989. *1992—The Struggle for Europe: A Critical Evaluation of the European Community*. New York: Berg.

Dahrendorf, Ralf. 1967. *Society and Democracy in Germany*. New York: W. W. Norton.

Darbishire, Owen. 1995. "Switching Systems: Technological Change, Competition, and Privatisation." *Industrielle Beziehungen* 2 (2): 156–79.

Däubler, Wolfgang, and Wolfgang Lecher. 1991. *Die Gewerkschaften in den 12 EG–Ländern: Europäische Integration und Gewerkschaftsbewegung*. Cologne: Bund–Verlag.

Deutschmann, Christoph. 1995. "Germany after the Unification: Industrial Restructuring and Labor Relations." In R. Hoffmann et al., 96–106.

Dininio, Phyllis. 1996. "New Patterns of Policy Innovation in Eastern Germany." *German Studies Review* 19 (February): 113–25.

Dobbin, Frank. 1994. *Forging Industrial Policy: The United States, Britain, and France in the Railway Age*. New York: Cambridge University Press.

Donges, Jürgen B. 1991. "Deregulating the German Economy." Occasional Paper, International Center for Economic Growth, San Francisco, Calif.

Dore, Ronald. 1996. "Convergence in Whose Interest?" In Berger and Dore, 366–74.

Dornbusch, Rüdiger, and Holger Wolf. 1992. "Economic Transition in Eastern Germany." *Brookings Papers on Economic Activity* 1:235–72.

Dorr, Gerlinda, and Stefan Schmidt. 1992. "Ostdeutscher Maschinenbau: Produktionsintelligenz—ein unterschätzer Faktor." *WZB-Mitteilungen* 58 (December), Wissenschaftszentrum Berlin, 7–9.

Edwards, Vincent, and Peter Lawrence. 1996. "Transition in East Germany: A British View." *Journal for East European Management Studies* 1 (1): 28–42.

Erickson, Christopher L., and Sarosh Kuruvilla. 1995. "Labor Cost Incentives for Capital Mobility in the European Community." In S. Jacoby, 35–53.

Ermischer, Irina, and Evelyn Preusche. 1995. "East German Works Councils: Between Cooperation and Conflict." In R. Hoffmann et al., 53–61.

Esping–Andersen, Gösta. 1985. *Politics against Markets*. Princeton, N.J.: Princeton University Press.

Ettl, Wilfried, and André Heikenroth. 1996. "Strukturwandel, Verbandsabstinenz, Tarifflucht: Zur Lage der Unternehmen und Arbeitgeberverbände im ostdeutschen verarbeitenden Gewerbe." *Industrielle Beziehungen* 3 (2): 134–53.

Ettl, Wilfried, and Helmut Wiesenthal. 1994. "Tarifautonomie in deindustrialisiertem Gelände: Report und Analyse eines Institutionentransfers im Prozeß der deutschen Einheit." Working Paper AG TRAP, Max–Planck–Gesellschaft, Arbeitsgruppe Transformationsprozesse in den neuen Bundesländern an der Humboldt–Universität zu Berlin, February.

European Commission, Directorate-General V/B/1. 1992–95. *Employment Observatory: East Germany*, nos. 1–16.

Evans, Peter B., Dietrich Rueschemeyer, and Theda Skocpol, eds. 1985. *Bringing the State Back In*. Cambridge: Cambridge University Press.

Ferner, Anthony, and Richard Hyman, eds. 1992. *Industrial Relations in the New Europe*. Oxford: Blackwell.

Fichter, Michael. 1991. "From Transmission Belt to Social Partnership? The Case of Organized Labor in Eastern Germany." *German Politics and Society* 23 (Summer): 21–39.

———. 1993. "A House Divided: A View of German Unification as It Has Affected Organised Labour." *German Politics* 2 (April): 21–39.

———. 1997. "Trade Union Members: A Vanishing Species in Post–Unification Germany?" *German Studies Review* 20 (1): 83–104.

Fichter, Michael, Michaela Hammerbacher, Hauke Laue, Holger Lengfeld, and Bodo Zeuner. 1996. "Programm der Beliebigkeit." *Gewerkschaftliche Monatshefte* 96 (4): 254–64.

Flaherty, Sean. 1983. "Contract Status and the Economic Determinants of Strike Activity." *Industrial Relations* 22 (Winter): 20–33.

Flanagan, Robert J., David W. Soskice, and Lloyd Ulman. 1983. *Unionism, Economic Stabilization, and Incomes Policies: European Experience*. Washington, D.C.: The Brookings Institution.

Frege, Carola M. 1996. "Union Membership in Post-Socialist Eastern Germany: Who Participates in Collective Activities?" *British Journal of Industrial Relations* 34 (3): 387–414.

———. 1997. "Workplace Relations in Eastern Germany after 1989: A Critical Review of the Debate." *German Politics and Society* 15 (Spring): 65–93.

Fuchs, Martina, Hans–Jürgen Uhl, and Werner Widuckel–Mathias. 1991. "Europäischer VW–Konzernbetriebsrat." *Gewerkschaftliche Monatshefte* 47 (November): 729–32.

Fuerstenberg, Friedrich. 1993. "Industrial Relations in Germany." In Bamber and Lansbury, 175–96.

Fukuyama, Francis. 1989. "The End of History?" *The National Interest* 16 (Summer): 3–18.

Fuller, Linda, and Annette Bridges. 1992. "Working-Class Politics during the 1989–1990 Revolution." Manuscript, University of Oregon, Eugene.

Giersch, Herbert, Karl–Heinz Paqué, and Holger Schmieding. 1992. *The Fading Miracle: Four Decades of Market Economy in Germany*. Cambridge: Cambridge University Press.

Gitlitz, David. 1994. "The Reich Reich: The Clinton Crew Has Embraced the German Model—Just as the Germans Have Realized It Doesn't Work." *National Review*, July 11, 44–50.

Golden, Miriam. 1993. "The Dynamics of Trade Unionism and National Economic Performance." *American Political Science Review* 87 (June): 439–54.

Goodhart, David. 1994. *The Reshaping of the German Social Market*. London: Institute for Public Policy Research.

Gorges, Michael J. 1992. "Interest Intermediation in the EC after Maastricht." Paper prepared for the conference "The Political Economy of the New Europe," Cornell University, Ithaca, N.Y., November 13–14.

Gourevitch, Peter. 1986. *Politics in Hard Times: Comparative Responses to International Economic Crises.* Ithaca, N.Y.: Cornell University Press.

Gowa, Joanne. 1989. "Bipolarity and the Postwar International Economic Order." In Katzenstein, 33–50.

Grabher, Gernot. 1992. "Eastern Conquista: The 'Truncated Industrialization' of East European Regions by Large West European Corporations." In H. Ernste and V. Meier, eds., *Regional Development and Contemporary Response*, 219–32. London: Bellhaven.

Gray, John. 1994. *Post–Communist Societies in Transition: A Social Market Perspective.* London: Social Market Foundation.

Hall, Peter A. 1986. *Governing the Economy: The Politics of State Intervention in Britain and France.* New York: Oxford University Press.

———. 1992. "The Movement from Keynesianism to Monetarism: Institutional Analysis and British Economic Policy in the 1970s." In Steinmo, Thelen, and Longstreth, 90–113.

Hancock, M. Donald, and Helga A. Welsh, eds. 1994. *German Unification: Process and Outcomes.* Boulder, Colo.: Westview Press.

Hanhardt, Arthur M., Jr. 1993. "The Collapse of the German Democratic Republic and Its Unification with the Federal Republic of Germany, 1989–90." In Huelshoff, Markovits, and Reich, 207–34.

Hans–Böckler Stiftung/IG Metall, eds. 1992. *Lean Production.* Baden–Baden: Nomos.

Hart, Jeffrey A. 1992. *Rival Capitalists: International Competitiveness in the United States, Japan, and Western Europe.* Ithaca, N.Y.: Cornell University Press.

Heckscher, Charles C. 1996. *The New Unionism.* Ithaca, N.Y.: ILR Press.

Heering, Wolfgang, and K. Schröder. 1995. "Vom Arbeitskolletiv zur Sozialpartnerschaft." In Schmidt and Lutz, 159–80.

Hegewisch, Ariane, Chris Brewster, and Josef Koubek. 1996. "Different Roads: Changes in Industrial and Employee Relations in the Czech Republic and East Germany Since 1989." *Industrial Relations Journal* 27 (March): 50–64.

Heilemann, Ulrich, and Reimut Jochimsen. 1994. *Christmas in July? The Political Economy of German Unification Reconsidered.* Brookings Occasional Papers. Washington, D.C.: The Brookings Institution.

Heilemann, Ulrich, and Wolfgang H. Reinicke. 1995. *Welcome to Hard Times: The Fiscal Consequences of German Unity.* Washington, D.C.: Brookings and American Institute for Contemporary German Studies.

Heinelt, Hubert, and Gerhard Bosch, eds. 1994. *Arbeitsmarktpolitik nach der Vereinigung.* Berlin: Edition Sigma.

Henzler, Herbert. 1992. "Managing the Merger: A Strategy for the New Germany." *Harvard Business Review*, January–February, 24–29 (Reprint 92103).

Herr, Hansjörg. 1992. "The New Federal States after the Shock of Unification." *Employment Observatory: East Germany* (European Commission DGV) 1:3–4.

Herrigel, Gary B. 1989. "Industrial Order and the Politics of Industrial Change: Mechanical Engineering." In Katzenstein, 185–220.

———. 1997. "Crisis in German Decentralized Production." In Turner 1997b.

Hickel, Rudolf, and Jan Priewe. 1994. *Nach dem Fehlstart—ökonomische Perspektiven des vereinten Deutschlands.* Frankfurt: S. Fischer Verlag.

Hinz, Andreas. 1996. "Arbeitswelt im Umbruch—Über den Orientierungswandel von Facharbeitern im ostdeutschen Werkzeugmaschinenbau." Ph.D. diss., Universität Göttingen.

Hirschman, Albert O. 1993. "Exit, Voice, and the Fate of the German Democratic Republic: An Essay in Conceptual History." *World Politics* 45 (January): 173–202.

Hitchens, D. M. W. N., K. Wagner, and J. E. Birnie. 1993. *East German Productivity and the Transition to the Market Economy.* Aldershot: Avebury.

References

Hobsbawm, E. J. 1995. "Guessing about Global Change." *International Labor and Working–Class History* 47 (Spring): 39–44.

Hoffmann, Jürgen. 1988. "Gewerkschaften in der Bundesrepublik: Zersetzungsprodukt oder strukturierender Faktor gesellschaftlicher Veränderungen?" In Walther Müller-Jentsch, ed., *Zukunft der Gewerkschaften: Ein internationaler Vergleich*, 18–44. Frankfurt/Main: Campus Verlag.

———. 1995. "The Reform of the Trade Unions in Germany—Some Critical Remarks concerning the Current Debate." *Transfer: European Review of Labour and Research* 1 (January): 98–113.

Hoffmann, Jürgen, Reiner Hoffmann, Ulrich Mückenberger, and Dietrich Lange, eds. 1993. *Jenseits der Beschlußlage: Gewerkschaft als Zukunftswerkstatt.* 2d ed., expanded. Cologne: Bund–Verlag.

Hoffmann, Reiner, Otto Jacobi, Berndt Keller, and Manfred Weiss, eds. 1995. *German Industrial Relations under the Impact of Structural Change, Unification, and European Integration.* Düsseldorf: Hans–Böckler Stiftung.

Hohn, Hans–Willy. 1988. *Von der Einheitsgewerkschaft zum Betriebssyndikalismus: Soziale Schließung im dualen System der Interessenvertretung.* Berlin: Edition Sigma.

Hollingsworth, J. Rogers, Philippe C. Schmitter, and Wolfgang Streeck. 1994. *Governing Capitalist Economies: Performance and Control of Economic Sectors.* New York: Oxford University Press.

Huber, Bertold. 1991. "Work and the Unions." *German Politics and Society* 23 (Summer): 40–46.

Huelshoff, Michael G., and Arthur M. Hanhardt, Jr. 1994. "Steps Toward Union: The Collapse of the GDR and the Unification of Germany." In Hancock and Welsh, 73–92.

Huelshoff, Michael G., Andrei S. Markovits, and Simon Reich, eds. 1993. *From Bundesrepublik to Deutschland: German Politics after Unification.* Ann Arbor: University of Michigan Press.

Hyman, Richard. 1995. "Industrial Relations in Europe: Theory and Practice." *European Journal of Industrial Relations* 1 (March): 17–46.

———. 1996. "Institutional Transfer: Industrial Relations in Eastern Germany." *Work, Employment, and Society* 10 (4): 601–39.

Iankova, Elena Atanassova. 1997. "Social Partnership after the Cold War: The Transformative Corporatism of Post–Communist Europe." Ph.D. diss., School of Industrial and Labor Relations, Cornell University.

Immerfall, Stefan. 1996. "Germany's Social and Industrial Order: Will It Weather European Integration and Economic Globalization?" Working Paper 7.14, Center for German and European Studies, University of California at Berkeley.

Industrial Democracy in Europe (IDE) International Research Group. 1981. *European Industrial Relations.* Oxford: Clarendon Press.

———. 1993. *Industrial Democracy in Europe Revisited.* Oxford: Oxford University Press.

Jacobi, Otto, Berndt Keller, and Walther Müller–Jentsch. 1992. "Germany: Codetermining the Future." In Ferner and Hyman, 218–69.

Jacoby, Sanford M., ed. 1995. *The Workers of Nations: Industrial Relations in a Global Economy.* New York: Oxford University Press.

Jacoby, Wade. 1995. "The Politics of Institutional Transfer: Two Post–War Reconstructions in Germany, 1945–1995." Ph.D. diss. in Political Science, MIT.

Johnson, Chalmers. 1982. *MITI and the Japanese Miracle: The Growth of Industrial Policy, 1925–1975.* Stanford, Calif.: Stanford University Press.

Jowitt, Ken. 1992. *New World Disorder: The Leninist Extinction.* Berkeley: University of California Press.

Jürgens, Ulrich. 1994. "From Socialist Work Organization to Lean Production: Continuity and Discontinuity in the Transformation." Draft paper, Wissenschaftszentrum Berlin.

Jürgens, Ulrich, Larissa Klinzing, and Lowell Turner. 1993. "The Transformation of Industrial Relations in Eastern Germany." *Industrial and Labor Relations Review.* 46 (January): 229–44.

Jürgens, Ulrich, Thomas Malsch, and Knuth Dohse. 1989. *Moderne Zeiten in der Automobilfabrik: Strategien der Produktionsmodernisierung im Länder– und Konzernvergleich.* Berlin: Springer–Verlag.

Kädtler, Jürgen, and Gisela Kottwitz. 1990. "Betriebsräte zwischen Wende und Ende in der DDR." *Berliner Arbeitshefte und Berichte zur sozialwissenschaftlichen Forschung* 42 (October), Zentralinstitut für sozialwissenschaftliche Forschung, Freie Universität Berlin.

———. 1994. "Industrielle Beziehungen in Ostdeutschland: Durch Kooperation zum Gegensatz von Kapital und Arbeit?" *Industrielle Beziehungen* 1 (1): 13–38.

Kädtler, Jürgen, Gisela Kottwitz, and Rainer Weinert. 1997. *Betriebsräte in Ostdeutschland.* Opladen: Westdeutscher Verlag.

Katz, Harry C. 1985. *Shifting Gears: Changing Labor Relations in the U.S. Automobile Industry.* Cambridge: MIT Press.

———. 1993. "The Decentralization of Collective Bargaining: A Literature Review and Comparative Analysis." *Industrial and Labor Relations Review* 47 (October): 3–22.

Katz, Harry C., and Thomas A. Kochan. 1992. *An Introduction to Collective Bargaining and Industrial Relations.* New York: McGraw–Hill.

Katz, Harry, and Charles F. Sabel. 1985. "Industrial Relations and Industrial Adjustment in the Car Industry." *Industrial Relations.* 24 (Fall): 295–31.

Katzenstein, Peter J. 1985. *Small States in World Markets: Industrial Policy in Europe.* Ithaca, N.Y.: Cornell University Press.

———. 1987. *Policy and Politics in West Germany: The Growth of a Semisovereign State.* Philadelphia: Temple University Press.

Katzenstein, Peter J., ed. 1978. *Between Power and Plenty: Foreign Economic Policies of Advanced Industrial Societies.* Madison: University of Wisconsin Press.

———, ed. 1989. *Industry and Politics in West Germany: Toward the Third Republic.* Ithaca, N.Y.: Cornell University Press.

Keenoy, Tom. 1995. "Review Article: European Industrial Relations in Global Perspective." *European Journal of Industrial Relations* 1 (March): 145–64.

Kern, Horst. 1991. "Die Transformation der östlichen Industrien: Soziologische Reflexionen über die Ex–DDR." *Die Neue Gesellschaft: Frankfurter Hefte* 38 (2): 114–21.

———. 1994. "Intelligente Regulierung: Gewerkschaftliche Beitrage in Ost und West zur Erneuerung des deutschen Produktionsmodells." *Soziale Welt* 45 (1): 33–59.

Kern, Horst, and Charles F. Sabel. 1990. "Gewerkschaften in offenen Arbeitsmärkten." *Soziale Welt* 41 (2): 144–66.

———. 1991. "Between Pillar and Post: Reflections on the Treuhand's Uncertainty about What to Say Next." Draft paper, MIT.

Kern, Horst, and Michael Schumann. 1984. *Das Ende der Arbeitsteilung?* Munich: C. H. Beck.

Kerr, Clark. 1954. "The Trade Union Movement and the Redistribution of Power in Postwar Germany." *Quarterly Journal of Economics* 68 (November): 535–64.

Kielmansegg, Peter G. 1995. "How New Is the New Federal Republic?" Occasional Paper, Center for German and European Studies, University of California at Berkeley.

Kinzer, Stephen. 1994. "A Climate for Demagogues." *Atlantic Monthly*, February, 21–34.

Kittner, Michael, ed. 1991. *Gewerkschaftsjahrbuch 1991.* Cologne: Bund–Verlag.

———. 1993. *Gewerkschaftsjahrbuch 1993.* Cologne: Bund–Verlag.

———. 1994. *Gewerkschaften Heute: Jahrbuch für Arbeitnehmerfragen, 1994.* Cologne: Bund–Verlag.

———. 1995. *Gewerkschaften Heute: Jahrbuch für Arbeitnehmerfragen, 1995.* Cologne: Bund Verlag.

Knuth, Matthias. 1993. "Employment and Training Companies: Bridging Unemployment in the East German Crash." Manuscript, Institut Arbeit und Technik, Gelsenkirchen.

———. 1996. *Drehscheiben im Strukturwandel.* Berlin: Edition Sigma.

———. 1997. "Active Labor Market Policy in the East: The Role of Employment and Training Companies." In Turner 1997b.

Knuth, Matthias, and Ulrich Pekruhl. 1993. "Der Beitrag von ABS–Gesellschaften zur Bewältigung des Transformationsprozesses." In Wolfgang Pfeiffer, ed., *Regionen unter Anpassungsdruck: Probleme der Einheit*, 95–126. Marburg: Metropolis.

Kochan, Thomas A., Harry C. Katz, and Robert B. McKersie. 1986. *The Transformation of American Industrial Relations.* New York: Basic Books.

Koelbe, Thomas A. 1995. "The New Institutionalism in Political Science and Sociology." *Comparative Politics* 27 (January): 231–43.

König, Klaus. 1993. "Bureaucratic Integration by Elite Transfer: The Case of the Former GDR." *Governance* 6 (July): 386–96.

Kopstein, Jeffrey. 1995. "Chipping Away at the State: Workers' Resistance and the Demise of East Germany." Occasional Paper, Center for German and European Studies, University of California at Berkeley, February.

Korpi, Walter. 1980. "Industrial Relations and Industrial Conflict: The Case of Sweden." In Benjamin Martin and Everett M. Kassalow, eds. *Labor Relations in Advanced Industrial Societies: Issues and Problems.* Washington, D.C.: Carnegie, 89–108.

Kotthoff, Hermann. 1994. *Betriebsräte und Bürgerstatus: Wandel und Kontinuität betrieblicher Mitbestimmung.* Munich: Rainer Hampp Verlag.

Krasner, Stephen D. 1984. "Approaches to the State: Alternative Conceptions and Historical Dynamics." *Comparative Politics* 16 (January): 223–46.

Krause, Axel. 1991. *Inside the New Europe.* New York: HarperCollins.

Kühl, J., R. Schäfer, and J. Wahse. 1991. "Beschäftigungs-perspektiven von Treuhandunternehmen." *MittAB*, March.

Lane, Christel. 1995. *Industry and Society in Europe: Stability and Change in Britain, Germany and France.* Aldershot: Edward Elgar.

Lange, Peter. 1992a. "The Maastricht Social Protocol: Why Did They Do It?" Draft paper, Duke University.

———. 1992b. "The Politics of the Social Dimension." In Sbragia, 225–56.

Lange, Peter, George Ross, and Maurizio Vannicelli, eds. 1982. *Unions, Change, and Crisis: French and Italian Union Strategy and Political Economy, 1945–1980.* London: George Allen & Unwin.

Lange, Peter, Michael Wallerstein, and Miriam Golden. 1995. "The End of Corporatism? Wage Setting in the Nordic and Germanic Countries." In S. Jacoby, 76–100.

Langer, Axel. 1994. "Arbeitgeberverbandsaustritte—Motive, Abläufe and Konsequenzen." *Industrielle Beziehungen* 1 (2): 132–54.

Lankowski, Carl. 1996. "Ein Auslaufendes Modell? The German Social Market Economy in the European Union." Working Paper 7.16, Center for German and European Studies, University of California at Berkeley.

Lecher, Wolfgang. 1997. "Gewerkschaften und Industrielle Beziehungen in Frankreich, Italien, Großbritannien und Deutschland—Rahmenbedingungen für die EBR." Diskussionspapier Nr. 30, WSI/Hans–Böckler–Stiftung, Düsseldorf.

Lehmbruch, Gerhard. 1994. "The Process of Regime Change in East Germany: An Institutionalist Scenario for German Unification." *Journal of European Public Policy* 1 (June): 115–41.

Leibfried, Stephan, and Paul Pierson, eds. 1995. *European Social Policy: Between Fragmentation and Integration.* Washington, D.C.: The Brookings Institution.

Levine, David L. 1995. *Reinventing the Workplace: How Business and Employees Can Both Win.* Washington, D.C.: The Brookings Institution.

Liebert, Ulrike, and Wolfgang Merkel, eds. 1991. *Die Politik zur deutschen Einheit.* Opladen: Leske und Budrich.

Locke, Richard M. 1990. "The Resurgence of the Local Union: Industrial Restructuring and Industrial Relations in Italy." *Politics and Society* 18 (September): 347–79.

———. 1995. *Remaking the Italian Economy.* Ithaca, N.Y.: Cornell University Press.

Locke, Richard, and Wade Jacoby. 1997. "The Dilemmas of Diffusion: Institutional Transfer and the Remaking of Vocational Training Practices in Eastern Germany." In Turner 1997b.

Locke, Richard, Thomas Kochan, and Michael Piore, eds. 1995. *Employment Relations in a Changing World Economy*. Cambridge: MIT Press.

Locke, Richard M., and Kathleen Thelen. 1995. "Apples and Oranges Revisited: Contextualized Comparisons and the Study of Comparative Labor Politics." *Politics and Society* 23 (September): 337–67.

———. 1997. *The Shifting Boundaries of Labor Politics*. Cambridge: MIT Press.

Lodge, Juliet. 1990. "Social Europe." *Journal of European Integration* 13 (2–3): 135–50.

Luebbert, Gregory M. 1991. *Liberalism, Fascism, or Social Democracy: Social Classes and the Political Origins of Regimes in Interwar Europe*. New York: Oxford University Press.

Lungwitz, Ralph, and Evelyn Preusche. 1994. "Mängelwesen und Diktator?—Ostdeutsche Industriemanager als Akteure betrieblicher Transformationsprozesse." *Industrielle Beziehungen* 1 (3): 219–38.

Mahnkopf, Birgit. 1991. "Vorwärts in die Vergangenheit? Pessimistische Spekulationen über die Zukunft der Gewerkschaften in der neuen Bundesrepublik." In Westphal et al., 269–94.

———. 1993. "The Impact of Unification on the German System of Industrial Relations." Discussion Paper FS I 93–102, Wissenschaftszentrum Berlin für Sozialforschung.

Mahnkopf, Birgit, and Elmar Altvater. 1995. "Transmission Belts of Transnational Competition? Trade Unions and Collective Bargaining in the Context of European Integration." *European Journal of Industrial Relations* 1 (March): 101–19.

Maier, Friederike. 1993. "The Labour Market for Women and Employment Perspectives in the Aftermath of German Unification." *Cambridge Journal of Economics* 17:267–80.

March, James, and Johan Olsen. 1989. *Rediscovering Institutions*. New York: Free Press.

Markovits, Andrei S. 1986. *The Politics of the West German Trade Unions*. Cambridge: Cambridge University Press.

Markovits, Andrei S., and Christopher S. Allen. 1984. "Trade Unions and the Economic Crisis: The West German Case." In Peter Gourevitch, Andrew Martin, George Ross, Chris Allen, Stephen Bornstein, and Andrei Markovits, *Unions and Economic Crisis: Britain, West Germany, and Sweden*, 89–188. London: Allen & Unwin.

Markovits, Andrei S., and Philip S. Gorski. 1993. *The German Left: Red, Green, and Beyond*. Cambridge: Polity Press.

Markovits, Andrei S., and Alexander Otto. 1991. "The German Trade Unions and the Challenge of 1992." *Business in the Contemporary World* (Winter): 69–79.

Martin, Andrew, and George Ross. 1992. "Unions and the European Community: A Report to the Project on Labor in European Society." Draft paper, Harvard Center for European Studies.

McFalls, Laurence. 1992. "The Modest Germans: Towards an Understanding of the East Germans' Revolution." *German Politics and Society* 26 (Summer): 1–20.

———. 1995. *Communism's Collapse, Democracy's Demise? The Cultural Context and Consequences of the East German Revolution*. New York: New York University Press.

Mensa–Petermann, Ursula. 1996. "Die Verbetrieblichung der industriellen Beziehungen in Ostdeutschland als Herausforderung für das duale System." *Industrielle Beziehungen* 3 (1): 65–79.

Merkl, Peter H. 1994. "An Impossible Dream? Privatizing Collective Property in Eastern Germany." In Hancock and Welsh, 199–222.

Mickler, Otfried. 1994. "Modernization of East German Industry and the Development of New Structures of Industrial Relations in Enterprises—The Case of the Auto Industry." Working Paper, Institute for Sociology, University of Hannover, October.

Mickler, Otfried, Norbert Engelhard, Ralph Lungwitz, and Bettina Walker. 1996. *Nach der Trabi–Ära: Arbeiten im schlanken Fabriken*. Berlin: Edition Sigma.

Milkman, Ruth. 1991. "Labor and Management in Uncertain Times: Renegotiating the Social Contract." In Alan Wolfe, ed., *America at Century's End*. Berkeley: University of California Press, 131–51.

References

Mitchell, J. Clyde. 1983. "Case and Situation Analysis." *Sociological Review* 31:187–211.

Möller, Rolf. 1994. "Der ergänzende Haustarifvertrag als Bestandteil künftiger Tarifarbeit." *Die Mitbestimmung* 2:48–49.

Mosley, Hugh G. 1990. "The Social Dimension of European Integration." *International Labour Review* 129 (2): 147–64.

Mosley, Hugh, and Peter Auer. 1989. "Die soziale Dimension des Europäischen Binnenmarktes." *Internationale Chronik zur Arbeitsmarktpolitik* 37 (July): 3–6.

Müller–Jentsch, Walther, and Hans Joachim Sperling. 1995. "Towards a Flexible Triple System? Continuity and Structural Changes in German Industrial Relations." In R. Hoffmann et al., 9–29.

Muster, Manfred, and Manfred Wannöffel. 1989. *Gruppenarbeit in der Automobilindustrie*. Bochum: Joint publication of the IG Metall Verwaltungsstelle Bochum and the Gemeinsame Arbeitsstelle Ruhr–Universität Bochum.

Neef, Arthur, Christopher Kask, and Christopher Sparks. 1993. "International Comparisons of Manufacturing Unit Labor Costs. *Monthly Labor Review* 116 (12): 47–58.

Neumann, Franz. 1951. "The Labor Movement in Germany." In Hans J. Morgenthau, ed. *Germany and the Future of Europe*. Chicago: University of Chicago Press, 100–107.

Niedenhoff, Horst–Udo. 1990. "Der DGB baute seine Position aus: Die Betriebsratswahl 1990 in den Betrieben der Bundesrepublik Deutschland." *Gewerkschaftsreport* 24 (September): 5–17.

Nolte, Dirk. 1994. "Industriepolitik in Ostdeutschland am Beispiel des Bundeslandes Sachsen." *Aus Politik und Zeitgeschichte* 17:3–13.

Nolte, Dirk, Ralf Sitte, and Alexandra Wagner. 1993. "Strukturpolitik in Thüringen—das Konzept 'Entwicklung Industrieller Zentren.' " *WSI Mitteilungen* 46 (6): 402–5.

Northrup, Herbert R., Duncan C. Campbell, and Betty J. Slowinski. 1988. "Multinational Union–Management Consultation in Europe: Resurgence in the 1980s?" *International Labour Review* 127 (5): 525–41.

Ostry, Sylvia. 1996. "Policy Approaches to System Friction: Convergence Plus." In Berger and Dore, 333–49.

Pereira, Luiz Carlos Bresser, José Maria Maravall, and Adam Przeworski. 1993. *Economic Reforms in New Democracies: A Social–Democratic Approach*. Cambridge: Cambridge University Press.

Piore, Michael J., and Charles F. Sabel. 1984. *The Second Industrial Divide: Possibilities for Prosperity*. New York: Basic Books.

Polanyi, Karl. 1957. *The Great Transformation: The Political and Economic Origins of Our Time*. Boston: Beacon Press.

Pontusson, Jonas. 1992. *The Limits of Social Democracy: Investment Politics in Sweden*. Ithaca, N.Y.: Cornell University Press.

———. 1995. "Between Neoliberalism and the German Model: Swedish Capitalism in Transition." Paper presented at a seminar of the International Political Economy Program, Cornell University, Ithaca, N.Y., March 1.

———. 1996. "Labor Market Institutions and Wage Distribution in Sweden and Austria." Working Paper, Institute of European Studies, Cornell University, Ithaca, N.Y.

Pontusson, Jonas, and Peter Swenson. 1992. "Markets, Production, Institutions, and Politics: Why Swedish Employers Have Abandoned the Swedish Model." Paper presented at the Eighth International Conference of Europeanists, Chicago, March 27–29.

Poole, Michael. 1993. "Industrial Relations: Theorizing for a Global Perspective." In Roy J. Adams and Noah M. Meltz, eds., *Industrial Relations Theory: Its Nature, Scope, and Pedagogy*, 103–17. Metuchen, N.J.: IMLR Press/Rutgers University and Scarecrow Press.

Powell, Walter W., and Paul J. DiMaggio, eds. 1991. *The New Institutionalism in Organizational Analysis*. Chicago: University of Chicago Press.

Radice, Giles. 1995. *The New Germans*. London: Michael Joseph.

Röbenack, Silke, and Gabriella Hartung. 1992. "Strukturwandel industrieller Beziehungen in Ostdeutschen Industriebetrieben." Monograph AG 3/3, for the Commission for Research in Social and Political Transformation in the New States, Berlin.

Rossmann, Witich. 1994. "The Transformation of Industrial Relations in the German Computer Industry: IG Metall Battles at DEC and IBM." Paper presented at the conference "The Political Economy of the New Germany," Cornell University, Ithaca, N.Y., October 14–15.

Roth, Siegfried. 1992. "Japanisation, or Going Our Own Way? New Lean Production Concepts in the German Automobile Industry." Frankfurt/Main: IG Metall.

———. 1996. "Lean Production in the German Motor Industry." In European Foundation for the Improvement of Living and Working Conditions, *P+ European Participation Monitor*, 12:25–31.

Rueschemeyer, Marilyn. 1993. "East Germany's New Towns in Transition: A Grassroots View of the Impact of Unification." *Urban Studies* 30 (3): 495–506.

———. 1995. "The Social Democratic Party in Eastern Germany: Political Participation in the Former German Democratic Republic after Unification." Discussion Paper P95–002, Wissenschaftszentrum Berlin für Sozialforschung.

Rustow, Dankwart A. 1970. "Transitions to Democracy: Toward a Dynamic Model." *Comparative Politics* 2 (April): 337–63.

Sabel, Charles F. 1982. *Work and Politics: The Division of Labor in Industry*. Cambridge: Cambridge University Press.

———. 1993. "Can the End of the Social Democratic Trade Unions Be the Beginning of a New Kind of Social Democratic Politics?" In Stephen R. Sleigh, ed., *Economic Restructuring and Emerging Patterns of Industrial Relations*, 137–65. Kalamazoo: W. E. Upjohn Institute.

Sadowski, Dieter, Uschi Backes–Gellner, and Bernd Frick. 1995. "Works Councils: Barriers or Boosts for the Competitiveness of German Firms?" *British Journal of Industrial Relations* 33 (3): 493–513.

Sadowski, Dieter, Martin Schneider, and Karin Wagner. 1994. "The Impact of European Integration and German Unification on Industrial Relations in Germany." *British Journal of Industrial Relations* 32 (4): 523–37.

Sally, Razeen, and Douglas Webber. 1994. "The German Solidarity Pact: A Case Study in the Politics of the Unified Germany." *German Politics* 3 (April): 18–46.

Sandholtz, Wayne, and John Zysman. 1989. "1992: Recasting the European Bargain." *World Politics* 42 (October): 95–128.

Sbragia, Alberta M., ed. 1992. *Euro–Politics: Institutions and Policymaking in the "New" European Community*. Washington, D.C.: The Brookings Institution.

Schettkat, Ronald, and Michael Wagner, eds. 1990. *Technological Change and Employment: Innovation in the German Economy*. Berlin: Walter De Gruyter.

Schmid, Günther, ed. 1994. *Labor Market Institutions in Europe*. Armonk, N.Y.: M. E. Sharpe.

Schmidt, Manfred. 1992. "Political Consequences of German Unification." *West European Politics* 15 (October): 1–15.

Schmidt, R., and B. Lutz, eds. 1995. *Chancen und Risiken der industriellen Restrukturierung in Ostdeutschland*. Berlin: Akademie.

Schmidt, Vivien. 1996. "Review Article: Industrial Policy and Policies of Industry in Advanced Industrialized Nations." *Comparative Politics* 28 (January): 225–48.

Schmitter, Philippe, and Gerhard Lehmbruch, eds. 1979. *Trends in Corporatist Intermediation*. Beverly Hills, Calif.: Sage.

Schnabel, Claus, and Joachim Wagner. 1996. "Ausmaß und Bestimmungsgründe der Mitgliedschaft in Arbeitgeberverbänden." *Industrielle Beziehungen* 3 (4): 293–306.

Schor, Juliet, and Jong–Il You. 1995. *Capital, the State, and Labour: A Global Perspective*. Aldershot, U.K.: Edward Elgar.

Schroeder, Wolfgang, and Burkard Ruppert. 1996a. "Austritte aus Arbeitgeberverbänden." *WSI Mitteilungen* 5:316–28.

———. 1996b. *Austritte aus Arbeitgeberverbänden: Eine Gefahr für das Deutsche Modell?* Marburg: Schüren Presseverlag.

Schumpeter, Joseph A. 1942. *Capitalism, Socialism and Democracy*. New York: Harper Torchbook.

Seibel, Wolfgang. 1994. "Strategische Fehler oder erfolgreiches Scheitern? Zur Entwicklungslogik der Treuhandanstalt." *Politische Vierteljahresschrift* 35 (March): 3–39.

Selznick, Philip. 1949. *The Tennessee Valley Authority and the Grassroots*. Berkeley: University of California Press.

Shonfield, Andrew. 1969. *Modern Capitalism*. Oxford: Oxford University Press.

Silvia, Stephen J. 1988. "The West German Labor Law Controversy: A Struggle for the Factory of the Future." *Comparative Politics* 20 (2), January, 155–74.

———. 1991. "The Social Charter of the European Community: A Defeat for European Labor." *Industrial and Labor Relations Review* 44 (July): 626–43.

———. 1993. " 'Holding the Shop Together': Old and New Challenges to the German System of Industrial Relations in the mid 1990s." Berliner Arbeitshefte und Berichte zur sozialwissenschaftlichen Forschung, no. 83, Zentralinstitut für sozialwissenschaftliche Forschung, Freie Universität Berlin.

———. 1997. "German Unification and Emerging Divisions within German Employers' Associations." *Comparative Politics* 29 (January): 187–208.

Singer, Otto. 1992. "The Politics and Economics of German Unification: From Currency Union to Economic Dichotomy." *German Politics* 1 (April): 78–94.

Smyser, W. R. 1993. *The German Economy: Colossus at the Crossroads*. Second Edition. New York: St. Martin's Press.

Soskice, David. 1990. "Reinterpreting Corporatism and Explaining Unemployment: Co–ordinated and Non–co–ordinated Market Economies." In Renato Brunetta and Carlo Dell'Aringa, eds., *Labour Relations and Economic Performance*, 170–211. Proceedings of a conference held by the International Economic Association in Venice, Italy. IEA Conference Volume no. 95. Houndsmill, U.K.: Macmillan.

Soskice, David, and Ronald Schettkat. 1993. "West German Labor Market Institutions and East German Transformation." In Ulman, Eichengreen, and Dickens, 102–27.

Springer, Beverly. 1992. *The Social Dimension of 1992: Europe Faces a New EC*. New York: Praeger.

Stark, David. 1992. "Path Dependency and Privatization Strategies in East–Central Europe." *East European Politics and Societies* 6 (1): 17–54.

———. 1996. "Recombinant Property in East European Capitalism." *American Journal of Sociology* 101 (January): 993–1027.

Steiner, Viktor, and Florian Kraus. 1994. "Aufsteiger and Absteiger in der ostdeutschen Einkommensverteilung: 1989–1993." *ZEW Newsletter* 2 (December): 21–25.

Steinmo, Sven, and Kathleen Thelen. 1992. "Historical Institutionalism in Comparative Politics." In Steinmo, Thelen, and Longstreth, 1–32.

Steinmo, Sven, Kathleen Thelen, and Frank Longstreth, eds. 1992. *Structuring Politics: Historical Institutionalism in Comparative Analysis*. Cambridge: Cambridge University Press.

Stelzer, Irwin M. 1994. "Clinton's Dubious Role Model." *New York Post*, May 18, 17.

Story, Jonathan. 1990. "Social Europe: Adriane's Thread." *Journal of European Integration* 13 (Winter–Spring): 151–65.

Strauss, George. 1982. "Workers Participation in Management: An International Perspective." *Research in Organizational Behavior* 4:173–265.

Streeck, Wolfgang. 1984a. "Co–determination: The Fourth Decade." In Bernhard Wilpert and Arndt Sorge, eds., *International Yearbook of Organizational Democracy*, vol. 2, *International Perspectives on Organizational Democracy*, 391–422. New York: John Wiley & Sons.

————. 1984b. "Neo–Corporatist Industrial Relations and the Economic Crisis in West Germany." In John H. Goldthorpe, ed., *Order and Conflict in Contemporary Capitalism*, 291–314. Oxford: Oxford University Press.

————. 1987. "Industrial Relations and Industrial Change: The Restructuring of the World Automobile Industry in the 1970s and 1980s." *Economic and Industrial Democracy* 8 (November): 437–62.

————. 1989. "Successful Adjustment to Turbulent Markets: The Automobile Industry." In Katzenstein, 113–56.

————. 1991. "More Uncertainties: German Unions Facing 1992." *Industrial Relations* 30 (Fall): 317–49.

————. 1992. *Social Institutions and Economic Performance: Studies of Industrial Relations in Advanced Capitalist Economies*. London: Sage Publications.

————. 1996. "Lean Production in the German Automobile Industry: A Test Case for Convergence Theory." In Berger and Dore, 138–70.

————. 1997. "German Capitalism: Does It Exist? Can It Survive?" *New Political Economy*, forthcoming.

Streeck, Wolfgang, Josef Hilbert, Karl–Heinz van Kevelaer, Friederike Maier, and Hajo Weber. 1987. "The Role of the Social Partners in Vocational Training and Further Training in the Federal Republic of Germany." CEDEFOP Research Project No. 1236/1968, European Centre for the Promotion of Vocational Training.

Streeck, Wolfgang, and Sigurt Vitols. 1995. "European Community: Between Mandatory Consultation and Voluntary Information." In Joel Rogers and Wolfgang Streeck, eds., *Works Councils, Consultation, Representation and Cooperation in Industrial Relations*, 243–81. Chicago: University of Chicago Press.

Swenson, Peter. 1989. *Fair Shares: Unions, Pay, and Politics in Sweden and West Germany*. Ithaca, N.Y.: Cornell University Press.

————. 1991. "Bringing Capital Back In, or Social Democracy Reconsidered." *World Politics* 43 (July): 513–44.

Taylor, Andrew J. 1993. "Trade Unions and the Politics of Social Democratic Renewal." *West European Politics* 16 (January): 133–55.

Teague, Paul. 1989a. "Constitution or Regime? The Social Dimension to the 1992 Project." *British Journal of Industrial Relations* 27 (3): 310–29.

————. 1989b. *The European Community: The Social Dimension. Labour Market Policies for 1992*. London: Kogan Page and the Cranfield School of Management.

Teague, Paul, and John Grahl. 1989. "European Community Labour Market Policy: Present Scope and Future Direction." *Journal of European Integration* 13 (1): 1, 55–73.

————. 1990. "1992 and the Emergence of a European Industrial Relations Area." *Journal of European Integration* 13 (2–3): 167–83.

Thelen, Kathleen. 1991. *Union of Parts: Labor Politics in Postwar Germany*. Ithaca, N.Y.: Cornell University Press.

————. 1993. "West European Labor in Transition: Sweden and Germany Compared." *World Politics* 46 (October): 23–49.

————. 1994. "Beyond Corporatism: Toward a New Framework for the Study of Labor in Advanced Capitalism." *Comparative Politics* 27 (October): 107–24.

Thelen, Kathleen, and Sven Steinmo. 1992. "Historical Institutionalism in Comparative Politics." In Steinmo, Thelen, and Longstreth, 1–32.

Thurow, Lester. 1992. *Head to Head: The Coming Economic Battle among Japan, Europe, and America*. New York: Warner Books.

Tilly, Charles. 1995. "Globalization Threatens Labor's Rights." *International Labor and Working–Class History* 47 (Spring): 1–23.

Timmersfeld, Andrea. 1992. "Chancen und Perspektiven europäischer Kollektivverhandlungen." Ph.D. diss., Universität Trier.

Tomandl, Theodor, and Karl Fuerboeck. 1986. *Social Partnership: The Austrian System of Industrial Relations and Social Insurance.* Ithaca, N.Y.: ILR Press.

Torpey, John. 1992. "Two Movements, Not a Revolution: Exodus and Opposition in the East German Transformation, 1989–1990." *German Politics and Society* 26 (Summer): 21–42.

Trautwein–Kalms, Gudrun. 1990. "Workforce Transformation, Social Change, and New Challenges for the German Trade Unions." Draft paper, WSI/DGB, Düsseldorf.

Treverton, Gregory F., ed. 1992. *The Shape of the New Europe.* New York: Council on Foreign Relations Press.

Turner, Henry Ashby, Jr. 1992. *Germany from Partition to Reunification.* New Haven, Conn.: Yale University Press.

Turner, Lowell. 1991. *Democracy at Work: Changing World Markets and the Future of Labor Unions.* Ithaca, N.Y.: Cornell University Press.

———. 1993. "Prospects for Worker Participation in Management in the Single Market." In Ulman, Eichengreen, and Dickens, 45–79.

———. 1996. "The Europeanization of Labor: Structure before Action." *European Journal of Industrial Relations* 2 (November): 325–44.

———. 1997a. "Beyond National Unionism? Cross–National Labor Collaboration in the European Community." In Locke and Thelen.

———, ed. 1997b. *Negotiating the New Germany: Can Social Partnership Survive?* Ithaca, N.Y.: Cornell University Press.

Turner, Lowell, and Peter Auer. 1994. "A Diversity of New Work Organization: Human–Centered, Lean, and In–Between." *Industrielle Beziehungen* 1 (1): 39–61.

Ulman, Lloyd, Barry Eichengreen, and William T. Dickens, eds. 1993. *Labor and an Integrated Europe.* Washington, D.C.: The Brookings Institution.

Upchurch, Martin. 1995. "After Unification: Trade Unions and Industrial Relations in Eastern Germany." *Industrial Relations Journal* 26 (December): 280–92.

———. 1996. "German Unification and Its Implications for Modell Deutschland." Paper presented at the seminar "The Transition in Eastern Germany," European Research Centre, London, November 20.

Venturini, Patrick. 1989. "1992: The European Social Dimension." Luxembourg: Office for Official Publications of the European Communities.

Visser, Jelle. 1994. "European Trade Unions: The Transition Years." In Richard Hyman and Anthony Ferner, eds., *New Frontiers in European Industrial Relations*, 80–107. Oxford: Blackwell.

Voskamp, Ulrich, and Volker Wittke. 1991. "Aus Modernisierungsblockaden werden Abwärtsspiralen: Zur Reorganisation von Betrieben und Kombinaten der ehemaligen DDR." *Berliner Journal der Soziologie* 1:17–39.

Wagner, Karin, David Hitchens, and Esmond Birnie. 1995. "Entwicklung der Produktivität und Investitionstätigkeit ostdeutscher Industriebetriebe: Eine Fallstudienanalyse." *Zeitschrift für Betriebswirtschaft* 65 (4): 373–84.

Wallace, William. 1990. *The Transformation of Western Europe.* London: Royal Institute of International Affairs.

Webber, Douglas. 1992. "Kohl's Wendepolitik after a Decade." *German Politics* 1 (August): 149–80.

———. 1994. "The Decline and Resurgence of the German Model: The Treuhandanstalt and Privatisation Politics in East Germany." *Journal of European Public Policy.* 1 (2): 151–75.

Weiss, Manfred. 1991. "The Transition of Labor Law and Industrial Relations: The Case of German Unification—A Preliminary Perspective." *Comparative Labor Law Journal* 13 (Fall): 1–17.

———. 1992. "The Significance of Maastricht for European Community Social Policy." *The International Journal of Comparative Labour Law and Industrial Relations* 8 (Spring): 3–14.

Westney, Eleanor D. 1987. *Imitation and Innovation: The Transfer of Western Organizational Patterns to Meiji Japan.* Cambridge: Harvard University Press.

Westphal, Andreas, Hansjorg Herr, Michael Heine, and Ulrich Busch, eds. 1991. *Wirtschafts-politische Konsequenzen der deutschen Vereinigung*. Frankfurt: Campus Verlag.

Wever, Kirsten. 1994. "Learning from Works Councils: Five Unspectacular Cases from Germany." *Industrial Relations* 33 (October): 467–81.

———. 1995. *Negotiating Competitiveness: Employment Relations and Organizational Innovation in Germany and the United States*. Boston: Harvard Business School Press.

Wever, Kirsten S., and Christopher S. Allen. 1993. "The Financial System and Corporate Governance in Germany: Institutions and the Diffusion of Innovations." *Journal of Public Policy* 12 (3): 183–202.

Whyte, William Foote. 1994. *Participant Observer: An Autobiography*. Ithaca, NY: ILR Press.

Wiesenthal, Helmut, Wilfried Ettl, and Christiane Bialas. 1992. "Interessenverbände im Transformationsprozess." Working Paper AG TRAP, Max-Planck-Gesellschaft, Arbeitsgruppe Transformationsprozesse in den neuen Bundesländern an der Humboldt Universität, —October.

Wildavsky, Aaron. 1994. "Why Self–Interest Means Less Outside of a Social Context: Cultural Contributions to a Theory of Rational Choices." *Journal of Theoretical Politics* 6 (2): 131–59.

Wilensky, Harold L. 1983. "Political Legitimacy and Consensus: Missing Variables in the Assessment of Social Policy." In S. E. Spiro and E. Yuchtman-Yaar, eds., *Evaluating the Welfare State: Social and Political Perspectives*, 51–74. New York: Academic Press.

———. 1991. "The Nation–State, Social Policy, and Economic Performance." Working Paper #25, Institute of Industrial Relations, University of California at Berkeley.

Wilensky, Harold L., and Lowell Turner. 1987. *Democratic Corporatism and Policy Linkages: The Interdependence of Industrial, Labor–Market, Incomes, and Social Policies in Eight Countries*. Institute of International Studies, Research Series #69. Berkeley: University of California.

Wilpert, Bernhard, Ayse Kudat, and Yilmaz Ozkan, eds. 1978. *Workers' Participation in an International Economy*. Kent, Ohio: Kent State University Press.

Windmuller, John P. 1980. *The International Trade Union Movement*. Deventer, Netherlands: Kluwer.

Windolf, Paul. 1989. "Productivity Coalitions and the Future of European Corporatism." *Industrial Relations* 28 (Winter): 1–20.

Windolf, Paul, and Hans–Willy Hohn. 1984. *Arbeitsmarktchancen in der Krise: Betriebliche Rekrutierung und soziale Schließung*. Frankfurt: Campus Verlag.

Womack, James T., Daniel T. Jones, and Daniel Roos. 1990. *The Machine That Changed the World*. New York: Rawson Associates.

Zwickel, Klaus. 1992. "Verteilungskonflikte und Gestaltungsanspruch—tarifpolitische Perspektiven für die neunziger Jahre." *Gewerkschaftliche Monatshefte* 43 (October): 659– 67.

Zysman, John. 1983. *Governments, Markets, and Growth: Financial Systems and the Politics of Industrial Change*. Ithaca, N.Y.: Cornell University Press.

———. 1996. "The Myth of a 'Global' Economy: Enduring National Foundations and Emerging Regional Realities." *New Political Economy* 1 (2): 157–84.

Zysman, John, Eileen Doherty, and Andrew Schwartz. 1996. "Tales from the 'Global' Economy: Cross–National Production Networks and the Reorganization of the European Economy." Working Paper 83, Berkeley Roundtable on the International Economy, University of California at Berkeley.

Index

Index

Index

Index

Cornell Studies in Political Economy

EDITED BY PETER J. KATZENSTEIN

The Sovereign Entrepreneur: Oil Policies in Advanced and Less Developed Capitalist Countries, by Merrie Gilbert Klapp

Norms in International Relations: The Struggle against Apartheid, by Audie Jeanne Klotz

International Regimes, edited by Stephen D. Krasner

Disparaged Success: Labor Politics in Postwar Japan, by Ikuo Kume

Business and Banking: Political Change and Economic Integration in Western Europe, by Paulette Kurzer

Power, Protection, and Free Trade: International Sources of U.S. Commercial Strategy, 1887–1939, by David A. Lake

State Capitalism: Public Enterprise in Canada, by Jeanne Kirk Laux and Maureen Appel Molot

Why Syria Goes to War: Thirty Years of Confrontation, by Fred H. Lawson

Remaking the Italian Economy, by Richard M. Locke

France after Hegemony: International Change and Financial Reform, by Michael Loriaux

Economic Containment: CoCom and the Politics of East–West Trade, by Michael Mastanduno

Business and the State in Developing Countries, edited by Sylvia Maxfield and Ben Ross Schneider

The Currency of Ideas: Monetary Politics in the European Union, by Kathleen R. McNamara

Mercantile States and the World Oil Cartel, 1900–1939, by Gregory P. Nowell

Who Elected the Bankers?: Surveillance and Control in the World Economy, by Louis W. Pauly

Opening Financial Markets: Banking Politics on the Pacific Rim, by Louis W. Pauly

The Limits of Social Democracy: Investment Politics in Sweden, by Jonas Pontusson

The Fruits of Fascism: Postwar Prosperity in Historical Perspective, by Simon Reich

The Business of the Japanese State: Energy Markets in Comparative and Historical Perspective, by Richard J. Samuels

"Rich Nation, Strong Army": National Security and the Technological Transformation of Japan, by Richard J. Samuels

Crisis and Choice in European Social Democracy, by Fritz W. Scharpf, translated by Ruth Crowley and Fred Thompson

In the Dominions of Debt: Historical Perspectives on Dependent Development, by Herman M. Schwartz

Winners and Losers: How Sectors Shape the Developmental Prospects of States, by D. Michael Shafer

Ideas and Institutions: Developmentalism in Brazil and Argentina, by Kathryn Sikkink

The Cooperative Edge: The Internal Politics of International Cartels, by Debora L. Spar

Fair Shares: Unions, Pay, and Politics in Sweden and West Germany, by Peter Swenson

Union of Parts: Labor Politics in Postwar Germany, by Kathleen Thelen

Democracy at Work: Changing World Markets and the Future of Labor Unions, by Lowell Turner

Fighting for Partnership: Labor and Politics in Unified Germany, by Lowell Turner

Troubled Industries: Confronting Economic Change in Japan, by Robert M. Uriu

Freer Markets, More Rules: Regulatory Reform in Advanced Industrial Countries, by Steven K. Vogel

National Styles of Regulation: Environmental Policy in Great Britain and the United States, by David Vogel

The Political Economy of Policy Coordination: International Adjustment since 1945, by Michael C. Webb

The Myth of the Powerless State, by Linda Weiss

International Cooperation: Building Regimes for Natural Resources and the Environment, by Oran R. Young

International Governance: Protecting the Environment in a Stateless Society, by Oran R. Young

Polar Politics: Creating International Environmental Regimes, edited by Oran R. Young and Gail Osherenko

Governments, Markets, and Growth: Financial Systems and the Politics of Industrial Change, by John Zysman

American Industry in International Competition: Government Policies and Corporate Strategies, edited by John Zysman and Laura Tyson